THE BACK HOME SERIES

SERIES TITLES

Powder Plant
Carolyn Dallmann

Hound Dog
M.L. Liebler

Mostly Woodcock
Joe McKnight

In the Room at the Top of the World
Ben McCormick

Water Spell
Catherine Broadwall

An Ignorance of Trees
Jim Daniels

Our Bodies Are Mostly Water
Katherine Riegel

You Shoulda Been Here Last Week
Ted J. Rulseh

The Past Ten: An Anthology
Donald Quist, Kali White VanBaale, & Bailey Gaylin Moore (eds.)

Table Talk & Second Thoughts
Michael Martone

Points of Tangency: Essays
Scott Russell Morris

Lessons in Geography
Phillip Sterling

This Season, The Next
Casey Knott

Wildlifer
Neil F. Payne

We Come from Good Stock
Kay Oakes Oring

Squatter
Yolanda DeLoach

The Arc of the Escarpment
Robert Root

Soul of the Outdoors
Dave Greschner

From the Heart: The Story of Matrix
John Harmon

The Long Fields
Anne-Marie Oomen

Kick Out the Bottom
Erik Mortenson & Christopher Kramer

Wrong Tree: Adventures in Wildlife Biology
Jeff Wilson

At the Lake
Jim Landwehr

Body Talk
Takwa Gordon

The In-Between State
Martha Lundin

North Freedom
Carolyn Dallmann

Ohio Apertures
Robert Miltner

PRAISE FOR

Powder Plant

I couldn't stop reading this! Dallmann went looking for a summer job in 1966 and ended up with a 30-year career at an ammunition plant that made gunpowder for the Vietnam War. She tested nitroglycerin, survived antiwar bombings, and witnessed the slow environmental reckoning of a billion-pound propellant operation built on seized farmland. Finally, a woman who actually worked in America's military-industrial complex tells her story. It's gritty, fascinating, and completely absorbing. If you love memoirs that uncover hidden histories, don't miss this one.

—LINDA SAETHER
author of *What We Can't Forget*

The Powder Plant is a heartwarming memoir that provides a fascinating look into an often unheralded aspect of the Army's logistical tail that sustained America's soldiers through three Wars.

—RICHARD S. BROWN
author of *Going Off the Rails*

Read this book to find out some of the things that happen inside the fence at the Badger Army Ammunition Plant. Carolyn Dallmann writes as if she were talking to you about her many experiences working as a laboratory technician at the Badger Plant. She writes as if it were a personal conversation of her experiences. Carolyn discusses her work, the people she worked with and the many inside incidents at the plant during her employment. A very informative read!

—FRANK WOLF
Badger History Group

Carolyn Dallmann provides a poignant and authoritative narrative with an historical and personal perspective. Wisconsin farmland is commandeered for national defense. A generation of farm families and an entire community paid a price. Farms are lost, replaced by a massive ammunition plant that serves the country from WWII through Vietnam. Carolyn takes you inside the controversy and the community of North Freedom where she grew up. She puts you inside her experiences in the plant where she worked for thirty years. This is compelling Wisconsin history, skillfully written by someone who lived and researched it.

—L.E. ROGERS
author of the *Hard Knox* series

POWDER PLANT

Farmland to National Defense

CAROLYN DALLMANN

CORNERSTONE PRESS
UNIVERSITY OF WISCONSIN-STEVENS POINT

Cornerstone Press, Stevens Point, Wisconsin 54481

www.uwsp.edu/cornerstone

Printed in the United States of America.

Library of Congress Control Number: 2026931959
ISBN: 978-1-968148-48-5

Cover Photos: (top) The John and Elsie Shimniok farm on the Sauk Prairie before the government took their land to build the Powder Plant. (*Image:* Badger History Group, Inc.); (bottom) An overview of Badger Army Ammunition Plant taken from near where the property meets Devil's Lake State Park. (*Image:* Carolyn Dallmann, 2006)

Cornerstone Press titles are produced in courses and internships offered by the Department of English at the University of Wisconsin–Stevens Point.

Director & Publisher
Dr. Ross K. Tangedal

Executive Editors
Jeff Snowbarger, Freesia McKee

Editorial Director
Brett Hill

Senior Editors
Ellie Atlkinson, Paige Biever

Press Staff
Lilly Kulbeck, Brianna Loving, Eleanor Belcher, Asher Schroeder, John Evans, Aja Woolley, Christiana Niedzwiecki, Nathan Pearson, Jazmyne Johnson, Sophie McPherson, Sam Bjork, Madison Schultz, Autumn Vine, Andrew Bryant

To my husband,
David Dallmann,
with love for over sixty years.

ALSO BY CAROLYN DALLMANN:

North Freedom

Contents

Badger Army Ammunition Plant located in South-Central Wisconsin supported our military during World War II. The Badger plant produced ordnance, gunpowder. Badger shipped the material to other powder plants for packing. The facility closed after WWII but returned to operate during the Korean Conflict and the Vietnam War.

Image: What is Remote Sensing? The Definitive Guide to Earth Observation. (2024. June 16). Retrieved from https://gisgeography.com/remote-sensing-earth-observation-guide/

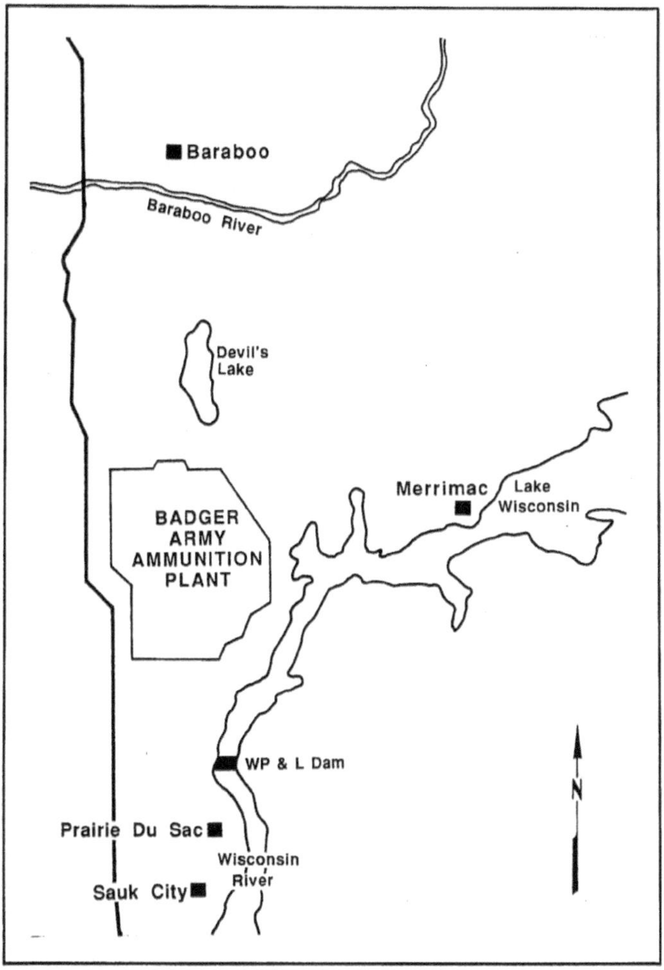

The map shows the relationship of Badger Army Ammunition Plant to landmarks in Sauk County, Wisconsin.

Image: U.S. Army Corps of Engineers, Fort Worth District, U.S. Army Materiel Command Historic Context Series, Report of Investigations, Number 2A, Geo-Marine. Inc., The World War II Ordnance Department's Government-Owned Contractor-Operated (GOCO) Industrial Facilities: Badger Ordnance Works Historic Investigation, February 1996

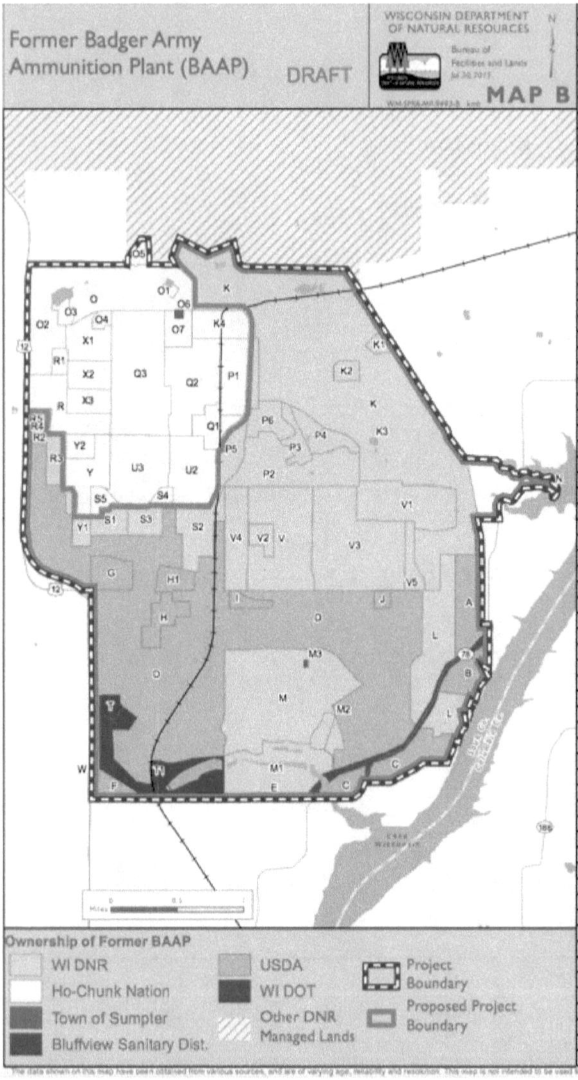

Parcel	Description	Acres
A	North River Corridor Buffer	88
B	South River Corridor Buffer	55
C	Southeast Corner	114
D	North and East Magazines	1,669
E	South Buffer	12
F	Southwest Corner	20
G	Conservation Club Area	45
H	Propellant Burning Ground	46
H1	Gate 16 Change Houses	30
I	Landfill # 2 Area	17
J	Inert Disposal Area	10
K	Northeast Corner	1,168
K1	Landfill #5	12
K2	Deterrent Burning Ground	17
K3	Wood Duck Pond	1
K4	East Ball Powder Pilot Plan	56
L	River Corridor	199
M	North Magazines	385
M1	Settling Ponds/South Magazi	161
M2	Geotube Laydown Area	18
M3	Thoelke Cemetery	1
N	River Pump	5
O	Northwest Corner	332
O1	Filtration Plant	4
O2	Miller Cemetery	0
O3	Ballistics Range	13
O4	Solvent Recovery Still	10
O5	Cannon Range	14
O6	Pioneer Cemetery	3
O7	West Ball Powder Pilot Plan	33
P1	Historic Shops Area	66
P2	Rocket Paste Area	161
P3	Old NG	30
P4	NG Pond Area	47
P5	Railroad Scale Area	78
P6	New Acid & New NG	43
Q1	Box Wash Area	43
Q2	B & C Line Rest Houses	145
Q3	B & C Line Central Area	238
R	Production Support and Labs	94
R1	Old Acid Area	14
R2	Well #1	1
R3	Maintenance & Salvage Area	36
R4	Administration Area	28
R5	Building 200	1
S1	Ball Powder Wet Line	35
S2	Metal Rest Houses	87
S3	Ball Powder Coating Line	40
S4	Ball Powder Dry Houses	10
S5	Ball Powder Rework	16
T	WWTP Area	15
T1	IRM/MIRM/Final Creek/SP1	147
U2	D&E Lines Rest Houses	100
U3	D&E Lines Central Area	131
V	West Rocket Production	209
V1	Landfill #6	137
V2	West Rocket Roll House	22
V3	East Rocket Production	272
V4	West Rocket Press Houses	62
V5	East Rocket Press Houses	29
W	Southwest Corner	47
X1	Open Space	56
X2	B Nitrocellulose Line	42
X3	C Nitrocellulose Line	37
Y	E Nitrocellulose Line	68
Y1	F Line Area	33
Y2	D Nitrocellulose Line	24

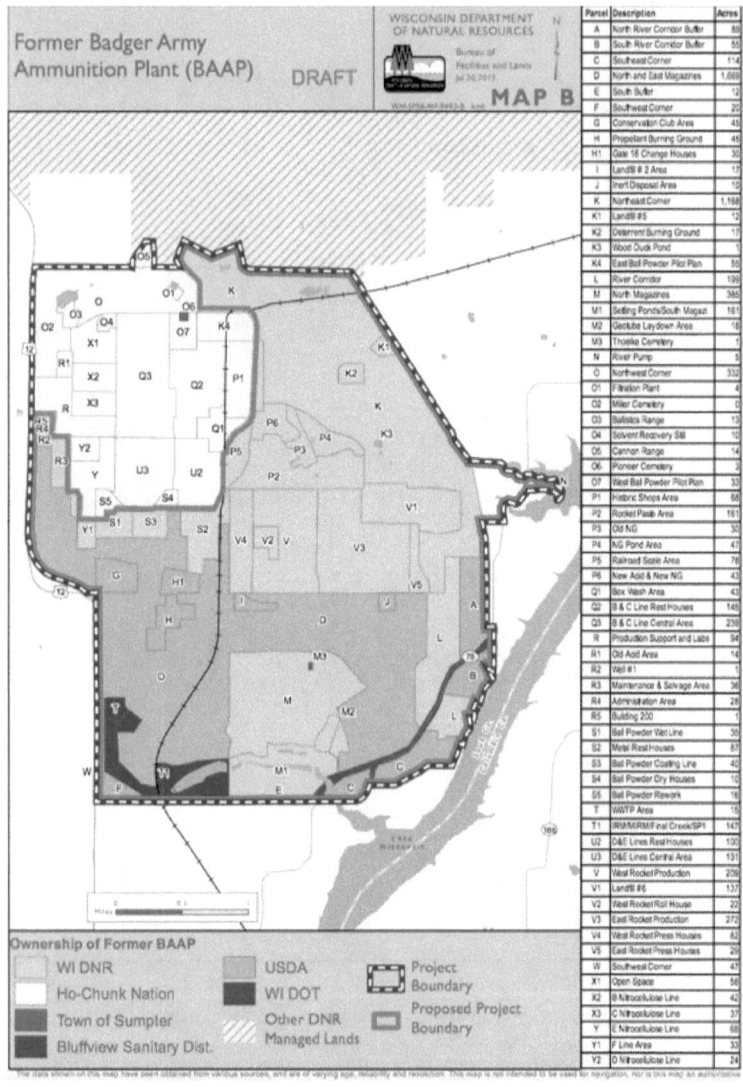

The map is a draft of the final version showing which agencies received Badger Army Ammunition Plant land after the Department of Defense determined they no longer needed the property. *Image:* Badger History Group, Inc.

KEY TERMS

Acid - A substance, usually a liquid, which contains hydrogen and can react with other substances to form salts. Acids have a pH less than seven. Some acids burn or dissolve other substances they come in contact with. Badger manufactured both Nitric Acid and Sulfuric Acid, as well as Oleum, highly concentrated sulfuric acid. Large volumes of these acids are used to manufacture propellent.
Badger Army Ammunition Plant - Badger, powder plant, plant, facility, BadgerAAP, BAAP
Badger Ordnance Works - BOW, Powder plants created in the 1940s were called "Works" if they did not manufacture a finished product. Powder plants making finished products were called "Plants." This nomenclature changed in 1963. Badger Ordnance Works was known as Badger Army Ammunition Plant after that date.
Base (laboratory term) - A substance that can accept hydrogen ions or donate hydroxide ions in aqueous solution. Bases have a pH greater than seven. They react with acids to form salts.
Base (manufacturing term) - Base is a term used for explosives manufactured at Badger. Badger manufactured two bases, Nitrocellulose or Nitrocotton (depending on whether cellulous/paper or cotton linters were used in the process) and Nitroglycerin.
BOO-U - University of Wisconsin - Baraboo/Sauk County
Building 200 - Administration Building, upfront
Building 2556 - Powder Lab (during the Vietnam War)

COD - Chemical Oxygen Demand. A procedure used for testing water

Commander's Representative - Top civilian employed by the US Department of the Army at Badger Army Ammunition Plant, CR

GSA - Government Service Administration. Served as the government's real estate agent when Badger land was no longer needed by the Department of Defense.

Gunpowder - Propellant, ammunition, ordnance, powder

Operating Contractor - The company awarded the government contract to operate BadgerAAP. Olin Corporation was the operating contractor during the Vietnam War and was tasked to manufacture propellant and maintain the facility in operating readiness until September 2004. The 'new' Environmental Contract's goal was, Demolition, Remediation, Restoration, and Turnover of Property to other Government Agencies, and was awarded to Specpro, LLC, October 2004. The majority of people working at Badger were employed by the operating contractor, not by the US Army.

PCBs - Polychlorinated biphenyls, a group of manmade chemicals widely used in industrial and commercial applications until their ban in the 1970s

pH - (power or potential of hydrogen) is a logarithmic scale from 0 to 14 that measures the acidity or alkalinity of a solution, where 7 is neutral. Lower pH values (<7) indicate increasing acidity, and higher values (>7) indicate increasing alkalinity (or basicity).

Remediation - The action of remedying something, in particular, reversing or stopping environmental damage

SMES - Superconducting Magnetic Energy Storage system used to control energy, like in northern Wisconsin where a series of SMES units enhance grid stability in a distribution loop or around the world for power quality control in installations, especially those requiring ultra clean power, such as microchip fabrication facilities.

UW - University of Wisconsin

VOCs - Volatile Organic Compounds, a broad group of carbon-containing chemicals that easily evaporate at room temperature and are released into the air from various sources

Vortex - A mass of whirling fluid (or air)

PREFACE

At age 18, I was not looking for a career in making things that go boom on a battlefield. In 1966, my search for a summer job led me to Badger Army Ammunition Plant, ten miles southeast of my home in North Freedom, Wisconsin. I wanted something different from being a nanny or waitress.

Working at Badger changed my life. It was a significant adjustment from the family farm and led to a career of over 30 years. During that time, I married my high school sweetheart, raised a family, and earned a very unconventional college degree.

Badger manufactured ammunition in support of our military during WWII, the Korean Conflict, and the Vietnam War. Considering we produced over a billion pounds of propellant for three wars, there were surprisingly few explosions at the powder plant. Three of those explosions affected me.

Activists dropped bombs on Badger while I worked at testing samples of gunpowder. Although the bombs did not explode, the event holds historical significance.

Challenges arose after the war, but before my retirement, when the government determined they no longer needed the powder plant.

I wrote this book because most employees never documented their day-to-day activities. I am also the only woman who was employed at Badger for both the production period during the Vietnam War and the demolition, remediation, restoration, and transfer of the property before the facility closed.

* * *

During high school, I had little interest in history and never thought much about the ammunition plant sprawling across 7,500 acres of the beautiful Sauk Prairie, ten miles from my family's farm. It was part of the original 10,500 acres taken by the government to build a powder plant after the attack on Pearl Harbor on December 7, 1941. However, my passion for farm life and knowing people who lost their property because of Badger's creation piqued my interest. Why was farmland taken when less fertile land was available?

World War I ended on November 11, 1918. H.G. Wells coined the phrase, "The war to end all wars." The Great Depression and Dust Bowl followed. But Wells' phrase was far from true. Fallout from WWI created unrest in Europe that spilled over into our country by the late 1930s.

The United States was in a dire situation by the fall of 1941. We were sending supplies and military equipment to war-torn European Allies through a Lend-Lease Program. Winston Churchill continually pleaded with President Roosevelt to provide more support for Britain following Germany's 1940 lightning invasion of Europe. Growing tension led us to evaluate our resources should England lose its fight with the enemy.

The War Department reported our country was woefully underprepared. We had nothing compared to Germany's juggernaut military. There was no national highway system to move equipment, supplies, or troops efficiently. We had only 400 lightweight tanks. Our artillery was mounted on wooden wheels designed to be pulled by mules or horses. We had guns. However, our stockpile of ordnance—ammunition—had dwindled to a critically low level. We had depleted our supply by sending it to the Allies.

A massive industrialization effort ensued. The manufacture of gunpowder was a high priority. Initially, our country planned to ramp up and expand the few existing powder plants. Then, in September 1940, over 200 were injured and 51 died in a series of explosions and fires at an existing plant in New Jersey. Almost 300,000 pounds of ordnance blew up.

The investigation showed that an initial explosion set off other explosions in adjacent buildings and more down a line of processing structures. But the need for propellant was critical. The government had the damaged facility up and running by April 1941, seven months after the disaster. Engineers designed safety features to mitigate the danger of the disaster recurring by doubling the distance between process buildings.

Plans changed. Rather than expand the few existing powder plants, the government decided to build several small facilities across the country. Locations in the Midwest and West would economically stimulate those areas and encourage further industrialization. Additionally, losing one of many small operations could slow production, but our country would not lose this overall resource. At least one powder plant would be in Wisconsin.

But where?

Two properties met the criteria. One was the fertile Sauk Prairie in Sauk County, home to successful farmers whose ancestors had settled the land for generations. The other, 40 miles to the north, was a flat glaciated wasteland of scrub pines in Adams County. Both had the required water supply, hydropower, and railroads nearby.

Concerned prairie farmers organized in the fall of 1941 under the leadership of the Sumpter Town Chairman, Garth Premo. This group represented pastoral, prosperous farms, not broken properties on barren Dust Bowl parcels like those on the Great Plains.

These farmers had recently agreed to raise 5.3 million more pounds of milk, 175 million more eggs, and 1.5 million more pounds of pork in 1942 than in 1941. In this manner, they supported our country's effort to help our Allies and people suffering from the Great Depression. The group sent formal protests to Madison, Washington, D.C., and everyone who could help them protect their property from being appropriated for an ammunition plant.

The contending Adams County Board, along with other community leaders, also organized. They spent two weeks drafting a telegram sent to President Roosevelt on November 24, 1941. It said Adams County wants the powder plant. The Adams property meets the same requirements as the Sauk Prairie. The land is cheaper, and the owners are less likely to resist the project.

So why did the federal government choose the bucolic Sauk Prairie and not the land in Adams County?

Opinions differed during the fall of 1941. The sadness of the farmers losing their property versus the delight of area businessmen thinking of quick profits. Locals who had been out of work because of the Great Depression were ecstatic to hear jobs were coming.

The Chicago and North Western Railroad ran through the Sauk Prairie. Like other railroads, it was suffering the effects of the Great Depression and was in receivership following bankruptcy. Roland L. "Bud" Williams, President of the C&NW railroad, contacted his friend, Leo T. Crowley, for help to save his company. Crowley was a lobbyist with a shady past whose business dealings were anchored in Wisconsin. However, he had national connections and influence.

Crowley spent much of his time in Washington, D.C., where he was known as "The President's Man" because of his close connection to Roosevelt. He was also known as "The Fixer." He and Bud Williams visited General George Marshall. Williams explained that his railroad ran through the Sauk Prairie. It could haul raw materials and employees into the plant and deliver finished products as well. "The President's Man" seated in his office created an impression on Marshall. William's wish was granted with little persuasion. The General's opinion to build the facility on the prairie carried weight with the President.

Japan attacked Pearl Harbor on December 7, 1941, intending to disable the U.S. Pacific Fleet. They anticipated a defeat at Pearl Harbor would be so devastating that the U.S. would give up rather than go to war. That did not happen. Roosevelt addressed the nation the following day, and Congress declared war on Japan. Three days later, Germany and Italy declared war on our country. We desperately needed ammunition.

Word soon followed that building the powder plant on the Sauk Prairie would commence. The decision saved the C&NW railroad. The prairie farm families were collateral damage.

Advertising far and wide, the Army searched for the thousands of employees needed to construct and operate the plant. There were not enough people in the rural area to fill the quota, which peaked at over 13,000. When employees arrived, there was nowhere to house them. To solve the issue, barracks-like apartments were built across from the main entrance of the plant. The new city, Badger Village, was constructed complete with a school, church, theater, and daycare. With gasoline and tires rationed, residents living across from the powder plant could walk to and from work. Expanding Badger Village continued throughout the production cycle.

When WWII ended in 1945, Badger closed abruptly. It operated again from 1950 to 1953 in response to the Korean Conflict. A few employees stayed until 1958 to build the ball powder production facility. The Army felt this new powder, used for small arms, would be a resource if our country became involved in another war. Ball powder production was unique to Badger. It was the only plant with the capability in the entire military industrial ammo base.

The facility sat idle until 1966 when it reopened in response to the Vietnam War. Protests took place throughout our country during the war. One random act of violence in Madison foreshadowed an attack on the ammunition plant. Following the signing of the Paris Peace Accords in 1973, the United States withdrew all combat troops from Vietnam, ending its active involvement in the war. With America's combat role ended, the Badger plant began shutting down and was converted to standby readiness.

Badger was a Government-Owned, Contractor Operated (GOCO) facility. I never worked for the Army. Olin Corporation hired me. They were a long-time operating contractor, but they were not the first or the last.

SpecPro LLC became the operating contractor in 2004 after the Army strategized that they needed only two of over 20 powder plants. SpecPro led the environmental project, which included demolition, remediation, restoration, and property turnover to other government agencies. The Department of Defense was transitioning the last of the property when I retired in 2014.

Leo T. Crowley © Wisconsin Historical Society. Used with permission.

The barn in the back left had belonged to one of the displaced farm families who were told in December 1941 to be off their property by March 1, 1942. Buildings, like this barn, were then owned by the Army and sold at auction. Some farmers bought back their buildings and removed them from what had been their property. Heavy equipment is already in place waiting for the ground to thaw so construction of the powder plant can begin. (*Image:* Dallmann Family Album)

The Rudolph Schlag home was moved from the prairie to 250 Holly Court in Prairie du Sac, WI, in 1942. (*Image:* Courtesy of the Sauk County Historical Society. As found in *Only in Sumpter* by Erhart Mueller, page 207)

The William Simon home was divided and moved to Prairie du Sac, WI. (*Image:* As found in *Only in Sumpter* by Erhart Mueller, page 226)

The Steidtmann home on the Sauk Prairie: Julius Steidtmann refused to leave the home he loved and the farm settled by his ancestors, who had purchased the land from the government. His son, Lewis, who also lived in the home, finally gathered his father in his arms and carried him to the car. The Steidtmann house was torn down and used for a house in Lime Ridge, WI, a portion of which was the Lime Ridge post office. The structure bore no resemblance to the original Steidtmann home. (*Image:* As found in *Only in Sumpter* by Erhart Mueller, page 205)

GUNPOWDER 101

The word *gunpowder* is interchangeable with ordnance, ammunition, and propellant.

Badger Army Ammunition Plant, first known as Badger Ordnance Works, manufactured propellant. The place was known colloquially by several different names to include Badger, the powder plant, the facility, and the ammunition plant.

Badger produced gunpowder using two explosives, also called bases: nitrocellulose, NC, and nitroglycerin, NG. Both explosives were manufactured at the facility because they are too dangerous to transport anywhere. Other materials were added to NC and NG in small amounts for stability and handling.

Badger also manufactured the large quantities of nitric and sulfuric acid required to make NC and NG because the acids are too hazardous to transport. Additionally, losing such an indispensable supply chain would stop production.

Gunpowder is made in little batches that are moved between small buildings as they are processed. Therefore, if there is an issue with a single batch, injuries are minimized and production is not shut down.

The composition of these small batches varies. That is why the powder laboratory tested samples of each. For simplicity, two of the many tests performed are addressed here.

Moisture and *surface area* significantly affect how gunpowder burns, thus affecting its performance when soldiers use it in the field or for training. The powder laboratory tested samples for these characteristics.

Process engineers analyzed the lab's test results to determine how to *blend* the small batches of gunpowder into increasingly larger batches to make final government lots that met military specifications. *Blending* batches of gunpowder is as critical as the *chemistry* of making it.

Technicians used a gun chronograph to measure the velocity of final lots at the ballistics laboratory.

Badger did not make bullets. They shipped propellant to other facilities for packing.

Glossing over elements of technical information in this book will not diminish my personal story.

* * *

The following pictures show the three types of propellant manufactured at Badger: smokeless, also known as single base, rocket, and ball powder. These grains of gunpowder were found in buildings or on the ground by work crews during demolition of the old facility; therefore, the grains are not pristine. Badger turned over such ordnance to other agencies for disposal.

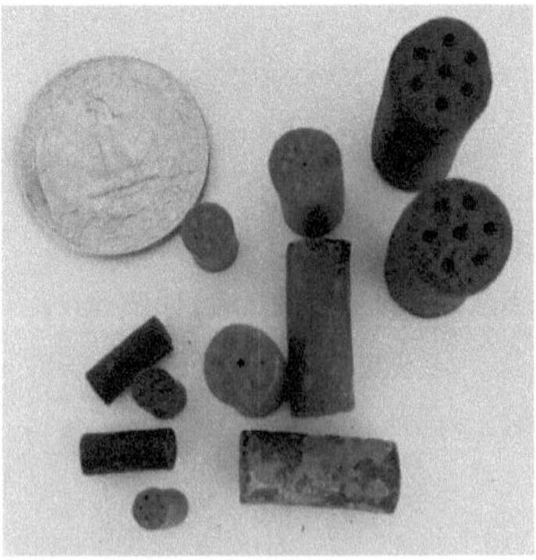

Image: Carolyn Dallmann

Smokeless gunpowder is also known as single base because it is made using only one of the explosives produced at Badger, NC. It was manufactured in different configurations. Notice the holes through the extruded grains. The holes increase the powder's surface area, thus affecting the burn rate. Smokeless was the first product manufactured at Badger. The military uses this versatile propellant in ground artillery on battlefields, to clear beaches, and in the 16" guns on battleships.

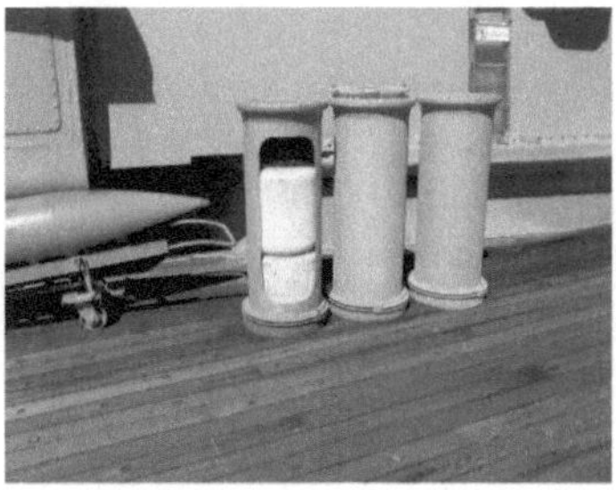

Image: Carolyn Dallmann

This mock staging on the deck of the *USS Missouri* models how bags of single base ordnance were used to propel missiles the size of the projectile on the left.

Image: Carolyn Dallmann

This photo shows guns firing from the battleship *USS Missouri.* One 16" gun can project a 2,700 pound missile 23 miles with pinpoint accuracy.

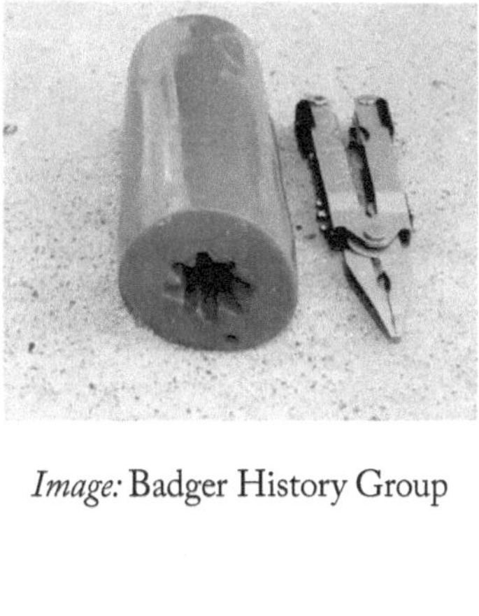

Image: Badger History Group

Whole rocket powder grains are three feet long, two and a half inches in diameter, and bright orange. An eight-pointed star runs through each extruded grain, increasing the surface area. Rocket powder is a double base propellant. It contains both NC and NG. The military uses rocket propellant to launch projectiles from ground artillery and helicopters.

Ball powder is a double base propellant. It contains both NC and NG. The size and shape of the tiny grains vary. The ball powder production facility was built after the Korean Conflict, making Badger unique. It was the only powder plant in the entire military industrial ammo base with the capability. Estimates indicate that ball powder propelled 90 percent of the small arms ammunition fired during the Vietnam War by our soldiers. Badger Army Ammunition Plant manufactured most of that powder.

Image: Carolyn Dallmann

1

MY FIRST YEAR AT BADGER

1965–1966

High School (1961-1965)

High school is roller skates, cows, a '56 Mercury, and David Dallmann. Whirling around the wood floor at the Rock Springs roller rink every Sunday evening is my social life.

Mom introduces my brothers and me to skating in 1961. I am 14 years old. My brother David is 13. Allen is 12. Randy, at five years old, is too young to skate.

I ride the bus seven miles from North Freedom, Wisconsin, to Baraboo High School in the fall. Mom and Dad say I must ride the bus home and cannot participate in after-school activities. Milking cows does not allow them time to drive back and forth between the village and Baraboo. This seriously limits my interaction with classmates.

It's not like I have a lot of time after school. I babysit for a family who has seven children. The couple often play euchre or sheepshead at nightly card parties and attend weekend dances. I am organist at St. Paul's Lutheran church in North Freedom, population 600. I had only six months of piano lessons when my parents volunteered me for that position. There was no one else in the small congregation with musical training. I must practice music for Sunday services at the church during the week. I also have farm chores.

One Sunday evening, Chully, the manager of the roller rink, asks me to play the Hammond organ to give the regular organist a break.

"I can't pay you," Chully says. "But I'll waive your admission fee, and you may use a pair of rental skates for free."

This is an offer I cannot resist. It is like getting paid for something I enjoy.

Skaters are from the surrounding area, mostly farm kids. I meet boys. One of the older boys, David Dallmann, catches my eye. He has serious skills on wheels including skating backward and doing dance steps while rolling across the floor. He is one of the guys Chully depends on to help beginners and monitor reckless racers on wheels.

I think about how nice it would be to skate with David and wonder how to approach him. Classmates on the school bus provide compelling tidbits of information.

The Dallmann family recently bought a farm three miles south of Rock Springs. Dave does not ride the bus because he drives his black and white 1956 Mercury two-door hardtop to school. As a graduating senior, he plans to attend Madison Vocational College. He wants to be a mechanic. That suits me. I enjoy our dairy farm. However, I do not want my life tied to a herd of cows.

David likely shares my thoughts. Our initial friendship and mutual interest in roller skating create the perfect setting for something more.

David graduates from vocational school when I am a junior. He has been picking me up in the Mercury on Sunday evenings for a year. It is a cheap date. We both skate for free because we help at the rink. He begins work at the Ford dealership in Baraboo and buys a new 1964 red Ford Fairlane with a black vinyl interior. I am impressed with the car and with David, too. Things are getting serious.

During my sophomore and junior high school summers, I work as a live-in nanny for a family with two young boys in Wisconsin Dells. It is easy work. The boys are well-behaved; I know my way around a kitchen and have the experience of caring for my youngest brother.

In my junior year, biology and geometry are my favorite classes. However, I opt out of taking chemistry as a senior because I am afraid of Mr. Felmlee. He is the only chemistry teacher and has a reputation for being stern. I sign up for home economics instead. I cook, bake, and help with canning at home. I crochet and embroider but have little experience with a sewing machine since Mom and Grandma Hilda are talented seamstresses. The class should be a breeze.

My third day in Mrs. Marking's home ec class is my last because Cole Felmlee strides into her room and asks, "Do you have a Carolyn Schroeder?" Mrs. Marking points to me in the back corner.

Felmlee walks to my desk, tells me to pack my things, and says, "You're coming with me." Too afraid to say anything, I follow him down the hall and up the stairs to his classroom. I am already two days behind in chemistry, and Mr. Felmlee took time away from teaching to fetch me. His other students stare as I take a seat. Nerves nettle my insides. To this day, I haven't found out what triggered the change. Mom says she had nothing to do with it.

Chemistry is a challenge. Felmlee's teaching style does not help. He has no patience with students who struggle. I ask him only one question, to which he replies, "I explained that in class," before he helps me. However, I would not be the person I am today had Cole Felmlee not dragged me out of home ec.

When I graduate high school, I think about becoming a biology teacher. Though due to the cost, college seems impossible. That changes when a guidance counselor directs me to a state scholarship. It covers my tuition. I must pay for room and board. All that babysitting and organ playing is finally paying off.

The summer of 1965, after graduation, my girlfriend and I rent a room in the Dells. The family I had lived with hire me to waitress at their Fireside Restaurant. Dave and I see each other on Sundays over those summers. It is my only day off because I play the organ for morning church services and at the rink.

I have been accepted at the UW-La Crosse in La Crosse, WI. It is 25 miles from Caledonia, Minnesota, Dad's hometown and where I was born. My parents are glad I will be close to relatives while attending classes 100 miles from the farm.

I qualify for a work-study job and land a 15-hour-a-week position as Assistant Secretary to the Dean of Men. It involves filing and typing. The few young men who visit the Dean are there because they are in trouble, usually academic.

David and I take this separation in stride. We write weekly letters. A couple of times each semester, he picks me up for a weekend with my family in North Freedom. We tiptoe through conversations about marriage; it will wait until I graduate. He will save toward a downpayment on a house.

Mom fusses about the money I spend attending college.

"I don't know why you're doing this," she preaches. "You'll just get married anyway." Mom's remark stings, but later, I will understand her reasoning. Dad says nothing. He is glad I am happy.

Money is dear to my parents. Their families farmed through the Great Depression. Their memories of those tough days stay with them throughout their lives, and they instill their thriftiness in my brothers and me.

I think about what Mom said, even though it upsets me. Life would be less complicated if I forgot about college and found a job. But that thought makes me uncomfortable. The opportunity to attend college might never come my way again.

College (1965-1966)

The university assigns my first roommate. We do not party like most girls in Baird Hall. We study together under a sad gray cloud, like characters in a Peanut's cartoon strip. She is homesick. I miss date nights with David. This is not the college life I expected.

She is a tiny ballerina from Illinois and sticks to me like glue. Her fragile frame hangs on our friendship. We say goodbye before Thanksgiving. Her father dies that weekend of an unexpected heart attack. Her family picks up her things before my return to school.

Her abrupt departure leaves a gaping hole inside of me, emphasized by her empty closet and the bare mattress on her bunk. We write, but I never see her again.

A letter from the university tells me my new roommate is an incoming freshman. She will arrive after winter break before I return.

I feel unbalanced without number one. Several high school classmates live on the upper floors of the dorm. They kindly stop by my room, which is just inside the lobby door on first floor. These girls are pleasant but do not linger. Like other first-year students, they established a circle of friends early in the semester. Rather than forcing my way into one of these groups, I continue being friendly but decide to enjoy the next few weeks alone.

However, what happens after winter break is unforgettable.

The smell of bleach and ammonia wafts through the lobby when I haul my laundry basket into Baird Hall. Sam the Sham and the Pharaohs belt "Wooly Bully" in the distance. The volume increases when I open the door to the first floor and realize the music is coming from my room. I peek.

Surprise! My new roommate has a stereo exactly like mine. Upon closer inspection, irritation replaces surprise.

"That's my stereo."

Startled, she turns with an infectious smile. "You weren't here. I didn't think you'd mind."

"Don't you have a stereo?"

"Not as nice as yours."

Her friendly chatter reveals the tight connections she has already forged with other early arrivals. They know nooks and crannies of the campus and have visited the popular college bars on Third Street.

"Come meet them. Let's go up to third floor." Her hand pulls mine away from unpacking. "That can wait." She drags me along like a little sister. We are giggling by the first landing.

Number two is a city girl from Milwaukee, pleasant enough but gregarious, especially compared to number one. She smokes. I am sure she did not read the Student's Handbook: dorm hours are monitored; boys are not allowed in girls' rooms. Every rule is a challenge. She does not shatter regulations but gets away with chips and cracks.

There are more parties and pranks. Your clean clothes disappear while you are in the shower. They are usually back in your dorm room, but streaking barefoot in a wet towel down a hall tracked with snow is chilling. Girls find soda crackers in their beds. Everything in your top drawer might be moved to your bottom and vice versa. I make a lot of friends. This is college life.

Late one night or early one morning, I wake to a flash of light from the hall and something being pushed between our bunks. "What's that?" I groan.

"I'm helping him through our window. It's too high to get him out on the third floor." Her whispers are hard to understand. I struggle to wake, then slam my eyes shut and feign sleep. I do not want to be a witness or confess to this smuggling.

"They wanted to see each other. Their friends had a party for them on third floor. They weren't doing anything. He leaves tomorrow. He enlisted."

I know the delightful couple and understand this good deed.

Enlist, the word sticks in my mind. There are no televisions in dorm rooms. A black-and-white portable plays in the lobby, but we seldom watch the news. I know the Vietnam War is happening on the other side of the world because some of my high school classmates signed up. Others received draft papers. Still, others chose to attend college to avoid the draft.

There is an antiwar protest in downtown La Crosse. News travels by word of mouth from downtown to the campus and through the dorm. Reactions range from proactive support to anguish or fear. I am glad I was not involved and keep jumbled thoughts to myself.

Friends frequent the college bars on Third Street. I tag along occasionally, but it is not my thing. That is because of David Dallmann, the skate boy from back home. My family calls him Dallmann to avoid confusing him with my brother David.

My boyfriend and I write weekly letters. Phone calls eat into my meager stash of coins, and conversations are public. Each floor of Baird has one pay phone mounted in the middle of the hallway. I must stand or sit on the drafty floor below the telephone while talking because the cords are short. Incoming calls are not possible.

On special occasions, Dallmann drives his new, red 1964 Ford Fairlane to La Crosse to pick me up for a weekend visit with my family in North Freedom. We giggle over a hug and quick kiss in the parking lot when he arrives at the beginning of spring break. My chatter about friends, work, and classes squeezes between his news from home, work, and family. Galloping through overlapping conversations makes talking while listening a challenge as we pack my things into the Ford.

David asks me to marry him that weekend. His proposal is serious and sincere. My reply is the same, but the giddy feeling inside of me is screaming and wild. We visit Goggin's Jewelry Store in Baraboo and look at engagement rings. Our plan is for me to return to UW-La Crosse in the fall and work toward my biology degree. He will continue work at the Ford dealership in Baraboo and save for a house.

I must return to the university Sunday evening. My work-study job allows me 40 hours of employment over spring break. I can use the money. Mom and Dad lend me their only car, a lavender and cream-colored Plymouth sedan with a pushbutton transmission. The dorms are closed, so I stay with Dad's cousin. Bernice and her husband Ole are empty-nesters and welcome me with open arms to their home south of the campus.

My funds dwindle as the semester ends. The scholarship will continue to cover tuition in the fall if I maintain my grades. But I need a summer job to pay for next year's room and board. Classmates talk about paid State internships in Madison. Some internships result in full-time positions after college. A summer job like that might allow me to transfer to UW-Madison in the fall. That university is half the distance from home compared to UW-La Crosse—closer to David.

An uneasy feeling wraps around me when I enter our farmhouse in North Freedom. I am home for the summer. It is May 1966. I turn 19 at the end of the month. My first year of college and the coveted work-study position ended yesterday. I need a job.

Last summer, I waitressed. I nannied the two summers before that. It's time to try something different, like being a summer intern for the state.

The arms of discomfort tighten when Mom says, "Badger's hiring because of the war. Why don't you apply?"

"I'm not working at the powder plant." My biting retort is left unsaid. Thoughts rumble through me. I have learned that my scholarship will transfer to other Wisconsin universities. It is time to broach the subject with Mom.

"My friends want to work as interns for the State this summer. So do I. May I use the car next week to go to Madison?"

My question catches Mom off guard. Her eyes betray her search for a response. "Let me talk with Dad." Mom's reaction is not surprising. She would prefer me to earn a wage rather than waste money on college. Her comment as I left for school last fall still stings.

I am amazed at how quickly Mom and Dad offer me their car. Is this a test?

Hired (1966)

Today is the day. My college friends have been coordinating their trip to North Freedom from Richland Center, 35 miles southeast of the village. Dad filled the car with gas before heading to the fields. Mom packed a Tupperware container of sugar cookies. She is anxious to meet my friends. I check the Madison city map one more time and jump when I hear gravel crunch on the drive.

My friends are apprehensive as they walk through the back porch of our farmhouse and into the kitchen. Where is their previous excitement about sharing an apartment and working for the State? Are they having second thoughts?

I introduce my classmates to Mom, who takes advantage of this last opportunity. "Why don't you stop by the powder plant? I hear they're hiring."

Eyes turn to me expecting a response that is not forthcoming.

I wonder why my mother keeps bringing up the ammunition plant. Doesn't she want me to be a state intern? Is she trying to keep me home by repeating what her father did to her? Mom was accepted to Platteville State Teachers College in 1943, but Grandpa Louie did not allow her to attend. She was an only child and he needed her help with farm work.

Our moods lighten when the girls see the lavender and white Plymouth. "I didn't know cars came in this color."

"My thoughts exactly when my parents brought it home. But it kind of grows on you."

We pile in, and I wheel the Plymouth out of the village.

The girls and I do not find work in Madison. Our arrival at the State office building without appointments is a problem. Conversations with registration people are not helpful. The girls admit they were already having second thoughts about spending money on an apartment.

The morning's bubble of anticipation deflates—flat as a pancake.

The quiet drive home takes us through Sauk City and past the small cemetery where SR 12 changes from two to four lanes. It's a short distance from there to the chain link fence securing the ammunition plant. The tall barrier continues four miles. It looks like a prison. I am embarrassed to bring up the subject. But I need a job.

"We're stopping here," I say, pulling off the highway toward the tall fence. "If I go home without work and tell Mom I didn't talk to these people, she won't let me use the car again."

"What is this place?"

"It's Badger Army Ammunition Plant. It was called Badger Ordnance Works, BOW, until three years ago. Most people call it the powder plant. It's a factory."

"What do they do?" The wary question comes from the backseat.

"They make gunpowder. It's reopening because of the Vietnam War."

The girls know nothing about the place.

"How do they make gunpowder? It sounds dangerous." My friends are bewildered.

"We don't need to know anything about gunpowder. We can apply for clerical jobs."

I am sure the Army will not offer us employment because we have no experience with manufacturing. Although I have clerical skills, how many secretaries would an ammunition plant need?

Mom's well-intended suggestion to stop at the plant grates on me. I don't like her telling me what to do. I do not want to work at Badger because of the Vietnam War. My parents brought me up to respect government leaders. But when our country sends soldiers, my classmates, to fight in this strange country so far away, it feels very wrong. Many people are objecting to our involvement.

I learned at home and in school that when you disagree with what government leaders do, you vote them out of office and elect different people. I am only 18 years old; 19 the end of this month. I cannot vote until I am 21.

Memories from childhood bombard me like current events. The ammunition plant was a topic of conversation in the early 1950s because Badger was operating in support of the Korean Conflict. Locals, including Mom, talked about hearing dishes rattle in cupboards. One loud boom was on July 19, 1945. Four men died that day when the Nitroglycerin Storehouse B exploded.

The day before I started grade school in 1953, Mom told me the father of one of my classmates died in the 1945 explosion. I think she realized that many of my classmate's parents, grandparents, and siblings worked at Badger. She preferred I hear about that sad event from her, not from someone at school.

I was over the moon about going to school and did not dwell on what Mom told me. However, I knew the boy and his family. Edwin "Eddy" Goff was my grade school classmate into high school.

Badger is part of my life: gunpowder, explosions, farmers forced from their homes. Living on a farm my entire life, I know firsthand how hard the people who lost their property on the Sauk Prairie worked for their livelihood. It was wrong for the government to take their land, not even for an ammunition plant to support World War II.

The topic came up often in my early years when neighbors got together. John and Elsie Shimniok owned the farm adjacent to my family's property in North Freedom. Before they lived next to us, John and Elsie had a farm on the Sauk Prairie until the government took it to build the ammunition plant.

John speaks of the cruel way he and 80 other landowners were treated. The government notified them in December 1941 that they had to be off their property by March 1, 1942—only two-and-a-half months to move during winter in Wisconsin.

Some landowners refused. But President Roosevelt issued an Executive Order on February 2, 1942, to seize their property.

"They gave us one dollar to make it legal," John remembers.

He and his brother Paul were among the majority who disagreed with the government's appraised prices. These landowners joined forces and hired a real estate lawyer. Ultimately, they each received more than the initial offer for their property. However, none received even partial payment until May 1942. Many were not paid in full until late 1944, when the war was almost over.

The Shimnioks, like other farmers, had to find a place to move their animals, machinery, equipment, and household goods in the middle of winter. At that time, they had received no money for the property they were forced to hand over to the government.

The family is in my thoughts when I turn off the highway.

Am I driving on land that was Shimniok's property?

Prairie flowers wave on tall stems and sturdy bull thistles with bulbous green heads, some bursting purple, brush under the car as I cross the expansive, overgrown parking lot of the ammunition plant. We stop by a plain-looking building with tan asbestos siding and a green shingled roof. An *Apply Here* banner sags from the eaves. An oversized hook and eye hold the open door in place.

Several men in white shirts and dark dress pants move authoritatively, like soldiers. One of them indicates we should sit in a row of straight-backed metal chairs with gray vinyl seats. A dozen men and women, all older than us, are already seated. The man grabs clipboards from the stack by the door. "Fill this out and give it back to me. Stay seated until you hear your name." The man's staccato voice matches his moves.

Glancing at each other, we stifle nervous giggles but quickly straighten up and complete the application forms. I slip copies of my high school and college transcripts under my paperwork and hand the clipboard to the man as he seats more people.

At tables in the far end of the room, three other men interview potential employees in muffled tones. I hear snippets of sentences, "rotating shifts...press house...acid...carpenters union." The words do not interest me. I quit straining to listen.

The spartan room has a faded poster of Uncle Sam tacked on one wall. The smell of musty, old dust fills the air. Pieces of notched wood prop open all the windows. One side of the room has no drywall, only studs. A warm breeze shuffles papers not weighted down. I expect to see people in military uniform. There are none.

"Carolyn Schroeder?" My name is a question. Startled, I sling my purse over my shoulder, tuck the folder of transcripts under my arm, and walk to the empty chair at the indicated table.

"What kind of job are you looking for?" the interviewer asks.

"I did clerical work at UW-La Crosse as Assistant Secretary to the Dean of Men. It's on my resume."

His eyes linger on my transcripts.

I prepare to get the boot.

"You have a strong science and math academic record."

"I'll be a sophomore in a biology program this fall."

"Would you be interested in a laboratory job?"

"Laboratory? I didn't know you had a laboratory."

"We have several. The powder lab is just opening. It might be a good fit if you're interested. We'll be hiring several laboratory technicians."

Thoughts whirl in my mind.

What does a laboratory technician do? Wear a white coat? Work in a sterile room? Peer into a microscope?

Lab work sounds more interesting than being a nanny or a waitress.

The man has my full attention when he says the job pays three dollars an hour. The wage is comparable to or better than anything

I dreamed of earning in Madison. The summer before, I earned seventy-five cents an hour plus tips for waitressing morning and lunch shifts in Wisconsin Dells. A waitress can earn two dollars an hour on busy days but rarely three. Many weekdays, it was tough to pass a dollar and a half.

Laboratory technician. It has a nice ring.

"When do I start?"

"It's all here. Report to this building for processing."

I tuck the envelope in my folder, unaware of the impact this day will have on the rest of my life.

The girls are downhearted. None received job offers. I say nothing about accepting a job in the powder lab.

My unexpected windfall soaks into me as we head to the farm. I hate to admit Mom was right. On the other hand, contemplating work as a laboratory technician feels good.

When I tell Mom I start work the day after Memorial Day, she is obviously pleased I am not moving to Madison. It's written all over her face.

David calls later that evening. "I'm as happy as your parents." I hear a smile in his voice.

"What do you think a laboratory technician does?" I question.

"I'll ask Dad and Grandma if they know lab people." David's father worked at Badger as a mechanic during the Korean Conflict. His grandmother also worked at the plant during the Korean Conflict and WWII. She was in rocket powder production. She told her grandson that employees she worked with suffered headaches caused by the product. Dave is relieved I am not working where his grandmother did.

My starting wage surprises him. "Maybe I should consider working at Badger."

His comment catches me off guard. "If you left the Ford garage to work at the plant and the war ended, we would both lose our jobs at the same time."

"I want to think about it," he adds. "But we could ride together if I worked at Badger." His comment settles me.

"Mom and Dad said I can use their car for a few days. But I'll have to find a ride with someone from the village soon."

"Can I pick you up tomorrow?" Dave asks. "How about six-thirty? We can go to the A&W and celebrate your new job. Maybe we'll drive out to Devil's Lake."

A feeling warms me. I want to feel his arms around me, but that will have to wait. We reluctantly hang up. I blow a kiss into the receiver.

The war is turning ugly. I hear it on the evening news and read it on the front page of the *Capital Times* and *State Journal.* My parents tell me seven of the eleven young men from my grade school class enlisted or were drafted. The war hits me like a sock in the gut.

Mom hands me last month's copy of the women's farm bulletin before trucking off to bed. I look at the recipe section to settle my thoughts before turning in for the night.

A historical article on the last page catches my eye. It is about the farmers living on the Sauk Prairie before the powder plant was built.

It's impossible to get away from rhetoric about Badger.

John and Elsie Shimniok's farm on the Sauk Prairie.
Image: Badger History Group, Inc.

First Day (1966)

The Sunday evening before I start work, my fiancé and I stop at the Dallmann farm on our way to the roller rink. His mother is cutting a rhubarb pie still warm from the oven. David pulls a gallon of Schoep's ice cream from the freezer and piles a double scoop on each plate. We discuss planting corn and tractor repairs around the early American-style table while we eat. Eventually, the subject turns to my new job.

"I lived on the Sauk Prairie before the powder plant was built." Harold, my fiancé's father, makes the statement like it's no big deal. It hits me like a ton of bricks.

"Our neighbors, the Shimnioks, lived on the prairie, too. The government took their land. What happened to your family?" I ask.

Harold explains, "Back in the 1930s, my father, Arthur, owned a farm across from the Valley of Our Lady Monastery on Old Bluff Trail in Sumpter Township. It was a half mile south of what became the main gate of the ammunition plant. That farmstead now belongs to a guy named Verlyn Mueller.

"When my dad, Arthur, got sick, we moved into Baraboo because he thought he was going to die. Uncle Charlie took over the farm. After a dentist pulled Dad's infected teeth, he recovered and wanted to return to farming. Charlie didn't want to let go of the property, so Dad rented a place on what would become Badger Ordnance Works."

My future father-in-law continues, "My brother, Donald, and I were just kids and went to school on the prairie. Two years later Dad bought a farm on the Old Lake Road south of Baraboo, and we moved."

Harold stops for a last bite of pie before he goes on, "Erhart Mueller farms in Sumpter and serves as the Sumpter Town Clerk; he's Verlyn's uncle. Erhart collects historical trivia and has written books about the prairie farmers and how the government took their property." Harold goes to the living room and returns with a green hardcover titled *Only in Sumpter*. "Mueller signed this book for us."

Stepping back in time, Harold opens the book and elaborates on one of the properties the government took.

Mrs. Ferdinand Magli is an elderly widow living alone. She is the first person the government men stopped to visit in the fall of 1941. They tell her she must leave her three-story, five-bedroom home with the lovely oak trim and sweeping staircase. Her husband, Ferdinand, and a hired man used crosscut saws to down the trees used for the building. His horses and a scraper dug the hole for the basement before they fashioned the cellar walls.

The men tell Mrs. Magli her house will become the headquarters of a massive powder plant. She does not believe them but soon hears the men have contacted others.

Only weeks after Mrs. Magli is forced to leave, her home becomes a temporary hospital for the plant. Dr. Howard Reed set it up after he left his practice in New York City. Within a short time, the medical equipment is removed, and the home becomes offices for contractors and Army personnel. Then, the office supplies are removed, and it again becomes a hospital. Mere months after the Army took the Magli home, it is no longer needed. They demolish it with bulldozers and burn the remains—collateral damage.

Mrs. Lewis Young, the Magli's daughter, lives a half mile away and witnesses the sad progression of events. She watches her parent's home, her childhood home, turn to ashes.

I want to hear more, but David is motioning me to hurry. Chully, the roller-skating rink manager, expects us to arrive on time. Harold insists I take the book. "Bring it back later," he says.

I speculate about Mrs. Magli's home and envision the powder lab while we fly around the wood floor of the skating rink. The two hours drag.

David knows I have an early work morning and cuts our goodbye short when he drops me at home. The Plymouth's car keys hang on their hook in the kitchen. Mom and Dad have retired.

I should sleep. But the book nags in my hand. Morning will come soon, but just a few pages won't hurt. While reading Mrs. Magli's story, I picture a 30-year-old Erhart Mueller kneeling by a console radio, taking in Franklin Delano Roosevelt's speech, declaring that his country is at war.

Considering the trauma of those days and the pain of the Shimnioks, my eyes fill with tears.

Trepidation suffocates me as I think of tomorrow.

In the morning, I descend the curves through the bluffs. Badger spreads south and east across the landscape as far as the eye can see, all the way to Lake Wisconsin.

Where is the powder laboratory in that vast expanse?

Nervous yet confident, I park by the building with the Apply Here banner. None of the men in white shirts and dark pants look familiar. And there are more of them. A young man sits at a desk by the door.

"I'm Carolyn Schroeder. I'm to report here today." The guy never looks up. "For work," I add. My confidence slips. I thought they would be expecting me.

"That changed. You need to go to the adjacent account." He continues writing.

"Sorry, I don't understand." Account? What's that?

He stops writing, looks directly at me, and points out the open window. "See that building? Go there."

"Thank you." My polite reply does not reveal my aggravation. A blush prickles up my neck to color my cheeks.

What a jerk. Why didn't he say that in the first place? He is young, about my age. His rude remark indicates he is unsure of himself.

This is my introduction to plant jargon. The accounting department maintains detailed records of everything the government owns at Badger, including construction costs for each building and its continued maintenance. These records are a resource throughout the history of the facility. The main accounts are known by number. Their function is mostly unnamed. For instance, we go to 200, not the Administration Building. Everyone, from tradespeople to lab techs to the janitor, knows 200 is the admin building. The powder lab is 2556.

Several deep breaths restore my composure. I open the door to the adjacent account and queue up, waiting my turn. The room looks eerily like the one next door.

"I'm Carolyn Schroeder. Reporting for work."

"What work did you apply for?"

"Laboratory technician." My confidence builds.

"Wait here and look this over." The man indicates a chair and hands me a small *Employee Handbook.* A legal-sized sheet of paper is folded into the back cover. It is a long list of do's and don'ts with associated repercussions. After reading for several minutes, I glance up. Everyone appears to know exactly where to go and what to do.

What have I gotten myself into? Is there a powder laboratory?

When he returns, the man explains that the lab is just opening, so my processing is taking longer.

"Do you have questions about that?" He points at the long list in my hand.

"Nothing yet." I pause, then add, "This room looks just like the building where I applied." Perhaps because I'm younger than other new hires and appear naïve, the man explains.

"Many of the buildings at Badger look the same, with tan siding and green-shingled roofs. The interior rooms are also similar. Most are painted the same two shades of green with a white ceiling.

"The Army minimizes construction costs by using the same materials at similar facilities nationwide. Most of the buildings at Badger were quickly constructed in the early 1940s to support WWII and meant to last ten years."

It's now 1966. No wonder things look so sad and decrepit. The Army surely updated the powder laboratory. *Didn't they?*

He pulls a separate copy of the long list I still hold and emphasizes a few of the more significant infractions. "No smoking is allowed within the facility. No smoking material is allowed within the facility. Termination is immediate and final for any employee breaking either of these rules."

Am I in the Army? It feels like it. But no one wears a uniform.

He continues covering general information. "You'll enter through the clock alleys for hourly workers. All employees pass by inspection stations just inside the alleys. Uniformed guards conduct random searches. If selected, guards look through your pockets, purse, lunch bucket, and any satchel you carry. Contraband is confiscated. Penalties for first, second, and third offenses for carrying contraband range from days off without pay to termination."

I want to leave. I'm just a kid. I shouldn't be here.

He drones on, "Cameras are not allowed within the facility. When needed inside the secure area, a camera requires a badge just like the person carrying it."

"Why can't someone have a camera at work?" I interrupt.

His eyebrows lift. Like he can't believe I asked such a question. Did I say something wrong?

"We work with gunpowder, explosives, and flammable material. The flash on a camera creates a spark, a significant safety hazard."

I knew that. Note to self—think before you speak.

His voice is patient, not condescending, as he continues. "Cameras are also a security risk. The Army does not want pictures of how our country manufactures ammunition available to the public, and they don't want those types of pictures falling into enemy hands."

Because of the camera rule, there are no candid or personal photographs of manufacturing or people inside the powder plant. The only pictures of work at Badger are those taken by the plant photographer for training or safety purposes or for the internal newspaper.

"Wear street clothes to and from work. You'll be issued lab clothes."

"What kind of clothes?" I am curious.

"I'm not sure. You're one of the first employees hired into that area. Since the powder laboratory is just opening, there's no information available. Pick up your clothes at stores."

Stores? I smile as I think about shopping the racks for my lab clothes.

"Lab people will take you through specific orientation. Go to the booth over there to get your badge. Check it and notify those folks of errors. Your employee number will be on the badge. That number is associated with your paycheck, insurance, and records at Badger. You need your badge on your person to get into work, throughout the day, and when you exit at the end of your shift."

I remember seeing rules about badges and penalties. None were good.

"Have a seat." A bright light flashes off the dome-shaped reflector around the bulb without warning. A short man wearing jeans and a plaid shirt hands me a piece of hard plastic. My picture, height, and weight are in bold type. H-14209 is the number that will identify me for over 23 years.

"Check it and wear it," Lenny says. His name is on his badge. He is the plant photographer.

I press the alligator clip and attach the badge to my blouse. Lenny points to an exit door.

Why do I need a badge? Is it to identify me in case the gunpowder, explosives, and flammable material blow me to smithereens?

I want to go home.

But I am curious.

The Dallmann farm was about a mile south of the Governor Phillips farm and Our Lady Monastery on Old Bluff Road. It was owned by David Dallmann's grandfather, Arthur Dallmann. Later owned by his great-uncle Charles. Still later, Verlyn Mueller, an employee at Badger and a relative of Erhart Mueller owned the property. (*Image:* circa 1930s. Dallmann family albums)

Mrs. Ferdinand Magli's home in Sumpter Township on the Sauk Prairie first became a hospital, then headquarters for Army and contractor personnel when construction of the powder plant began. (*Image:* As found in *Only in Sumpter* by Erhart Mueller, page 218)

Stores (1966)

I join a group of six new hires assembled in the morning sun. They are all older than me. I turned 19 last Friday, but I am just a kid compared to everyone at Badger. Some of my companions could be my parents; others are my grandparents' age. None of these people are going to the powder laboratory. Pleasantries are short. Apprehension floats in the uncomfortable silence as we wait for transportation to stores.

A long van pulls up. We pile in. The van's interior is cramped and stuffy. I hope it's a short ride because I am prone to motion sickness. The driver explains that processing people is bogged down. Everyone is a new employee, including those doing hiring and orientation.

We travel east then turn right before crossing the railroad tracks. Like an Army base, long tan buildings with green roofs parallel either side of the road. The driver stops at the far end of the structures and opens the sliding door.

"Will you be taking me to the powder lab?" I ask. I do not want to get lost in this strange place.

"You won't see me again today," the driver replies.

"How will I get to the lab?"

"Someone will stop by to drive you over. It's not far. Tomorrow, you'll take a bus from the clock alleys. They'll tell you."

Clock alleys? I've never used clock alleys. I feel like Alice falling down a rabbit hole.

Stepping into warm sunshine, I look back at the long building on the west side of the road. It appears to be a series of adjoined shops. Incrementally spaced signs indicate different trades: Carpenter, Pipefitter, Electrical, Paint, Riggers, and Plumbing. Opposite the trades building and to the east is a large open garage door. A sign next to the door says Stores.

This is not what I expected.

A high counter looms deep inside the building. A concrete floor large enough to park several pickup trucks stretches between the door and the counter. Two men behind the counter are assisting customers. Our little group strolls up behind them. A grandfatherly gentleman behind me answers my question about clock alleys while we wait our turn.

"It's easy," he says. "Just follow the crowd from the parking lot to the alley that alphabetically matches your last name. Your card will be in one of the slotted metal shelves. Take it and stick one end into the meter machine until you hear the click. Return the card to the correct spot. Everybody does it."

"What do you need, young lady?" the guy behind the counter asks. He wears jeans and a T-shirt.

"I'm not sure. I'm working in the powder laboratory."

"Not many folks have checked in for lab work. I'll have to ask." He dials the telephone.

Morning sun glares off the cement floor, reflecting heat into the cool building. Chicken wire fencing mounted behind the counter creates a barrier before what looks like a vast warehouse of shelves. A pungent chemical odor floats in the air.

Maybe I should reconsider and be a waitress.

"You need a lab coat. What size do you wear?"

"Size 12."

"Shoes, too. What size?"

"Eight, maybe bigger. I should try them on."

Answering these personal questions in front of strangers makes me squirm.

The man disappears behind the wire cage and returns with two putrid green lab coats. The heavy denim material resists as my arms push into the long sleeves. Lattice pockets on both sides of the garment are made of woven strips of fabric, creating openings that are two inches square. If you put coins into the pocket, they would fall to the floor. A handkerchief or anything personal could be seen through the holes. Why, I wonder? Sewing the lattice requires more time and money than regular flat pockets. Wasting time and money is not something the government does. But my question will wait.

The foreign aroma, more intense now, crinkles my nose. It reminds me of a new car when it is closed shut and sits in the sun—the smell becomes sickening.

Wrapped in green denim, I realize the obnoxious odor is coming from the lab coats. I anticipated chemical fumes from manufacturing processes. I did not expect them to be embedded in my protective clothing.

Three dollars an hour flashes in my brain.

Breathe through your mouth.

"The material is treated to repel harsh chemicals. The coats will protect you from acid splashes," the man explains. "They're also flame resistant. Don't take them home. Leave them at the lab at the end of your shift. Our laundry washes them onsite."

He plunks a pair of yellowish-brown oxfords on the counter. "Try these."

The shoes feel odd as I take several steps across the concrete. They are not pretty. And they do not feel like leather. The material is more like stiff cardboard that promises blisters. Wiggling my toes, I bend to feel where they hit at the front.

"They have steel toes," the man chuckles softly. His name is John, according to his badge. Another jerk.

"Should I keep these on?" My question is stoic.

"No. Wear your street shoes for now. They'll train you about your shoes at the lab." We look at each other, both knowing how uncomfortable the shoes are. Maybe John is not a jerk after all.

"I almost forgot. You need safety glasses. Do you wear a prescription?"

"No."

He hands me a pair in a clear wrapper. "There are splash guards." He takes the package from me, shakes two clear rounded pieces of plastic into his hand, and attaches the guards to the bows.

I wished I could wear glasses as a kid because they made my classmates look stylish. But when I hook them behind my ears, the lenses fog from humidity and sweat. The splash guards block the summer breeze from my eyes.

"Safety glasses are required here at Badger." John looks directly at me, checking how they sit on my nose. When satisfied, he finishes scribbling the list of the items issued to me on a form attached to a clipboard and hands it over for my signature.

When Badger closes at the end of the Vietnam War, I must return every item on the list or pay the cost unless I have paperwork to show its replacement or loss. That's one way the government accounts for their property.

Shoving the ugly lab coats under my arm and hooking my fingers into the heavy shoes, I say goodbye to John. The expanding throng of new employees now lines from the counter to the large open door.

What do I do now? I am about to turn back when I hear, "Someone going to the powder lab?"

My hand shoots into the air like I am on a deserted island, and an airplane appears in the sky. I slide into the pickup truck and stack my coats and shoes next to a young man my age plus a couple of years.

"Carolyn?"

"Yes, I'm Carolyn Schroeder. I'm supposed to go to the powder lab."

"That's where we're headed. I'm Jack."

"It's a relief to meet you, Jack. I live on a farm ten miles west of here but have never been inside the plant until now. I'm glad you know where to go." We drive past gas pumps, maintenance bays, and banks of compressed gas cylinders secured with chain link fencing. Then, we turn east and head deeper into the facility.

Bluebirds flit in front of the truck, beckoning us forward with their colorful dance. A meadowlark follows. More tan structures and green roofs appear in the distance.

"Everything looks the same," I wonder out loud.

"Buildings are identical on the inside, too," Jack says. Both the powder lab and the acid lab are opening. I don't always know which building I'm in," Jack laughs at himself. His light conversation and humor put me at ease. "The Army uses one floor plan for each type of building, not just at Badger but at other ammunition plants, too. Each floor plan is unique to the operation inside. This streamlines construction and maintenance, which minimizes costs. Also, process changes are more easily implemented at multiple facilities throughout the country."

"Where did you learn this?"

Jack explains that it was part of his orientation.

Why wasn't it part of my orientation?

I stifle my question and ask, "How long have you worked here?"

"I hired into the powder lab two weeks ago. I was a student at UW-La Crosse. Graduated with a degree in chemistry."

"I was at UW-La Crosse, too, in a biology program. I'll be a sophomore this fall."

I gawk as Jack drives. Pipes hang along and above the narrow, unmarked roads. Some pipes are small, others large and ominous as they spit puffs of steam like lazy dragons taking a snooze. The only identifying landmarks are the imposing brick powerhouse by SR 12, the railroad tracks, two white water towers, and the Baraboo Bluffs to the north. We see no people.

Powder Laboratory (1966)

Dancing brown eyes hide any apprehension Jack feels about working in this strange place. His carefree attitude reminds me of my brothers.

We approach a building with a freshly painted, neatly lettered wooden sign that says Powder Laboratory 2556. The structure is about 180 feet long with dirty, single-hung windows. Prairie grass and weeds grow through cracks in the cement parking lot.

"Here we are. Take your things."

The change from bright sunlight to the dark interior diminishes my vision. I stumble into Jack when he stops in the hall to glance at an official-looking black book with maroon binding. It lies open on a small, freshly painted shelf. Chips of the former green color lay in ancient dust on the floor.

Incandescent bulbs, some burned out, cast dim light. A superficial sweep of dirt and grime is evident. The grunge remains. We are alone in what appears to be a deserted building. This is not the pristine atmosphere I expected.

Is this a lab?

Maybe Jack stopped at the wrong building. He is a new employee.

Should I be scared?

Three dollars an hour. Remember, three dollars an hour.

The black book is the operations log for the powder lab. Supervisors check it at the beginning of their shifts and document significant happenings during work hours. Like Pavlov's dogs, they look at it every time they enter the building.

There will be many similar books over the next eight years. We use these and green hardcover workbooks to document testing procedures, variables, and results.

A quick left down another hall takes us between banks of drab Army green lockers. Three at the far end have names written on masking tape stuck at the top. Jack stops at a nameless door. "Put your things in here and find some tape." I toss my shoes inside and pile my lunch bag and coats on the high shelf. Tape must wait. Jack is far ahead.

At the end of the hall, two desks sit askew in a corner room filled with late morning sunshine. Dusty shafts of light stream through windows filled with cobwebs. A black rotary telephone sits on one desk in the otherwise vacant space. Soon, two secretaries will occupy this office.

Jack nods at a closed door as he drags in a straight-backed metal chair with a gray vinyl seat. "You may wait here. Mr. Thiede will be out shortly." He disappears as mysteriously as he appeared at stores. I stand alone between the desks.

The office has broad views to the east and south. Open fields of prairie grass sway all around. Red-winged blackbirds grip sturdy, tall stalks. 200 yards to the east, a light green van drives on the opposite side of three small garage-like structures. It parks by a larger building on the same road. A red fox scampers from a ditch beside the van and bounds toward the lab on a walking path between the two buildings. Its den has likely been disturbed by recent human activity.

To the south, the building ends at a large parking area surrounded by low shelters, like little carports. Further south and beyond a crossroads are impressive, two-story buildings sitting side-by-side as far as I can see. Pipes both large and small, snake in, out, and alongside these structures.

Bored, I look back down the hall. A long room is visible. I didn't notice it earlier because it is behind a bank of lockers. Inching my chair forward reveals half a dozen young men, including Jack, sitting around tables piled high with books and ledgers. They are recent college graduates with degrees in chemistry, learning the procedures for testing gunpowder.

These young chemists receive a deferment from military service because they work at Badger. Soon, they will be assigned to a rotating shift to supervise laboratory technicians. Most lab techs will be women, old enough to be their mothers or grandmothers—others, young enough to be their wives.

Many young men enlisted or were drafted into the military. Skilled men work out of the many trade shops at Badger. Others work beside women on production lines. Some of those men are supervisors who, from stories I have heard, only observe. A few hazardous tasks are assigned solely to men.

Before WWII, women were considered too fragile for production work. However, with most eligible men fighting the war, management reluctantly assigned previously designated male jobs to women. The 1940s launched the era of Rosie the Riveter. Women proved they were as capable as men to work in production.

Most women I know farm alongside their husbands. They operate machinery during harvests and do animal chores in barns or corrals. Their strong hands and arms show muscles and veins just like their male counterparts'. I wonder if production work is more challenging or physical than farm work.

Because of access restrictions at Badger, I never see the entire manufacturing process. Most employees don't. However, I learn that production involves mixing small batches of cotton linters or wood pulp with acids, water, and solvents to make propellant, gunpowder. Production line supervisors send samples of these small batches to the powder lab, where technicians break down the material and test it.

The small batches appear the same when we log them into the lab. However, they vary because of the way they are put together.

Supervisors and engineers study test results before directing line workers to blend the small batches into final government lots. The physical *blending* of batches is as critical as the powder's *chemistry* in the manufacture of propellant.

The powder lab tests final government lots to confirm the propellant meets Army specifications. Lastly, the velocity of each final lot is tested at the ballistics lab with a gun chronograph to ensure the propellant fires as it should when used by our soldiers in the field or for training.

The door opens, and Bob Thiede steps out of his office. He is about my height and of average build. Coarse gray sprinkles his short, dark hair. The yellow hard hat under his arm contrasts his white shirt and black pants. Thick lenses make it difficult to see his eyes, but when ours meet, I feel he wonders why I am sitting alone outside his office.

A different, slightly older Jack appears as if on command. His feet shift in an awkward dance as he formally introduces me to the lab manager. I later learned that Jack Two is supervisor to Jack and the other young chemists. Two leans towards his boss, anticipating his next important assignment.

"Nice to meet you," Thiede says to me.

"Get on with her orientation," he tells Jack Two and strides down the hall. A forlorn look melts across Two's face.

I am sure the lab manager does not remember my name. He probably did not remember most new hires' names because he meets many employees daily.

In the future, Mr. Thiede will don his spanking-clean green lab coat and walk through testing rooms doing white glove inspections. Counters and workspaces are seldom clean enough to pass such scrutiny, especially when production ramps high and hundreds of samples come into the lab daily. Deadlines trump clean counters on those busy days.

Windows are propped open during the hot summer as well as during cool, even cold, weather. The lab is overly warm due to heating apparatuses used for testing. Brownish-gray coal smoke from the powerhouse pours in year-round because production requires steam. It becomes so thick some days, it takes your breath away. It leaves a gritty black residue on every surface. Mr. Thiede understands this but expects his employees to run the cleanest lab possible.

Jack Two, perturbed at his new assignment, picks up the phone and meekly says, "I have a new hire—yes, to do an orientation—well, okay, as soon as you can."

He does not talk like a supervisor. I wonder who is at the other end of the line.

"Where do I find masking tape?" I ask. His face sinks lower. He does not know.

Minutes later, a wisp of a woman in her 50s flies like a hummingbird into the room. "I'm Verna. Do you have a lab coat? Shoes? You won't need that." She points at my purse. Verna is an old-timer who worked at Badger during WWII and the Korean Conflict.

"My locker…"

Verna cuts me off with a turn and heads down the hall. She is short, tiny, and very fast. "It's here," she adds.

I notice the locker next to mine has her name on it.

"I need masking tape, but Jack…" She raises her hand, halts my request.

Verna rolls her eyes and pulls a small roll from her lattice coat pocket.

What a Boy Scout.

This woman commands respect. She knows more about Badger than Jack Two. That's why Jack Two talked to her the way he did. He's afraid of her.

Verna's instructions snap my thoughts.

"You must wear your shoes, coat, and glasses while you work in the lab. Put them on when you arrive and leave them in your locker at the end of your shift. If you go out in the area, wear a hard hat. They hang on hooks at the north end of the hall."

I coax the stiff material of my coat into place and roll the long sleeves above my wrists while Verna's foot taps impatience.

"Don't roll those too high. You want that coat to protect you," she says. I copy Verna's sleeves.

As my feet settle into the ugly shoes, those spots where they already left their mark are noticeable. Steel resists my toes. I wish I had stashed Band-Aids in my purse. I didn't know then that personally treating work-involved injuries is unacceptable; this includes Band-Aids for blisters. It is one rule I ignore.

"Step on the conductivity meter," Verna commands. "The needle must be in the correct range before you start work. Debris builds up on the soles and makes your shoes ineffective. Scuff your feet on the dry floor if that happens and try again. If the needle still points out of range, pick up a new pair at stores." I make a mental note to avoid breaking in new shoes.

Verna continues, "It's critical that stray voltage doesn't build up and cause a shock because the resulting tiny spark around powder and flammables could be disastrous." Being a farmgirl, I understand stray voltage or sparks can start a fire in hay or cause an explosion in a dusty grain bin.

"We're going to the government lab," Verna explains as she takes off down the hall. I race after her. The young men studying in the room behind the lockers are a blur.

"Do we need hard hats?" I holler as she flies out the door.

"No, only when you leave the lab area."

We are on a makeshift walk of broken asphalt to an adjacent building. A huge pipe hangs so low over this path that even Verna must duck to avoid bumping her head. The size of the support beams holding the pipe rivals that of hundred-year-old oaks. Verna disappears in tall grass and bull thistles, already shoulder high and swaying in the breeze.

HISS. Mist from a steam release sinks into my coat, warm and moist on my back. A startled scream sticks in my throat; no noise comes out. I bolt toward Verna, who is holding the door, waiting for me.

Three dollars an hour, I remind myself. Three dollars an hour.

"Government auditors use the north and east wings of this lab. We don't go there. We use the south half," Verna explains. The floor plan is exactly like the powder lab.

A decade of dust lays thick on either side of the hall floor. Footprints track down the center. Spiders skitter deftly into the darkest corners when we pass their home. They live in layers of old webs attached from walls to floor. I glance at the ceiling. No spiders. Only two working bulbs provide dim light.

"The riggers just unlocked this building. They'll clean it tomorrow," Verna tells me.

Creepy. I want to leave. Now.

Three dollars an hour.

A hinge screeches to a flash of outside light. BANG. A door hits a wall. My heart skips a beat. I follow Verna when she turns into a room where a slightly built woman named Donna hefts two wood carriers that were fashioned onsite by trade workers. Each carrier holds six quart-sized Ball mason jars full of dark gray gunpowder.

I first think Donna is a man. I never saw a woman wear a hard hat before. She is also an old-timer, albeit younger than Verna. She worked during the Korean Conflict. Protruding muscles in Donna's tan arms indicate the carriers are heavy. She is strong despite her size and used to physical work.

"Time for lunch," Donna pipes up. Verna starts pulling jars from the carriers.

I am torn between the two women.

"This can wait," Donna adds pointedly. Verna continues placing samples on the counter.

"I'm Donna." Her hand reaches for mine in a friendly gesture. Her grip is firm.

"Carolyn Schroeder," I reply.

"I hope you brought something for lunch. We get 30 minutes and can't leave." Donna heads for the door but looks back when I do not follow. "The lunchroom is in the powder lab," she explains. I follow, but only after Verna nods approval.

As we duck under the hissing pipe, we spot Jack Two ushering a middle-aged woman carrying her shoes and green coats into the lab. I see the woman bump into him when he stops to check the operations log.

Donna and Verna (1966)

Donna's brown eyes twinkle. "I'll grab my lunch and meet you." She's gone in a flash.

The brown paper bag in my locker is flat. I find it squished against my second lab coat.

Donna sits on a high stool in the first lighted room down the hall. She is already eating. Her hardhat is perched beside her on a stool of its own. The tall table is two massive wooden squares shoved together. I situate on another high stool and pull a soggy sandwich and crumbled cookies on to brown paper toweling. Donna frowns at my food. "There's a refrigerator in the corner for your lunch."

Ignoring her comment, I inquire, "Is Verna coming?"

"Probably not. She doesn't usually eat with us." She rolls her eyes, emphasizing *us*. I do not ask questions.

Donna tells me her husband manages the Sauk Prairie Airport. The runway is in their backyard. They do not have children. Her conversation is interesting. Her laugh contagious. "I want to be on D shift," she says. "Have you heard anything?"

"No." Her question catches me off guard. "How long before that happens?" I ask.

"Which supervisor do you want to work for?" Donna answers my question with a question. I think she's fishing for information I do not have.

"I've only met Jack. He picked me up at stores."

"Ah, the cute one." Donna's right. Jack is more cute than handsome. Someone fun to be around, same as Donna.

"Where do those guys eat?" I am curious.

"In the room next to Thiede's office. Verna eats back there, too. At a separate table."

"What's D shift?" I naïvely ask.

"The plant runs 24/7. No interruptions. Three shifts each work eight hours while one is off. They're A, B, C, and D. They rotate weekly. Days off move every rotation," Donna explains.

"What about weekends?"

"Your days off usually fall in the middle of the week. They're on Saturday and Sunday every seven to eight weeks."

I do not respond as I absorb this information. I'll never see David, my family, or my friends.

"Go back to the government lab when you finish. I'll catch up." Donna tosses the remains of her lunch in the garbage, grabs her hard hat, and runs after the young men headed out the door.

I wonder where Donna and the men are as I walk under the hissing pipe. Verna has logged the samples and is arranging them next to a lead sink when I arrive. "Your first job is to dry ball powder."

Minutes later, Donna bangs through the outside door, smiles, grabs the carriers, and heads for the pickup truck. A faint odor lingers in her wake.

"She went out for a smoke with the supervisors," Verna explains, even though I did not ask. "The men drive to 200, the administration building, for a quick cigarette after lunch. Donna tags along when she can. The guys dropped her off on their way back." I don't comment. Unlike Verna, who is all business, Donna is more complex.

"We set the samples in chronological order." Verna barks orders like a little Colonel as she demonstrates. "Their numbers are on the chains of custody wired to the jars. Remove the first chain of custody and place it in front of the first receptacle." Six metal cylinders sit in front of six receptacles hanging inside a hood.

Verna deftly transfers the sample from a jar to the first cylinder using a spatula. I see fine mesh at the bottom. This ball powder only slightly resembles the gray grains my family uses for hunting. It hangs in wet clumps to the sides of the jar and emits a solvent smell. Verna shoves the sample into the first receptacle and clamps it in place.

She talks as she works. "Badger adds acids to paper or cotton material to make explosives. Solvents and water are added during the manufacturing process. We must remove that liquid before testing." I like how Verna explains what we do and why each task is essential.

"Don't rinse propellant down the sink. Cleaning a drain plugged with gunpowder is messy and dangerous. The plumbers don't like it." She uses a jug labeled *Tap Water* to rinse powder from the spatula and jar into a waste powder bucket lined with black plastic conveniently placed at our feet.

"Do your work over this large tray. It makes cleanup easier. Ball powder flies all over when it's dry." She hands the spatula to me.

I remove the second chain of custody and place it on the counter in front of the second receptacle. The spatula, awkward in my hands, slips. A clump of grains splats on the tray. Verna rolls her eyes.

After I clamp the sixth receptacle under the hood, Verna lowers the sash and flips the switch, which starts the blowing of warm air through the cylinders.

The six chains of custody laying on the counter are wired to six clean jars and placed, in order, in front of the hood while the samples dry. "If sample custody is broken or lost, sample results are meaningless," Verna stresses the point as she transfers the first dry sample to its corresponding jar. I do the other five.

"Cleanup is done with water, brushes, and brooms." A long handheld brush with four-inch bristles hangs on a nail head beside the sink. "Sweep powder from the counter and floor to the dust-pan and dump it in the waste powder pail down here." Verna's steel toe bumps the small, galvanized bucket. "Add water each time the plastic bag is changed. Powder doesn't burn or explode when it's wet."

"Where's the vacuum?" I ask.

Verna shoots me a look that means "dumb question," but does not state the obvious. "There are no vacuum sweepers. First, they need to be plugged in. Conventional plugins create a spark and are not allowed. A no-spark adapter must be installed when equipment requires an electrical hookup. Second, sucking gunpowder, an explosive, into a bag, especially if the bag is inside a metal container, is like making a pipe bomb. A bag full of gunpowder could do serious damage."

I should have known that.

I find supervisors and experienced coworkers open and receptive to questions. If they do not know the answer, they find someone who does. Most employees know specifics about their tasks and work area. Few, if any, know the entire operation for several reasons. First, the facility is expansive. Access to the over 1,400 buildings is restricted. The second is security. The government does not want firsthand knowledge of how our country makes gunpowder available to the public. Another reason is safety. Unique safety rules apply to each work area. Employees are not allowed out of their work area for their well-being. Consequently, they learn little about what is happening in the rest of the plant.

"You need a driver's license," Verna blurts out of the blue. "One of the men will draw up paperwork."

"I already have a driver's license." *How young does she think I am?*

"Yours doesn't allow you to drive inside the plant. You need a plant license. There's a written test. They'll tell you." Verna is serious. "Not many people are allowed to drive inside Badger." I do not ask questions because it sounds like having a plant license is a privilege.

"Most employees clock in, change into provided work clothes, and board an assigned bus that takes them to a building where they spend eight hours. The bus arrives at the end of their shift and returns them to their change house. Buses drive the same routes each shift. Most employees see only that part of the facility along their route the entire time they work at Badger. The number of vehicles is minimized because hazardous material is constantly moved between buildings via narrow gauge railroads, trucks, or mules, those small, motorized tractors."

Does she explain this to each new hire? Or does she think I am exceptionally naïve because of my age?

This hood was used to dry ball powder. Notice the three no-spark electrical outlet receptacles on the left, the large tray on the counter, and the stud/slat partition board walls in the background. (*Image:* Badger History Group, Inc)

Screens (1966)

Verna plows on, never coming up for air. "Next, we screen the powder." She has a stack of eight round, ten-inch metal screens. Each is an inch deep. The mesh of individual screens is incrementally smaller from the top of the stack to the bottom. "The purpose of this physical test is to measure the surface area of each sample of ball powder. Surface area affects the sample's burn rate."

Memories of general science and geometry flashed in my head. "Are we looking for the diameter of the grains in each sample?" I ask.

A smile tugs Verna's mouth. She realizes that I understand basic math. I think she is the interface between supervisors and new hires. I wonder if she is why I qualify for a plant driver's license.

Verna pours a small cup of ball powder onto the top screen and covers it. SWISH. Tiny grains slip-slide through the mesh.

"We clamp it on the shaker-pounder machine." She demonstrates, then flips a switch. The deafening banging of metal against metal ensues for five minutes. When it stops, she sets the stack next to a double beam balance. "Have you used one of these?"

"I saw my chemistry teacher use one, but the pans were smaller. The object goes on one pan, then weights are added to the other until the needle between them stops at the center." I am thrilled to be using something I learned in high school chemistry. I wish I could tell Mr. Felmlee.

Verna points to a testing workbook, showing me her notes from calibrating the balance earlier in the morning. She points to the letters *VH* next to the record. "You must initial everything you write in workbooks." I make another mental note of Verna's instructions.

"Readings are written in the space next to the corresponding screen. Let me see you weigh the top one."

With the heavy screen on the left pan, I pick up the sturdy tweezers and reach for a medium-sized weight. Verna stops me. "They're heavier than that." She points to the biggest. After I position the cumbersome weight on the right pan, I add smaller weights until the needle is close to the center. It is excruciatingly slow to settle.

"Moving air keeps the needle moving." Verna closes both doors into this closet-sized room partitioned off the hall. It has no windows. "See, now it's still." I record the numbers and proceed.

Gary, a supervisor, taps on the window in the door and waits until Verna nods. The middle-aged lady from earlier and a young woman wedge into the small room. "Audrey and Sandy are new techs. Get them started." He nods at Verna and retreats without entering.

We turn simultaneously, when Donna barges through the outside door, hoisting another heavy load. "D Line wants me back immediately," she hollers. She logs in the twelve samples and leaves.

Now, what do we do? I feel like we're in the chocolate factory with Lucy and Ethyl.

"Carolyn, you show these ladies how to dry samples. I'll take over weighing. I'm in here if you have questions." Verna hustles us out of the stuffy little room and closes the door.

How did Verna do this?

Adrenaline, or fear, kicks in. I start my first training spiel. "We sort the samples chronologically by the numbers on the chains of custody." I demonstrate as I talk. "Set the first chain of custody next to the first cylinder." I am sure Verna is listening through the thin wall of partition board separating the two rooms.

Concentrate. Do not make a mistake.

"Transfer the sample with the spatula." I feel myself becoming Verna when I hand the spatula to Audrey. Her moves are awkward. A clump of grains splats on the tray. I do not roll my eyes.

Audrey and Sandy grasp the nuances of drying powder and keeping numbers straight before Donna returns with another 12 jars. "These are the last for today," she announces as she scribbles in the logbook. She does her quick introduction, grabs a second spatula, and jumps into the action.

Verna barks at me, "Start another screen test and fasten it to the shaker-pounder. Then go back to weighing." The afternoon flies as we become comfortable with our tasks.

Audrey is from a small town west of the plant. "I was working at the county farm. I hated to leave those people. Many residents consider me their family," Audrey's voice quivers. She did not need to explain the Sauk County Home. The facility, west of North Freedom, cares for people who have nowhere else to go.

Sandy pipes up, "After high school, I started waitressing at a café in Reedsburg. That was two years ago. The money here is a lot better. I thought I'd be on a manufacturing line."

Ten samples remain next to the sink at the end of the day. Others are dry and wait for the screen test. Verna delivers one last command, "We start here tomorrow." We do not roll our eyes at the obvious.

Shrugging off the heavy lab coat, I lean against my locker to untie the ugly footwear. One sock sticks to my skin. Blood. A blister burst above my heel. Toes wiggle freely, happy to be in canvas tennis shoes.

My first day was not what I expected.

Verna's words echo as I drive back to the farm. I want to live up to her example. It is not a pristine job. But it is precise work. The variety makes time fly. Will I learn more tests tomorrow?

Mom is inquisitive. I think she wishes she would have had such an opportunity. The farm got in her way. I share a bit with her but hold back details.

Later, my phone call with David is a play-by-play. Mom likely hears most of it. Our only phone sits on a tall shelf in the centrally located dining room of our farmhouse.

"Verna Hackett was my trainer. She knows a lot about the plant."

"I know her sons. She had her hands full when they were at home."

"I pity anyone that crosses her," I laugh, thinking of Verna as a little general keeping her boys in line.

"Donna mentioned shift work."

"When does that start?" my fiancé asks.

"I don't know. No one else talked about it. She wants to be on D shift."

"Why?"

"She didn't say. Donna left with the supervisors. There's a place where smoking is allowed. They must inhale the whole thing in one breath because they were not gone long."

We are reluctant to hang up. However, it is getting late, and morning comes fast.

Satisfied with my first day, sleep comes quickly. In dreams, my mind repeats the rhyme of the lab until the morning alarm interrupts.

After clocking in, drivers sort us into buses for our short ride. Heat and humidity increased overnight. My lab coat blankets my body. The broken blister under the Band Aide burns like fire. Steamy mist greets me as I duck under the ominous pipe over the path to the government lab.

I find Audrey transferring a sample. Donna heads out the door with the carriers—no Verna. There is not a breath of air, so the doors to the balance room are both open when I start weighing screens. Perspiration fogs my safety glasses in the stillness.

It could be worse, I remind myself. *Three dollars an hour.*

When Verna arrives, she first peers over Sandy's shoulder then Audrey's. The little general checks my workbook and leaves. No orders.

Donna returns with more samples. "Break time. We get 15 minutes," she exclaims before rushing toward the powder lab.

In the lunchroom, Donna stuffs a doughnut in her mouth and follows the supervisors out the door. Sandy and Audrey raise their eyebrows. I explain what just happened over coffee. Sandy is curious, but I cannot answer her questions.

Room three, next to the lunchroom, is the only air-conditioned part of the lab. Yesterday, I met Don Peterson, who works with instruments in the cool room. He is another old-timer from the Korean Conflict. The girls and I stroll by the first of the cool room's two swing doors, hoping for relief from the heat. Feeling none, Sandy jumps ahead and gives the second door a hefty shove. We freeze, soak up the refreshing air, giggle, and rush toward the exit as Don shoots an eagle eye in our direction.

Our routine remains unchanged until the following week.

Cute Jack is waiting in the lab when our bus drops us at the door. "Carolyn, we need you in prep. You too, Audrey," he says.

We hear laughing and talking echo from down the hall as Jack ushers us to the south end of the powder lab. "These ladies will show you what to do." Eight new hires sit in little groups around a high table. They are cutting grains of smokeless powder, single base, with scissors. The grains look like the extruded rabbit pellets my brothers fed to their bunnies on the farm.

Audrey knows Anne, and introductions begin. Anne hands us a quart jar of smokeless and two small pans. The ladies smirk as we grab the last two scissors. "They're dull. You'll get blisters." Audrey and I look at each other and laugh along with the others. We are now the new people—stuck with crappy scissors. The grains, little extruded cylinders, each have seven holes through them. *Why?*

The ladies groan when a production worker sets two dozen incoming quart jars of smokeless on the table. Then chuckle. The atmosphere in this room is different from the government lab's quick, organized pace. It is a coffee klatsch without coffee.

The ladies range in age from 20 to 60 and act like they have been friends for years. They are discussing previous employment, families, recipes, aches, and pains.

The reason we are here is not mentioned. The war is not discussed.

Like me, maybe these new hires have been so busy learning tasks over the past week that they have not had time to think about the war.

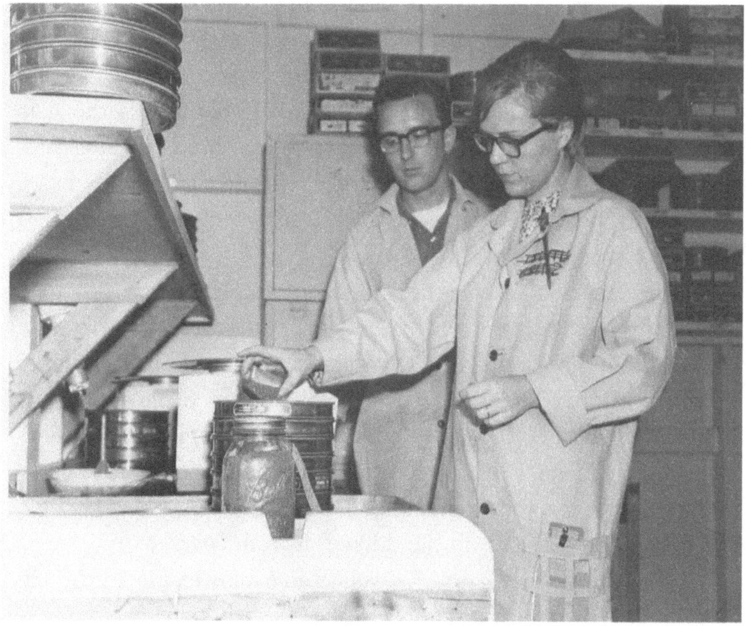

Lab technicians perform a screen test to determine surface area. The woman transfers ball powder from the Ball mason jar into the top of a stack of eight screens. Studs, slats, and partition board walls show in the background. Notice the technician's badge attached to the lattice pocket of her lab coat. (*Image:* Badger History Group, Inc)

D Shift (1966)

Anne and Audrey cautiously eye the six thick, flat sheets of bright orange material on the cutting room table when we return from lunch.

"What's this?" Anne asks.

Verna appears like the genie conjured from the magic oil lamp. "That's rocket powder from a cut and slitter house," Verna says with authority. Gary stands next to her. He is wearing latex gloves.

"Could I have your attention?" He speaks like he is trying to calm his nerves.

"Samples of rocket powder will come from the production area in two forms: flat sheets like these from process lines and chunks of finished grains. Both are bright orange."

"This is a chunk of a grain of rocket powder." A piece of solid material fits in the palm of Gary's gloved hand. It is the size and color of an orange. "Whole grains are three feet long and two-and-a-half inches in diameter. There's an eight-pointed star through the center. They're used to launch rockets from ground artillery and helicopters."

He glances at Verna, seeking her approval. Her nod encourages Gary to proceed.

"All gunpowder is primarily nitrocellulose and nitroglycerin with a few added plasticizers and stabilizers. Smokeless is mostly nitrocellulose. Ball powder is ten percent nitroglycerin. Rocket powder is 33 percent nitroglycerin. This combination makes rocket especially dangerous to handle," Gary looks at the orange chunk covering the palm of his hand like it is from Mars.

"Nitroglycerin is a drug, as well as an explosive. Doctors use it to treat certain heart conditions," he speaks like he is reciting a learned script. Several ladies nod.

Verna intercedes. "A person taking this drug places a tablet under their tongue instead of swallowing it. It's absorbed into your system faster through skin than the digestive tract."

Gary regains control of the narrative. "Always wear gloves when handling rocket powder. Change your gloves often. Nitroglycerin permeates latex as well as skin."

He sets two boxes of gloves on the table. "We have non-latex for anyone that's allergic. Dispose of used gloves in the waste powder pails."

"Any questions?" Gary asks.

"Can it blow up? I saw NG on television." Anne's worried look is shared.

"I asked a similar question," Gary admits. "All gunpowder is dangerous if you don't follow procedures. Handle it correctly, and you'll be fine."

Verna cannot help but interject. "Wear gloves whenever you touch rocket powder. And change your gloves often. Every couple of hours."

"What happens if I don't change my gloves?" A small voice comes from the far side of the table. Nancy was hired in yesterday.

Gary answers. "You may get a headache."

"We called them NG headaches. They're nasty. I know from experience," Verna adds.

"More questions?" Gary asks.

The room is strangely quiet.

"Is he exaggerating?" Anne asks after Gary leaves.

"No." Verna's response is quick and firm. "Follow directions. Wear gloves when handling rocket powder, and you'll be fine. I started picking up samples in the early 1940s during WWII. I dried, cut, and ground gunpowder. Did every test. I worked through the Korean Conflict. There were no explosions in the lab." Verna's eyes flash directly at Anne.

I think Verna has recently educated the young supervisors about handling gunpowder. Gary is nervous because he has learned about the chemistry of our products at university. That chemistry conveys danger. Verna has years of experience handling gunpowder at the ammunition plan. She has confidence in the manufacturing and testing processes designed to mitigate danger and keep employees safe.

I think of our farm. People from our village fear equipment used to plant and harvest crops. Farmers are not afraid of these machines or activities because each generation trains the next about how to use the equipment and prevent injuries.

Verna respects the young supervisors. The respect is mutual. I have picked up on how the young men make a statement and then look to her for approval.

We cannot cut the thick round grains of rocket powder with scissors. They are the consistency of a tire. A guillotine reduces rocket and big smokeless grains into smaller pieces. Anne shows me how to lock the long slicing arm of the guillotine in an upward position and place grains in the dies. When released, the arm easily pulls down until the integrity of the grains resist the heavy, broad blade. Circles shave off when the outer surfaces break. We cut, then grind these circles to a smaller size in a Wiley mill because they are too large for testing.

Cute Jack interrupts our cutting and walks five of us to the room next door. "We're out of clean sample jars. The Ball Mason Company wasn't expecting huge government orders. The next shipment is three weeks out."

Unwashed quart jars line the long counter on both sides of a wash sink. Four three-tiered metal carts are also stacked. Spider webs from the Korean Conflict, maybe even WWII, cling inside some of the cloudy glass.

"People on the production lines are too busy to continue washing jars," Jack adds. "It's our job now. Get 25 into the drying oven for the night shifts. Here's the wash protocol." Jack lays a piece of paper in a protective plastic sleeve by the sink.

Our assembly line follows the steps listed for washing, rinsing, and drying.

In exuberance, Sandy splashes Anne. Anne splashes back. We all jump into the sloppy action. Everyone is soaked through their lab coat after eight hours. But there are enough clean jars for the night shift and the next day.

Most new hires are sent directly to wash and cutting rooms because they need little training for these labor-intensive tasks. Natalie, a new tech, had been driving school bus. She is old enough to be my mother. She and Sandy are instigators in the wash line. They initiate new hires by christening them with subtlety directed squirts of suds. Feigning innocence, they blame me or another tech.

Natalie blows her cover when laughter spurts through pursed lips. Her hand covers her mouth, too late.

Sandy has weaseled herself under Donna's wing. They squeeze beside supervisors in the van for a smoke during morning break. Natalie plays the role of mom to the young lady. "Why are you doing that? It's not good for you. You're such a pretty girl," she makes her point good-naturedly.

Sandy's eyes twinkle. Her face lights up. She grabs the half-eaten doughnut from Natalie's hand and skedaddles out the door after the men.

After lunch, Audrey is the first to ask, "What's the meeting about?" The notice was posted on the chalkboard while we ate.

"I heard we're starting shift work," Sandy announces. I think the supervisors told her.

Over 20 people are in the lunchroom at three that afternoon. Jack Two reads from a list. He mentions wet chemistry work and titration tests being brought online. He stresses safety.

"New signs posted at every door show the maximum number of people and pounds of propellant allowed in each room. Anyone exceeding those limits is subject to having a letter issued to their permanent record. Supervisors, as well as safety inspectors, and government auditors will be monitoring."

Jack Two drones on.

"All work-related injuries must be reported. A plant doctor is at the hospital during the day. There's at least one RN plus other nurses working every shift.

"Wear gloves when handling NG. We've already had one headache reported."

"Shift work starts next week. Stop in the office if you need a specific shift. Otherwise, you'll be randomly assigned. Helen, the secretary here, can help you." An older lady with silver gray hair and a conservative navy dress nods with a smile. The room is abuzz.

Natalie winks at me, her hand over her mouth. Donna pokes my ribs. Her arm links with Sandy's. Four of us follow Helen toward her office, leaving the others behind.

D shift works from midnight to eight in the morning beginning the following Wednesday. Switching from day to night work is strangely disorienting. Natalie and Donna are already on the dimly lit bus when I arrive. Sandy jumps on last.

Cute Jack, our supervisor, is in the lunchroom when we arrive. Donna and Sandy are not subtle. They tell him they want to ride upfront with him for smoke breaks. He does not respond to their request as he awkwardly assigns work. It is obvious, he has never managed people.

The smokers stay in the powder lab. Natalie and I are off to dry powder and weigh screens next door.

Natalie's husband is a major with the 115th Fighter Wing of the Air National Guard at Truax Field in Madison. We are night owls by nature. Conversation keeps us awake until darkness overwhelms us. Peering through dirty windows at stars in the dark summer sky, we pray for daylight. At four o'clock, it's lunchtime.

Jack and the girls are already gone. A smokey aroma follows them into the breakroom when they return.

Jack answers my question by explaining that the holes through smokeless and the star through rocket grains increase the powder's surface area. The grains burn from both the outside and the inside, optimizing effectiveness.

He smiles when we suggest a potluck on Sunday. It is the last of the five nights of our midnight shift.

Image: Badger History Group, Inc.

The guillotine reduces the size of large smokeless and rocket powder grains. The slicing arm is raised and locked. Grains are placed in dies located behind the slicing arm. The arm is lowered to cut thin circles off solid grains. The arm is again raised. A turn of the crank at the bottom bumps the grains forward for another slice. The circles are further reduced by cutting and grinding.

The Wiley mill reduces propellant samples to a size appropriate for testing. The rectangular sieve in front of the mill is inserted into a slot (not visible) on the right and secured with tabs to hold the flat glass plate over the sieve. The funnel is placed directly over the sieve. The large protective metal shield covers the entire mill, with only the funnel barely sticking through the hole on the top. Pieces of powder are fed into the funnel. A full-face shield is required while the mill is operating. A large piece of plate glass mounted in a stand (not visible) is pulled in front of the mill during operation. (*Image:* Badger History Group, Inc.)

Injury (1966)

My fiancé applies for a mechanic position at Badger in July 1966.

Over 70 people now work in the powder lab. There are 14 on D shift. Newly hired runners deliver hundreds of propellant samples from production lines daily.

Like others hired early, I have experience at most workstations in the lab. We become trainers. Our assignments fluctuate to accommodate a smooth workflow. Titrations consume much of our workload. These wet chemistry tests require one solution to be added to another to obtain a color change.

Jerry joins Jack as a second supervisor on D shift. He is tall, blond, and recently married. Jack is a bachelor. They stop to banter with us during breaks or lunch. Otherwise, we see little of them. They post test results from our workbooks to paper forms and on a huge blackboard mounted on wheels in the back office.

These numbers determine how small batches of propellant will be blended into government lots. Blending batches is as important as the chemistry for making gunpowder. Technicians in the ballistics lab use a gun chronograph to measure the velocity of huge final government lots before they are shipped to other facilities for loading and packing.

Jack and Jerry are always up for a potluck unless we work the day shift. Sweetcorn mysteriously appears with loads of butter. Watermelon, too. I do not know where it comes from, and do not ask. Natalie quizzes Sandy and Donna. Those two are in on the secret but won't tell. Jack's eyes twinkle. Jerry unsuccessfully tries to suppress a knowing grin.

Natalie and I discover a small, galvanized garbage can under the outside steps to the lab attic. Someone has painted the letters SC on it. The instigators fess up. Cute Jack uses it to cook sweet corn, SC, over steam heat.

The supervisors keep the story hush-hush until their boss, Jack Two, finds the little SC garbage can and hauls it to his office thinking it might be of use in the lab. The quick-thinking shift guys diffuse the situation.

"We use that can to trap rats on the late shift," Jack explains. Jerry strains to keep a straight face.

Jack Two's eyes drift to the floor around his desk looking for rat scat. He does not resist when the young men remove the SC can. He will avoid it like the plague in the future because he does not want to be the one to tell Mr. Theide there are rats in the lab.

One night, the titration ladies run low on a solution. Jerry prepares it.

I am weighing screens in the government lab when I hear the siren and see the swirl of red lights at the north door of the powder lab. Shivers go down my spine when the medical people haul someone out on a stretcher and load them into the ambulance.

What happened?

I had not heard an explosion. Who got hurt? We stay away—continue working.

After the safety people leave, Jack calls us together.

"Jerry has chemical burns on his legs and feet," our boss explains. "He was combining chemicals in a five-gallon glass carboy sitting on a metal cart. He planned to move it to the titration room when the solution cooled." Jack takes an uneven breath.

"A significant amount of heat is expelled when these chemicals mix. Jerry stirred the solution with a long glass rod to evenly distribute the chemicals and avoid hot spots. We use glass because it doesn't react with the chemicals or contaminate the solution." Another breath.

"The glass container may have had a flaw that caused it to break from the stress of the heat or a touch of the stirring rod, maybe both." Jack is all business as he continues. I think he has already explained everything to high-ups and answered many questions.

"Jerry's lab coat, rubber gloves, and safety glasses protected him. The full-face shield he wore prevented splashes that could have burned his face and eyes.

"However, when the carboy broke, the hot solution saturated his pants from the knees down. It caught and collected in his shoes and socks, securing them to his skin. Blisters opened."

Techs suck in air. Gasps escape.

"Fortunately, he was by the sink in Room 2 and hoisted himself immediately. He sat on the sink ledge with his legs in the basin and turned on the cold water. He peeled off his shoes and socks and yelled for help. A nurse cut off his pant legs."

The seriousness of the situation momentarily breaks as a nervous laugh emanates around the room. We picture tall Jerry perched on the edge of the sink with his long, naked legs dangling under running water.

Jack takes a long, deep breath. "Jerry's injuries are serious, not life-threatening."

We are quiet as we absorb the implications of what happened to Jerry, we know that it could happen to us.

"Are there questions?" Jack's usual happy-go-lucky personality has disappeared. "There will be a formal safety meeting and training session for all lab personnel about what happened to Jerry. Attendance is required."

We quietly return to work. I ponder the dangers that are part of my job.

Three dollars an hour hangs in my mind.

Jerry returns to the day shift within 24 hours and is assigned desk duty until he heals.

After that, the large glass carboys are set in the deep, wide sink in the little janitor's room while chemicals combine. A short time later, two young men, George and Jerry Two, are hired to prepare all testing solutions. They work a straight day shift.

Jerry's accident is the topic of the following safety and training session. We all attend and sign off that we participated.

One night, Jack announces our wages will go up to a whopping five dollars an hour. We hear later that it had something to do with a union. The lab is not a union shop. However, many trades are represented at Badger. Several techs are married or related to trade workers. Gossip is rampant.

We plan a potluck to celebrate.

As an afterthought, Jack adds, "The minimum hiring age for technicians will be raised to 21."

PANIC. I'm 19 years old.

I wait until everyone leaves before asking. "If I return to the university in September, can I get my job back next May?"

Jack will check with Mr. Theide.

I want to return to the lab next summer. I have learned so much.

I need to talk with my fiancé.

David started work as a mechanic at Badger two weeks ago. We eke out social time but seldom with friends. Instead, we coordinate outings with my coworkers around our mismatched schedule. Family is a fading memory.

My fiancé could have stayed on days but chose D shift so we could ride together. We are working from midnight to eight in the morning when I learn about my raise.

I jump into the red Fairlane. "They're going to pay us five dollars an hour," I burst with the news.

"Whoa, that's a huge jump," he says wide-eyed.

"The hiring age for lab work has changed to age 21." My voice echoes stress.

"So?" David does not grasp my dilemma.

"What if I can't return to the lab next summer?" I fuss. "Jack is checking with Thiede."

"We'll cross that bridge when we come to it." He is tired. My concern is not urgent. It is tossed aside.

I bite my lip. Depending upon what Theide says, there may not be a problem.

My usual solid sleep comes in fits and jerks. *Five dollars an hour—age 21—university*, float through intermittent dreams as golden opportunities, then melt into sinister warnings.

I avoid bringing up the elephant in the car while we drive to work under the stars the following evening. As we walk to the clock alleys, warm summer air lingers from the day's heat.

At the lab, Jack asks me into the office and addresses my question directly. "If you return to college this fall, you'll be considered a new hire next summer. You'll not be eligible for lab work. You'll be too young.

"However, as long as your work record is clean, you may stay in the lab. You're grandfathered in."

YIKES! I had not thought I might have to transfer from the lab to another department because of the new 21-year-old age requirement.

I thank Jack and mull his words. If I return to college this fall, my options for returning to work at Badger next summer are dismal. I could be a secretary or do production work. Neither appeals to me.

Natalie and I measure single base powder to determine the surface area that evening. I read from calibrated marks under the microscope's lens. She records the numbers. She repeats them back to me for confirmation. I am glad we cannot talk while we work. I think Natalie intuits my predicament but says nothing.

Five dollars an hour—college degree—David—my mind runs in circles.

Everything spills over when I get in the car.

"You need to return to college. Don't worry about the money," my fiancé reassures.

"I like my job. And the people." I do not add—and the money.

"Don't say anything yet. Work needs only two weeks' notice before you leave." His words minimally relieve the crushing weight on my shoulders. We are silent as he drives.

When the Fairlane pulls from the driveway, I walk toward our quiet farmhouse in the fresh morning air. Exhausted, I sleep.

The following evening, Jack asks me into the office again.

PANIC.

Now what?

Natalie Hendrickson and Mary Hein measure the surface area of smokeless, single base, propellant. The recorded numbers are up to seven digits long. Although one technician could do this job alone, two usually worked together. They regularly changed positions during a shift. Notice the Ball mason jar of smokeless grains. The bulky no-spark outlet powers the light on the microscope. This small testing room had a limit of four people: i.e. two technicians, one supervisor, and one transient, who could be a second supervisor, janitor, electrician or other trades worker, or government auditor. (*Image:* Badger History Group, Inc)

Short-timers, Acid, and Gordie (1966)

I worry Jack will tell me I must leave the lab because I am only 19 years old. But that does not happen.

"Do you want to change to the day shift?" His question catches me off guard. I'm startled.

"Yes—Yes, I do," I stutter. "There were two people ahead of me in seniority."

"They both turned it down. You start next shift change."

My mind swirls. I feel off-balance with these changes happening so fast. I'm just a kid. I wish David would have stayed on the day shift. What about riding to work? Will I regret this decision?

Jack interrupts my quandary. "I'll let the office know."

"I won't be working for you," I blurt.

"We'll be around every couple of weeks," Jack's eyes twinkle.

Memories of the past two months fly in my mind. The potlucks. Sweetcorn appearing like magic. Farmers renting land inside Badger to grow corn will surely notice a smaller yield this year. I'll miss the laughter. My friends who replaced my family—I'll miss them.

I tell Dave with strangely mixed emotions.

"I'll put in a request for day shift," he has trouble sleeping the rotating hours and welcomes the change.

"We can ride together every third week while you work D shift," I say. If he remains on rotating shift, his weekends will not fall on Saturday or Sunday until September.

Where will I be then?

When I start the day shift the following week, more than a dozen women cut powder. I forgot how different cutting is from testing.

Testing involves reading and recording numbers from calibrated equipment. It is quiet work because conversation interrupts concentration and causes errors. Testing stations allow four to five people at most in a room. The number of people allowed in cutting rooms is much larger. I jump into a conversation with the rowdy group.

This room is at the south entrance of the lab, where tradespeople come and go, and deliveries arrive. Foot traffic is constant. Visitors often holler greetings at us when they pass the door.

We hear about employees caught with smoking material, fender benders, romances, weddings, coworkers looking to join a carpool, and sundry other tidbits.

There is little talk of the war. Either folks are reluctant to share their opinions or have heard enough about it in the news.

The fact that Badger supplies materials for the Vietnam War does not pose a moral dilemma for me. Mom and Dad raised me to support our country, including the decisions made by elected leaders. Voting is how situations change.

I support our soldiers. Some are my classmates.

Badger will continue to produce gunpowder until the war ends, whether I work here or not.

Occasionally, new hires leave Badger after working one day or only a few days. Some give notice—others do not. The cutting ladies have opinions about that.

A few short-timers said they were against the war.

"Why would anyone consider working at Badger if they were against the war?" one tech asks.

"They took the job because of the pay but couldn't reconcile their work with its role in the war," another speculates.

The banter continues in the lunchroom. Several women have sons, husbands, boyfriends, or relatives serving. Many of those men did not willingly choose to join the military. These women explain that working at Badger is one way they can support their men.

"Maybe short-timers are afraid," Audrey says. "They didn't realize lab work involved handling large amounts of gunpowder when they applied for the job."

Another opinion, "Their intent might be malicious. They want to blow up Badger to end the war. Protests and riots are on the news every night. They chicken out once they hear the rules and go through security."

The comment raises concern because we work with explosives and flammables. Engineers and chemists have designed safety features into our tasks. But it is precise work.

The cutting ladies are watchful because most new hires are first assigned to work with them.

Three days later, Don Peterson stops at the door, looks at me, and says, "You're coming with me, Kid."

Don supervises the instrument group in Room 3, the only air-conditioned room in the lab. He is a big man with a deep, growly voice. He calls everyone 'Kid,' even the other supervisors. But not Mr. Theide or higher-ups.

I have longingly peered into the instrument room all summer. I am now headed there on one of the hottest days of the year. Excitement bubbles inside me.

PANIC.

I know nothing about the instruments. Being assigned different tasks within a week to keep the workflow smooth is not unusual. But the instruments?

What an opportunity for a 19-year-old kid.

"We're bringing the polarograph online. It might replace some of the more time-consuming wet chemistry tests." Don adds a qualifier. "It's not been done before." A chuckle bubbles through his thick neck.

The chemists continually attempt to streamline or replace labor intensive, traditional wet chemistry tests using the instruments. They receive a cash award if their idea is implemented. Don successfully brought other time-saving procedures online over the years and is confident his idea will work. He hands me a manual, tells me to set up the polarograph, and follows the other men to the van for a smoke break.

I like a challenge and tackle this new responsibility with determination.

After two weeks of trial and error, the polarograph proves inadequate for quantitative testing. I return to sample prep, but not before Don says there may be another opportunity for me to join his group.

"Start in titration tomorrow," Gary informs me.

Donna Two is my partner in the morning. We have worked together before. She is fast and accurate, but her quick movements are messy. Patches from acid burns cover her lab coat. Some patches have new holes.

"Darn it." She wipes a splat of clear liquid from the counter. Water or acid? They look the same.

"I shake," she explains. Her infectious laugh draws me in, makes me comfortable. Donna Two has three children. She smokes. When she's sleep and nicotine deprived, her shaking is more noticeable.

"I need to change my gloves." Donna Two steps off the narrow board after taking a high-level meniscus reading. "One glove leaked last week. Acetic acid seeped in. I don't want that to happen again." She tugs on the latex, protecting her hands.

I'm curious. "What happens with acetic?" I want to know before handling it. "I've worked with sulfuric and nitric. Those acids create a warm feeling on my skin—before a burn gets serious. That feeling gives me time to dilute the spot and rinse it with water."

Donna Two explains, "Acetic acid is different. There's no warning. You don't feel it at first. I didn't know it got into my glove. It absorbs into your skin. By the time you notice a burn, the damage is done.

"There were blisters on the pads of my fingers between my knuckles and fingertips at the end of the day. They didn't hurt until I got home. Either the acid kept burning, or the blisters swelled, maybe both. I iced my hands—then used a needle to drain the fluid. They're still tender."

"That sounds terrible. What did the doctor say?" I'm concerned.

"Are you kidding," she laughs. "I didn't report it." Donna Two said she did not tell anyone and shot me a look that said—"Don't even think about it."

"The blisters are drying. No infection. I'm careful." She pulls on new gloves with a smile.

I scrutinize the five-gallon carboys of titration solutions on the shelf above my head. They remind me of what happened to Jerry's legs and feet. He had been preparing a solution for this room when the glass carboy broke.

I like wet chemistry work because it requires concentration and a bit of physical agility, such as stepping up and down to take meniscus readings from the tall glass burettes. However, I do not take the dangerous acid and base solutions for granted.

At the weekly safety meeting, we listen to the list of injuries that happened throughout the plant. Donna Two shoots me a look that says, "There's no accident to report."

At the end of the meeting, we are reminded that the lunchroom has warming ovens. Food should not be heated in testing rooms. The comment is directed to everyone but meant for Gordie, an older gentleman on a rotating shift who happens to be working days.

Gordie brings full dinners wrapped in separate aluminum foil packages. He strategically lays them on steam heaters in testing rooms to ensure the individual items cook to perfection by lunchtime. By eleven o'clock, an enticing aroma wafts down the hall—meatloaf, casserole, escalloped potatoes, lasagna. By noon, we're all drooling.

The packages often leak meat juice, cheese, butter, and spices, which continue to cook on the heaters after Gordie removes his food. The drippings burn to a crisp. By afternoon, they stink.

Supervisors chastise Gordie and make him clean his mess. He smiles as he scrubs with steel wool. The next day, he does it again.

Paul, a fussbudget supervisor, spies on steam heaters up and down the hall like it is the most essential job in the world. Paul grabs the old man's packages early and takes them to the warming ovens in the lunchroom. But those ovens are not hot enough to cook food. Gordie fusses when he can't find his lunch or when it is not fully cooked to his liking. Sometimes, he has nothing to eat.

One day, George and Jerry Two, the solution guys, decide to help Gordie. They watch Paul carry the foil packages from the heaters to the lunchroom before leaving the lab. The boys stroll into the lunchroom, grab Gordie's food, and sneak it back to the heaters. They only want to help the old man and pull one over on Paul.

The guys plan to return the food to the lunchroom after it has fully cooked but before it drips on the steam heaters. And before Paul finds it. If their plan goes astray, they assume Gordie's natural, pleading innocence will be convincing and add to Paul's frustration. Getting the old man in trouble is not their intent.

Natalie and I know the prank and assist George and Jerry Two by watching for Paul. We know he'll check the heaters when he gets a whiff of cooked food.

At eleven o'clock, Nat sees the supervisors pile out of the van in the parking lot and alerts the boys. George and Jerry Two fumble the hot packages down the hall to the lunchroom like jugglers.

Their jostling causes steamy, greasy juices to drip through their fingers to the floor.

They barely escape the lunchroom when Paul comes through the north door. They head to the testing room, where Natalie and I wait. George has an oily stain streaking the front of his lab coat. Jerry Two wipes greasy juice from his steel-toed shoes. Natalie helps the boys clean their mess while laughter spurts from her pursed lips. My jaws clench, stifling guffaws until I hiccup. Tears drip from my chin.

Later, we hear Paul giving Gordie the business about how he cooked his food.

A gentle soul, Gordie, just listens—with this big shit-eating grin.

Others speculate about Gordie getting fired, but that doesn't happen. Cooking food on steam heaters is not on the long list of dos and don'ts. Production workers likely cook their food the same way because most employees don't have access to warming ovens, and steam heat is available throughout the plant.

Gordie is a good employee. He does assigned work, albeit at his own pace. He is either very smart or very naïve because he cooks his food on steam heaters throughout the war. Paul continues to fuss at him to no avail.

Laboratory technicians stand in front of titration stations in the early 1950s during the Korean Conflict. Notice the 5-gallon glass carboys of titration solution on the shelves above their heads. A tank of compressed air is behind the gentleman on the right. Some titrations were done under inert gas. The technicians in the back row stand on one of the narrow plank steps they used to take upper-level meniscus readings. (*Image:* Badger History Group, Inc)

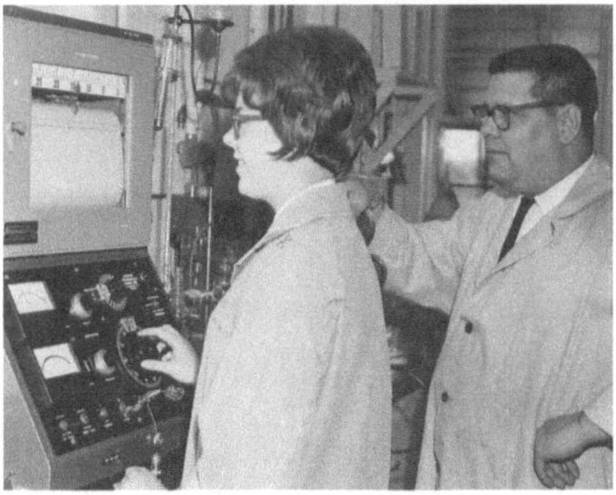

Carolyn Schroeder operates the polarograph, as Don Peterson observes. The small vessel containing mercury in the ring stand above Carolyn's head is part of the dropping electrode test. Don has his hand on a compressed air tank. Inert gases were required for many tests. (*Image:* Badger History Group, Inc)

Decision (1966)

Should I return to university? Or should I keep my lab job at Badger? The decision continuously nags at me. I say nothing at work.

Our farmhouse is quiet on Wednesday, the first day of my fiancé's weekend. A thought wrestles my mind. I pick up the phone. David's voice is in my ear after the first ring. We have not talked since Sunday evening because of our mismatched work hours.

"We should talk to our parents." My voice is decisive. I have avoided going down this rabbit hole. However, Mom was right about me applying at Badger. I need her opinion now.

My fiancé says nothing. I panic. I should not have addressed the subject head-on.

"That's a good idea," his late coming reply. "Do you want me to stop by in about an hour? Will your parents be home?" His response settles me.

"Yes, that'll be fine. We can tell them we're thinking about getting married and me not returning to college. We'll see how they react."

A comfortable feeling I have not had for a long time enfolds me.

Dave arrives as Dad descends the basement stairs to wash up and change into clean overalls after milking cows. Mom is preparing leftovers for their supper. A plate of warm-from-the-oven date bars and homemade gingersnaps sit on the kitchen table. My youngest brother Randy and I ate earlier. My brother David is at the trap range. Allen attends a Lutheran high school in Watertown, 80 miles southeast of North Freedom. He is spending a few days with another classmate's family.

We sit on the sofa in the living room and ponder a calendar while my parents eat. Our weekends fall together on Saturday and Sunday at the end of September.

It seems forever before Mom and Dad meander to their overstuffed rocking chairs across from us.

I start. "We're thinking about getting married this fall. I might not return to school." A smile widens Mom's round face. Her planning gears kick in and prioritize. The farm is at the top of her list.

"October would be after third-crop hay and before corn harvest." She's pragmatic, not emotionally demonstrative. A "Congratulations" from her would have been lovely—a hug, totally unexpected—neither happened.

Dad stands and formally shakes my fiancé's hand. He wraps his arm around my shoulders. The familiar tobacco and Old Spice floats between us. "Well, Susie, I'm happy for you," Dad always calls me Susie because the song "Susie Q" was popular when I was a child.

I find out later David had already approached Dad about us getting married.

"Randy, come down here," Mom calls upstairs to my little brother.

"Yeah, whad' you want," he is an antisocial ten-year-old.

When he finally appears, I announce, "We're getting married."

Randy frowns. "Does that mean you won't be my sister anymore?" He is dead serious.

"I'll still be your sister. That won't change just because I'm married." One corner of Randy's mouth lifts forming a tilted smile.

I look at Mom. "We were thinking the end of September. Maybe the 24th. My Dave has normal weekends then." I smile at Dallmann. I often revert to his last name around my family.

Mom's eyes widen, "Eight weeks—plenty of time to plan a wedding."

David and I say goodbye to my family. We want to talk to his parents tonight to preclude the village grapevine notifying them before we do.

Butterflies churn my stomach as the Fairlane bumps along the quarter-mile gravel driveway to my fiancé's family farm.

Harold sits in his captain's chair at the maple, Early American table. Virginia, who goes by Jean, pulls sweet corn from a steaming pot to go with leftover meatloaf for their supper. Their son anxiously makes the announcement before we take a seat.

"We're talking about getting married. Carolyn may not return to school." It sounds different when he says it. Uncomfortable.

Harold and Jean react more slowly than Mom and Dad.

"That's wonderful," Jean's response is formal, but her hug is quick and meaningful—Harold's measured and awkward.

"What are your plans?" she asks.

David jumps in, "We're still trying to decide. We just talked with Carolyn's parents."

I explain that I cannot return to my lab job next summer if I return to college this fall. I would be too young. But I am grandfathered in if I stay.

His parents understand my quandary over losing the scholarship. They are also concerned about the chaos on college campuses.

Jean changes the subject. "It's wonderful news." She smiles at her oldest son and me.

The following afternoon, my fiancé picks me up from home shortly after I return from work. After celebrating with burgers and fries at the Baraboo A & W, we settle at a picnic table at Devils Lake south of Baraboo.

"Mom has a guest list prepared. She showed it to me when I walked in the house. Dad's ten brothers and their families are on it. Then there is Mom's family. She's an only child. However, you know most, but not all, of my great aunts and uncles. There are friends from church and the village. It's a long list. I wish she'd slow down."

"You said this would happen," Dave says with a smile. "We don't need to rush."

"I want to get married now." My words fall into the summer air like a restless melody.

David looks happy—surprised—but happy.

"I don't want to live in North Freedom. You know how Mom and the neighbors critique new brides." My pent-up thoughts spill.

"Apartments are hard to come by with Badger operating. Do you want to drive by some I found?" my fiancé queries. "I only looked in Baraboo," he adds.

"Can I see now? Before it gets dark?" I didn't know he was already looking for apartments. He smiles. He anxiously heads the Fairlane toward town as the sun falls behind the west bluff.

Night is already throwing long shadows when we park in front of an old clapboard house just off the city square. From the street, I see light blue paint peeling around a globed bulb by a front entrance door. The place looks shabby. It is not what I was expecting.

"A one-bedroom space will open next month. It's in the attic. Up those outside stairs under the overhang. The apartment is good sized." Initially excited with his find, my fiancé reads my expression.

"There are two more," he quickly adds. "We can look again tomorrow night."

"I don't want to be picky, but maybe something newer."

"There is a newer duplex built into a hill on the south side. The lower level is a small one-bedroom apartment next to a single-car garage. The owner uses the garage. But there is space to park."

"Let's look even though it's getting dark."

A streetlight brightens the duplex. It is painted yellow with neat white trim. A long, wooden balcony runs the length of the upper three-bedroom unit. The little apartment on the lower level looks perfect. David signs a rental agreement the next day.

I address a significant change on my weekend. "I plan to transfer my membership from St. Paul's Lutheran Church in North

Freedom to your church in Baraboo. I've been thinking about it for some time. Mom's list sealed it. My church could barely hold everyone for the service. The basement's tiny kitchen and dining area are too small for the reception. We're both Lutheran, so the change should not be complicated."

"You want to get married at St. John's in Baraboo?" he asks.

"Yes. It'll be our church."

A sense of regret rifles through me and settles with a tingle on the back of my neck. "Let's wait until next week to talk with your pastor at St. John's. I want to tell Mom and Dad first."

David returns to work the following day. I tell Mom and Dad Sunday afternoon. They say nothing. But I see disappointment in Dad's eyes. Mom, on the other hand, switches planning gears. I tell them David is making an appointment with the pastor in Baraboo. The big church fellowship hall will accommodate the guests. I have my fingers crossed that the September date is available.

Mom says, "I think the reception should be at Jimmie's Del-Bar."

I'm stunned. Did I hear her correctly?

Have Mom and Dad ever been to Jimmie's?

This well-known supper club in Wisconsin Dells was established in 1943, a year after the ammunition plant first opened. Jim and Alice Wimmer bought a small roadside restaurant and grew it into a famous steakhouse known all the way to Chicago.

"Jimmie's Del-Bar?"

Mom's eyes twinkle. "Yes. Alice Wimmer said their restaurant doesn't open until four o'clock. They'll prepare a private buffet luncheon for us at noon."

"Dave and I plan to pay for the reception. We thought the Ladies Aid at St. John's would give us a quote for ham and turkey sandwiches." Dallmann and I know general family finances on both sides. We make more money than our parents.

Mom is not letting go. "We think the reception should be at the Del-Bar. If you get married at eleven, you can have pictures taken and be at Jimmie's by one. Your Dad's brothers live in Minnesota. Most are farmers. They would have time to milk cows in the morning, drive to Wisconsin for the wedding, eat lunch, and drive back to Minnesota for late milking. The Del-Bar will serve coffee and lemonade with the food. The bar will be closed."

Oh, my goodness. She has thought of everything.

Mom shows me the quote. It's more reasonable than I expected.

"What made you think of Jimmie's?" I ask.

"I looked at other supper clubs in the Dells. The Del-Bar has a good reputation." Mom's only concerns are whether the supper club will be large enough to hold the crowd and will there be enough food. Dad's ten brothers and their families add up fast. Minnesota weddings serve hearty meals. Mom is competitive when it comes to food—quality and quantity count.

"Alice Wimmer said many on the guestlist would be no-shows. I disagreed—gave her an estimate of 215 and told her not to run out of food."

Mom does not mince words.

What must Alice Wimmer think of Mom?

"Let me talk to Dallmann."

My fiancé is shocked when I report the news. His parents have never been inside the Del-Bar. Neither of us have been to the restaurant.

"Should we eat there sometime?" he asks.

"It's expensive, from what I've heard. Let's wait. We need to save money. Mom and Dad said they would pay upfront for the reception. We can pay them back later."

I'm not surprised Mom calculated cows into our wedding plans. The beasts rule a farmer's every move. Their milk is the primary source of income. They give less milk when daily schedules change. Therefore, cows are as important as any guest attending our wedding—including the bride and groom.

The date will be September 24—the reception at Jimmie's Del-Bar.

By mid-August, we've booked Mrs. Steinhorst, the well-known wedding cake lady from Reedsburg. We'll save money by moving the cake ourselves. But will the large layers fit in the Fairlane?

Photographer. Attendants. Invitations. Flowers. To save money for the reception, I borrow my dress from a coworker. The powder lab is all atwitter. D shift friends are on the guest list.

A Strange Sensation (1966)

Two weeks before our wedding, I sit at a double beam balance weighing screens in the stuffy little squared-off room in the government lab. Scenarios of the big day race through my mind. However, our wedding is not what I will remember about September 8, 1966.

I feel something strange—a foreign sensation that is hard to describe—something I will never forget.

Several things occur in short order at ten o'clock in the morning, but I can't remember their sequence. A jarring sensation emanates up through the floor. Something nudges me—every part of my body. A deep, foreboding sound—a boom and thud—penetrates my eardrums and consumes me.

The balance shakes on its marble mount. Lights go out. Deafening silence follows when the stack of screens on the shaker-pounder machine abruptly stops.

Whatever happened—it can't be good.

Technicians look at each other, surprised and confused. Some run to the west windows.

Nothing.

The powder lab?

Sandy and I slowly walk the hall to the south door, afraid of what we might see.

Nothing. The powder lab looks fine. We return to the others and report.

Shortly, Gary arrives. "There's been an explosion in a building on one of the production lines directly south of the powder lab," he says. There's no other information. He tells us to continue working as best we can.

I should have returned to college.

I never should have stopped at Badger in the first place.

I'm just a kid. What am I doing here?

A more sobering feeling jars me. PANIC.

D shift is working daytime hours.

David. Where is he? He is assigned to maintenance and can be called out when mechanical issues occur.

What if?

Oh no. My hands shake when I recall the power of what I just experienced. I whisper to Sandy that I'm going to the lab office.

My fiancé meets me at the hall door.

He is fine.

Our nervous laughter is contagious. The other techs clap when we kiss. We hold on to each other, to make sure we are not dreaming. I do not want to let go.

David leaves as quickly as he arrived because he is not supposed to be at the lab.

With the hoods and pounder machine out of commission, we can do little work.

Speculations fly around the room in the eerie dim light. Each of us contribute what we felt and heard. Our stories are similar.

However, not seeing the event or knowing what happened creates speculation.

How big was the building? Was it occupied? Were people hurt?

Did anyone die?

The explosion happened close to the lab and the main garage where my fiancé was working, about a half mile from either of us. He was in a wash bay when the impact and boom hit him.

"Debris was flying in the air," David later tells me. He scrambled to see what happened. Wide-eyed, he watched as "rubble, some burning, fell all around, like a war zone." He watched "a plume of smoke" billow skyward and was relieved his supervisor didn't select him to carpool to assist at the site.

David was equally concerned about me. His coworkers "saw the bushel basket-sized motor hurtle" from the building and fly high in the air before landing directly in front of the line office where I sometimes collected samples. The motor broke through the asphalt and "was completely buried in the ground." The office secretary was sitting at her desk when the explosion happened. She was not hurt, but word was she had to exit through a window. Debris blocked the door.

Shirley, a young woman who married Dave's classmate, worked with the materials control group when the explosion happened. Her team was processing fifty new hires when she and coworkers felt and heard the explosion. Shirley said that without explanation or comment, "a whole bunch of new hires walked out of the building." They intended to leave the plant. To her knowledge, "they never returned."

Jim Mattei was a young accountant and, like several chemists, a recent graduate of UW-La Crosse. He was in a meeting with two old-timers when the explosion happened. He later said the gravity of the situation was evident when "the men's faces went white." The three climbed into a car and arrived at the site to see the plant's firefighters in action.

The accounting department monitored costs and Jim said he sometimes wondered what the fire chief, Percy Loomis, did to earn this salary. Seeing Percy in action, Mattei said, "he never questioned Loomis' pay again because Percy earned all of it and more that day."

A still, a large vat, in a ball powder hardening house exploded because of a mixing and blending problem inside one in a line of stills. Explosives, solvents and other chemicals are blended in hardening houses. The blast destroyed the building along with an ethyl acetate storehouse. Eleven workers were injured. Fortunately, there were no fatalities.

The blast shook the guard shack at the front gate, a mile away. It rocked mobile homes in Bluffview, the trailer park across SR 12, formerly Badger Village. Windows rattled in Baraboo. Dishes clattered in Sauk City and Prairie du Sac. The towns were each seven miles away. A gray mushroom cloud rose and floated above the plant.

Jim, one of our chemists just off the midnight shift, was relaxing with coworkers in an establishment on the south side of the square in Baraboo when the blast happened. Several buddies asked, "What was that?"

"Something at the ammunition plant blew up," Jim replied off-handedly.

Engineers designed redundancy into the ball powder plant, just like the rest of the facility. The explosion delayed but did not stop production. Within days, work crews were reactivating another in a line of hardening houses. They brought it online in less than a month. Greater volumes of ball powder manufactured during the next three months made up for the lost output in September.

The investigation did not reveal a specific cause of the explosion. However, summarizing what preceded the event provides insight.

Ball powder production equipment was a new design built at Badger in the mid-1950s following the Korean Conflict. It had never operated at maximum capacity. Then, the new equipment sat idle for a decade until 1966. It was brought online for the Vietnam War. When Badger opened, equipment was quickly ramped to capacity because of the critical need for the product.

Ball powder production was unique to Badger. It was the only plant with the capability in the entire industrial ammo base. As noted later in an article by Michael Goc, "It has been estimated that 90% of the small arms fired in Vietnam was propelled by Ball Powder. Nearly all of that Powder was manufactured at Badger."

During the days after the explosion at the hardening house, the seriousness of what happened sinks into me. My thoughts fluctuate between "I should have returned to college" and "I hope I keep my job."

Since my first day at Badger, I have compared the dangers of working at the powder plant to dangers on the farm. Serious injuries occurred to farmers in our area: broken bones from falls or a cow kick, a concussion from being knocked down by a broken belt, lost fingers and a mangled hand caused by hydraulic equipment. One man suffocated in a grain bin.

Each of those farm injuries had happened to one person, usually because they were in a hurry and did not follow common safety practices.

The explosion was different because a group of people were involved.

Like the hardening house, a group of technicians work in the lab.

To calm my apprehension, I recall Verna's rationale. If my coworkers and I follow laboratory safety rules, we will be safe.

The explosion directly affects the lab. The ball powder production line where it occurred was a major sample source. The change is dramatic.

There is no work.

They'll send me home—I'll have no job.

But that does not happen.

The Army does not want to lose trained workers because finding employees in our rural area is increasingly difficult.

We process samples already at the lab in less than a week. Supervisors tell us to look busy. We wash sample jars and glassware, change out tubing for various tests, and dry desiccant for future use. Desiccant takes moisture out of the air. It looks like colorful little stones, which change color from blue to pink when they absorb moisture from an environment. Once pink, desiccant can be dried by heating, which changes the color back to blue for reuse.

When those tasks are done and redone, we washed grimy windows and sills and organize drawers that hold labware not used since the Korean Conflict. We do anything to keep busy. My friends on D shift talk about how hard it is to stay awake during the wee morning hours.

Everyone is relieved when samples begin arriving a month after the explosion.

Hardening House 9501-2 is a duplicate of Hardening House 9501-1, which was the building that exploded on September 8, 1966. This photo of the northeast corner of Ball Powder Hardening House 9501-2 shows us what 9501-1 looked like before the explosion in Hardening Still #4 destroyed this part of the building. (*Image:* Badger History Group, Inc)

Ball Powder Hardening House 9501-1 after a problem with the process in Hardening Still #4 caused the contents to explode. Although this building still stands in this photo, it was damaged beyond repair and had to be demolished and replaced with a new building. Most of the equipment in this building was used in a 'new' building. Hardening House 9501-3 went into service thirty days after this explosion. (*Image:* Badger History Group, Inc)

Ball Powder Hardening House 9501-1 and the ethyl acetate storehouse after a problem with the process in Hardening Still # 4 caused the contents to explode on September 8, 1966. (*Image:* Badger History Group, Inc)

Wedding (1966)

Friends express concern for our well-being because of the hardening house explosion. Some ask if we are seeking employment elsewhere. Others pray for our safety. The attention becomes a little much for me. My resolve to continue working at Badger is polarized. Wedding plans continue.

Friday afternoon, the day before the wedding, my soon-to-be husband and I load the middle two cake tiers into the trunk of the Fairlane. I sit on the floor of the backseat to balance the thin fiberboard holding the foundation of the extravaganza. It is three large, heart-shaped cakes, tips pointing to the center. The lady warns that the board bends from the weight. We must keep it level, or the hearts will break. The pedestals to mount the layers are in a brown paper bag on the seat.

My knees brace against the bottom of the heavy, awkward piece. The top layer, adorned with three fragile sugar bells, sits by my shoulder in a tall, narrow box propped level. I hold it steady with one hand. David slowly pulls into traffic and heads to the Del-Bar for our first-ever visit. Mom scheduled our appointment with Alice Wimmer.

It's a hot and sticky day. Like most cars, the Fairlane is not air-conditioned. The windows are open only an inch to prevent insects or road dust from getting on the cake. Beads of perspiration dampen my hair and coalesce into drops on my face. Holding this awkward position numbs my legs.

I do not feel like a bride.

Alice and Dave exchange introductions at the door of the restaurant. I remain on the floor in the backseat until the waitstaff helps move the bottom layer off me. We transfer the rest of the cake on our own and assemble it on a table partially hidden behind a screen in the lower dining room.

A chunk of one of the sugar bells lies in pieces at the bottom of the box. We cannot fix it. DRAT. To hide the faux pas, we position the top tier so the broken bell is on the wall side of the cake.

Early diners arrive when the doors open at four. Patrons are dressed in Sunday's best. We wear everyday clothes. I have smudges on my tan cutoffs from the floor of the car.

"Let's sneak out through the kitchen," I whisper to David. But Alice surprises us during our escape.

"Would you like to stay for the buffet?"

She intuitively interprets our panicked expressions. We have no idea how much the buffet costs.

"Please, be our guests. A wedding treat." She is sincere.

I look down. "We aren't dressed for—."

Alice stops me. "You're fine. Come along." We obediently follow the gracious lady.

I feel like a cindermaid at the ball. But the feeling evaporates as we indulge in the delicious meal. The buffet is extraordinary. The food appears arranged for royalty. We wonder if tomorrow's luncheon buffet will look and taste the same.

A cloudy sky greets me early on September 24, 1966. Rain is forecast later in the day. I have an appointment at a beauty shop in Baraboo to have my hair done. I fuss the humidity will make the stylist's smooth, sleek waves bounce into tight curls by the time the wedding starts at eleven.

My fiancé is having problems of his own. David cannot find the keys to the Fairlane. He had them last night after the rehearsal party when he finished polishing the car and drove it into the garage.

But the keys are nowhere to be found. He is sure someone took them. Someone is playing a mean trick on his wedding day.

His mother has him sit. They diligently go over his steps since last night.

He eventually finds the keys in the gap between the top sandstone step by the back door and the foundation of the house. The keys must have slipped from his grasp as he carried in wedding gifts brought to rehearsal.

My morning is a blur until I meet Mom and Dad and my attendants at the church. The fall-colored mums in their bouquets compliment my bridesmaid's moss-green satin gowns. The two flower girls wear matching gold satin dresses sewn by Grandma Hilda. David and the men are in black tuxedoes.

The church is full, from the pews in the back to the white, gothic altar in the front. Two other Daves sing the "Wedding Song." They are counter-parts of the Davey Trio. Those guys will ask my Dave to sing at their weddings in the future.

It is over too soon.

Our moms, dads, and grandparents greet us in the narthex of the church. An awkward happiness fills the space. My family holds moments like this deep inside instead of being openly demonstrative. Mom reminds us to come directly to the Del-Bar after pictures.

"The crowd will be waiting."

The Del-Bar is bursting at the seams by the time our wedding party arrives. Guests squinch together so we can enter. Everything is perfect. The food is as attractive as it was the night before. In my elegant attire, I feel like Cinderella.

David and I share a bite of wedding cake after the meal. We spy the broken bell. A silent smile bounces between us.

Light rain is falling when we bid our guests adieu and depart the restaurant for a cruise in the Fairlane. Friends have attached streamers to the car. The wedding party follows behind us. We honk at every car we meet. In the interest of time, we had put off this traditional event. Now we party.

About 200 people attended the wedding. The Del-Bar bill was $750.00. Mom was pleased with the meal. And there was plenty of food.

By the end of the year, we repaid the total amount to my parents.

Best man Gary Dallmann and maid-of-honor Carolyn Myers look on as David and Carolyn Dallmann share their wedding cake at Jimmie's Del-Bar in Wisconsin Dells, Wisconsin, on September 24, 1966. The broken bell is visible on the top tier of the wedding cake. (*Image:* The Dallmann Wedding album, Ronald Rich, photographer)

David and Carolyn Dallmann and their attendants enjoy a wedding luncheon at Jimmie's Del-Bar in Wisconsin Dells, Wisconsin, on September 24, 1966. (*Image:* The Dallmann Wedding album, Ronald Rich, photographer)

Nitroglycerin (1966)

David and I are lucky to get a couple of days off, albeit without pay, to enjoy a short honeymoon. It was my first trip to Milwaukee. We strolled through the domes at the Michell Park Conservancy, Whitnall Gardens, and the Milwaukee Zoo.

The lab is swamped when I return.

Being proficient at most lab tests, supervisors jostle people like me from job to job to keep samples moving and the workflow smooth. Being assigned to several workstations within a week is not unusual.

Unseasonably warm temperatures and humidity return during late October. We call this part of fall Indian Summer. Steam baths pour additional discomfort into the room, where I prepare samples for titration.

Will I ever get another chance to work with the instruments?

I am thinking of the air-conditioning in Room 3 when Don Peterson appears in the doorway.

"You're coming with me, Kid," his friendly growl no longer intimidates me. I follow him with cautious optimism.

"We want to use the instruments to find how much nitroglycerin is in the powder. We're currently using a titration procedure. Using the IR-spectrophotometer will save time."

I know IR means infrared wavelengths, but nothing more. I am resolved to learn.

Ruth smiles. I think she is happy I am back.

"Well, Kid, the first thing I need you to do is drive to the nitroglycerin area and pick up some NG."

Where's that? I do not ask.

I thought I would be "testing" for NG, not picking it up from where they make it.

Don stops by the now familiar polarograph. He unlocks a padlock that secures a sliding wooden door with a yellow sign showing a large number four. The padlock caught my eye, as did the sign, the first time I worked for Peterson.

Production buildings at Badger are numbered one through four. Those with a four are the most dangerous. When I asked Ruth about it, she explained there was standard material in the cupboard.

Don pulls two wooden boxes from the enclosure. Each is half the size of an ordinary shoe box.

"You'll use these to transport the nitroglycerin." He sets the boxes on the counter.

Is he serious?

Transport?

Nitroglycerin?

Did I hear correctly?

Reality sinks in.

Jeez. Nitroglycerin. That stuff blows up. I saw it in the movies and on television.

I say nothing. Just watch and listen—very carefully.

"You see, Kid, this is a unique little box." Don is not at all concerned. "The shop guys designed it."

He flips wooden latches on the sides of one box, allowing the handle to move from vertical to horizontal. A curved groove fluidly guides the motion. With the handle in its low position, he gingerly removes the cover.

Inside are two small plastic bottles with green rubber stoppers. They are about four inches tall and an inch and a half in diameter. They sit snuggly in perfect holes cut into a solid block of wood.

Don's dexterity indicates his experience with this task. He removes one of the bottles and holds it to the fluorescent light in his gloved hand. The small container rests on his pinky while his three middle fingers and thumb control a grasp.

A tiny bit of clear liquid at the bottom of the bottle shows through the plastic.

"Ya see, Kid, we're getting low on NG. We plan on testing actual samples using IR to compare results with the titration method. We need new linear regression graphs to get started.

"The lady in the nitroglycerin lab is preparing the raw material for us.

"One of the solution guys will take you up the hill. You pick it up, and he'll bring you back. Pay attention to where you go. Next time, you'll drive yourself."

Don puts the small bottle with the trace of NG in the second box and secures it in the cupboard. An empty bottle remains in the box on the counter. He tells me to give it to the NG lady.

"Now, let's see you open and shut this thing." His growly voice adds a dimension of seriousness.

I flip wooden latches, opening and closing the box until my proficiency is deemed satisfactory.

"Do you have questions?" Don asks.

"I do. I know nitroglycerin is dangerous. It can explode."

Don seems amused, but his answer is serious. "The danger is negligible when a stabilizer is added. The NG you pick will have the stabilizer in it. Be sure the wooden carrier is securely closed before you start driving. The NG will be okay. It won't hurt you. The biggest problem is getting an NG headache if it gets on your skin. But you already know that."

I climb into the truck with Jerry Two, who is not at all concerned that we are picking up nitroglycerin. Two miles straight east, we make a slight jog to the right, then a quick left up the only hill on the prairie part of the plant.

Jerry Two was an upper classmate in high school, an intelligent kid. He explains, "This knoll is a moraine caused by a glacier, the same glacier that created Devils Lake."

He adds, "NG is manufactured on a hill. Open-air wooden toughs move it to the loading station. It's made on demand and in amounts specific to powder batches."

Will I see this? I do not ask.

We stop at a small building, not much bigger than a latrine. A wooden sign labels it the NG Laboratory. Stepping out with the box in my hand, I notice the road ahead curves sharply around what appears to be a formidable bunker of grass-covered soil. A small building within this bunker is all but hidden, like it was dropped into a hole.

"Hello. You're Carolyn?" My attention returns to the job at hand. "I hear you need some nitroglycerin." Macy is the tech working in the NG lab. She rides my bus.

"Yes. I've never been this far from the powder lab." My eyes wander to the bunker and all the pipes going in, out, and around the sunken building.

"That's where the glycerin is nitrated. We don't go there," Macy smiles. I follow her inside the small lab and watch. She is familiar with this transferring task, which increases my comfort level.

Saying goodbye to Macy, I walk my special package to the truck. Handling the little wooden box carefully, I climb in and place it between Jerry Two and me. There are no seatbelts.

At the lab, Don removes and inspects the plastic container. It's over half full of yellow liquid.

"The stabilizer accounts for the color," he explains. Then, he shows me how to evaporate the stabilizer with compressed air. We monitor the liquid as yellow fades to clear.

"The solution is now pure nitroglycerin," Don explains. "Ruth will show you how to prepare the standards.

"Do you have questions?" he asks, like an afterthought.

"I do."

Who is he kidding? I'm nineteen and working with pure NG. Of *course, I have questions.*

"The nitroglycerin is no longer under the stabilizer. How dangerous is it now?"

"Well, Kid, that depends on how much you have."

Is he avoiding my question? I like specifics. I conjure a scenario.

"Let's say I put a drop of NG on the cement step at the north door of the lab and whack it with a hammer."

Don's eyebrows raise above his broad face.

"Well, Kid, hitting NG with a hammer is never a good idea. But to answer your question, there would be a considerable jolt of energy.

"It probably wouldn't hurt the building, but it sure wouldn't do the step any good."

If Don was laughing on the inside, he did not show it. He paused and looked at me as I pondered his explanation.

"Does that answer your question, Kid?" he asked.

I nodded confirmation.

Don Peterson
Image: Badger History Group, Inc.

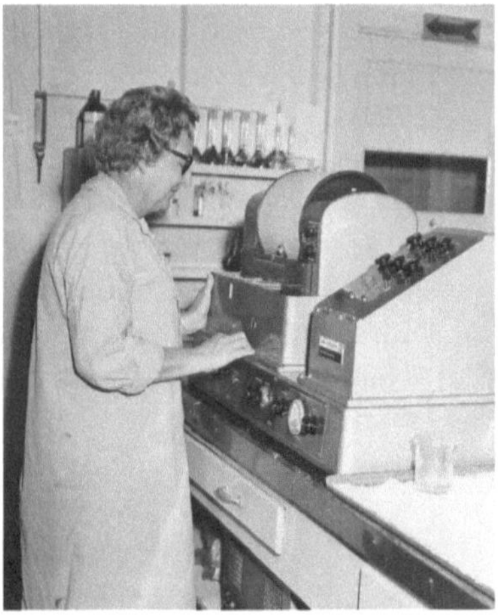

Ruth Keith runs the IR-Spectrophotometer
Image: Badger History Group, Inc.

Notice the little cupboard with the padlock and the big number 4 on the sliding door to the left of Carolyn Dallmann's head. This cupboard is where the nitroglycerin used to prepare testing standards was stored at the powder lab.

Image: Badger History Group, Inc.

Two nitroglycerin carriers, fabricated of wood by trades workers at Badger, were used to transport NG from where it was manufactured at the facility to the powder lab. This NG was the standard material needed to prepare linear regression graphs used for measuring the concentration of NG in gunpowder samples. *Images:* Carolyn Dallmann, 2020.

Image: A picture of a photo at the Museum of Badger Ammunition.

This building is the one Carolyn saw at the nitroglycerin manufacturing area. The NG Neutralizing House is pictured from the top of the north barricade. The small roof at the right covers the NG Gutter between the NG Nitrating and Separating House.

Nitroglycerin was made in small batches as needed. A worker pushed an "Angel Buggy," like the one pictured, containing NG from where it was made down an openair, wooden Wheeling Walk, which had a framed roof cover, to the Rocket Paste Pre-Mix House or the NG Transfer House. A batch of NG was transferred via small tractors called mules to the ball powder area. The guards and safety staff incrementally cleared traffic from roads during the transfers. *Image:* Badger History Group, Inc.

2

BADGER DURING THE VIETNAM WAR

1967–1974

The Lump (1967)

The explosion at the hardening house is the focus of weekly safety meetings until there is nothing new to report. Different topics take the floor: safe driving, fire prevention, and annual physicals by the plant doctor.

The ladies buzz about seeing the Army doctor. New hires detail their experience.

"He just goes through the motions. Doesn't do any medical stuff," one reports. "He's old and fat," she adds.

Another woman rolls her eyes and grimaces, "You have to take off your bra and hold a towel over your boobs."

The safety guy schedules appointments.

I tell him, "Dr. Pearson is my family physician. I saw him last month. He can submit my medical records."

Pearson has been my doctor since I was a kid. He made a house call to our farm when my brothers and I had the mumps. We were three, four, and five. He sewed my eye together after a barbed wire fence incident on our farm.

The safety guy does not acknowledge my comment. "Your appointment is at 11:15 tomorrow."

When I arrive at the hospital, the nurses are all business. They line us up like soldiers. When it's my turn, I sit alone in a makeshift cubicle constructed of moveable metal frames with fabric stretched across the middle. I hold the towel in front of me.

The Army doctor weasels between the frames. He compares paperwork to my badger number. "H14209," he mumbles.

"Yes."

"How do you feel?" He does not look up.

"Good."

Doc sticks a wooden spatula into my mouth. He does not peek in. The spatula flips into the trash bucket at his feet.

He sticks a new cap on the eargazer thing. The gazer enters each ear. Again, Doc does not peek in. The cap arcs the same trajectory as the spatula.

Looking to his left, he pulls down the towel. With the backs of his hands, he administers a light slap to the outside of each of my breasts. I look to his left to see what is so interesting—only fabric.

He disappears, leaving me to think about what just happened.

The exam started when he asked how I felt. It ended when I said, "Good."

The rest was—superficial—degrading—disgusting.

Everything I heard about this guy is true.

I tell Natalie when she gets on days.

"He's taking advantage because you're a pretty young thing," Nat razzes good-naturedly. "He won't be interested in an old lady like me," she insists. She's barely 40; her ivory skin, coal-dark hair, and ruby-red lips are striking.

"Watch out for him," I tease back. "He's not after youngsters like me. He's more into foxy ladies—like you." In the end, Natalie experiences the same treatment as the rest of us.

The doctor is the topic of the day. The general feeling is, "Get rid of this joker."

I cannot let it go and bring it up at lunch.

"What if someone is legitimately ill and depends on this guy for medical help? Some people won't pay to see a real doctor if one at work is free."

"Or, their husbands won't let them," Sandy pipes up. Several ladies stop chewing and look knowingly at the young lady.

Others are less courteous with their criticism. "I wouldn't take my dog to that man—my horse—my mother-in-law. He's a veterinarian, not a people doctor."

In the Army doctor's defense, there are over 5,000 employees at Badger. He is the only physician on the payroll. Considering he works 40 hours a week, annual physical exams alone are a heavy load. Plus, he handles injuries.

I feel a lump in the lower outside quadrant of my right breast the week after New Year's 1967.

It can't be. I'll ignore it.

There it is, again.

It'll go away.

Women talk about self-breast exams—quietly—among themselves.

My husband and I are members of the local Jaycee and Jaycette organizations. The groups are independent but work together on community service projects. Members must be 36 or younger. The new self-breast exam brochure handed out at the last meeting is still in my club notebook. I read it thoroughly.

I am scared.

David knows. But it is an embarrassing thing for a 19-year-old newlywed.

"Make an appointment with Pearson," he says.

"I'll wait. Next week, if it's still there," I procrastinate.

It's part of me now, the size of a slightly inflated 50-cent piece. No pain.

Audrey, Dr. Pearson's receptionist, answers the phone. She is my North Freedom classmate's mother. "This is Carolyn Dallmann. I need an appointment."

Audrey cuts me off. "Doctor is indisposed. He is referring patients to Dr. Hansel." She gives me the number.

DRAT. Three physicians check my boobs within a month. Mortifying.

My family saw a doctor only if we were sick. Annual physicals are new to me.

Mom says, "Follow up with Dr. Hansel. Pearson is dealing with his own medical issues." Pragmatic by nature, Mom approaches problems logically. Worrying wastes time.

I confide in Natalie and swear her to secrecy. She insists I see a doctor, not the Army doctor.

Nat's daughter, Cynthia, is my age. I think Natalie sees Cynthia in me.

I call Pearson's replacement for an appointment.

Dr. Hansel, younger than the other physicians, is mildly concerned, "It might go away. It's best not to be aggressive with treatment because you're so young. I'll see you in two months."

Mom is confident in Hansel's assessment.

Not Natalie. I wish I hadn't told her.

"See my doctor," Nat encourages. "I'll make the appointment."

"No. I'll wait. I'd like to see Dr. Pearson. He's a surgeon. I'll want him to do the procedure if it comes to that."

David is concerned but agrees with my decision. Pearson is his family physician, too.

I want the lump to go away. The new guy says it might.

Eight weeks later, I follow up with Dr. Hansel.

"No change," he says. "It's not bigger. But it's not smaller either. The lump needs to come out now. Don't put this off." My false sense of hope shatters like crystal on cement.

Hansel is not a surgeon but explains, "Dr. Pearson will return to his practice in two weeks. We'll make an appointment for you to see him."

I should have listened to Natalie. I want this thing out now.

I swear it is growing.

The two weeks drag by, giving me time to invent all sorts of terrible scenarios. The lump starts to itch.

Or am I imagining?

Dr. Pearson hums through the exam. It is his nature. I dress and wait for the dreaded verdict.

"It appears the lump hasn't changed for two months. That's good. I want to see you in six weeks."

"The other doctor said it should come out now," I inform him.

Six weeks? That can't be right. What kind of illness did doc have? A stroke.

"Breast surgery at your age subjects you to scar tissue issues later in life. The tumor may shrink or go away. I'll see you in six weeks."

Pearson has the last say.

Six weeks later, I check into St. Clare's Hospital in Baraboo and have a benign tumor removed from my right breast, but not before signing paperwork consenting to a total mastectomy. I am 19 years old. We will celebrate our first wedding anniversary in four months.

Dave and I are relieved. Our parents and Natalie, too.

I tell Jaycette friends about my lump. They ask me to share my experience at a meeting. "It'll compel other young women to do regular self-breast exams and seek a doctor's help," they encourage.

I decline. I am one of the youngest members. Additionally, I don't feel qualified to speak.

The girls ignore my reluctance and ask the local clinic to provide information. "We know members who are ignoring lumps because they're convinced they have cancer. If you share your story, we might be able to persuade them to see a doctor."

I am intimidated. It is an awkward subject.

My friends do not give up. They wear me down.

I consent, albeit with considerable trepidation. A nurse or doctor from the clinic will attend and bring pamphlets.

Nervous jitters turn my words wispy as I begin to speak. Breathe, I tell myself—start over. The curious eyes of women I know urge me to continue.

I do not expect the overwhelming response when I finish. Members openly express how much they appreciate my candid story. It gives them a platform to talk to others, especially their mothers.

Relief replaces nervous energy. An unexpected sense of confidence—and pride—follows.

I did it.

But it does not end here.

I stewed over the Jaycette event with Natalie for days. She continually egged me to do it and is anxious to hear the group's response.

"I told you," she exclaims with raised eyebrows and a knowing grin. "Introduce an awkward subject. People are more comfortable discussing it.

"You should give your talk here at work."

"No way. Once is enough. I've been a wreck," I wail.

I have created a monster. I am not doing this again.

"Doris and Lois told me they have lumps. They haven't told their husbands. They're scared to see a doctor," Nat informs me. "Lois was sure the Army doctor would find her lump. He didn't. Now she thinks she's okay."

My opinion of the plant doc drops another notch.

"I'll talk to them one-on-one," I volunteer. "Speaking to a group of women my mother's and grandmother's age makes my knees knock."

Natalie confesses, "I can't tell Lois and Doris you'll talk with them alone. I promised I wouldn't tell their secret."

What? If Nat didn't keep their secret, who did she tell about my lump?

Note to self: *A secret told to one person is no longer a secret.*

The more I hold back, the more Natalie insists. She pokes me at the end of the weekly safety meeting when employees are encouraged to submit topics relating to safety or health. Turning toward the safety guy, she raises her voice, "You need to do this, Carolyn. Nobody can talk about the subject like you because they haven't gone through it."

The safety guy is more than a little interested in what he overhears.

The topic for the following safety meeting is Self-Breast Examination. I will tell my story. The Army doctor will be present for support and to take questions. Men and women will attend. The meeting will be repeated for each shift.

Nat cocks her head in my direction with a satisfied smirk.

The supervisors. The Army doctor. *The horror!*

"Why did you get me into this? Now, there'll be men there, too. I can't do it. It's so embarrassing," I rant at Natalie. She giggles behind her cupped hand.

"Men have wives and girlfriends that may have a lump. If women find the subject difficult to discuss, imagine what it's like for men. Men have breasts. They can get breast cancer, too." Natalie cuts me no slack.

"How do you know so much about this?" I squint, daring her to back down.

"I know men can get breast cancer." Nat does not waver.

"Are you sure?" I challenge again. "I've never heard of that."

Natalie is sure.

I am a nervous wreck as almost forty people file into the lunchroom: safety guys, supervisors, Mr. Theide and his boss, Howard Foster, the Army doctor, the day and D shift technicians. Some drag chairs from workstations to accommodate seating.

My hands shake. I cannot catch a deep breath. Gurgling noises emulate deep in my belly. Blood swirls up my neck and prickles red splotches on my sweaty face.

Remembering the Jaycette program, I take a breath and begin. Nerves fade as I speak and answer questions.

I did it. Again.

My relief melts to a soothing calm like a cool breeze after a storm.

Coworkers, including men, thank me for addressing the awkward subject.

Later, one young tech told me she found a lump that went away after a few weeks, but she had seen her doctor. Natalie convinced Doris to talk to her husband. Lois, too.

One of the young chemists, a newlywed, told his wife about my experience. She had not told him about a lump she found. Surgery for her benign tumor was successful.

I turn twenty the week before the last presentation.

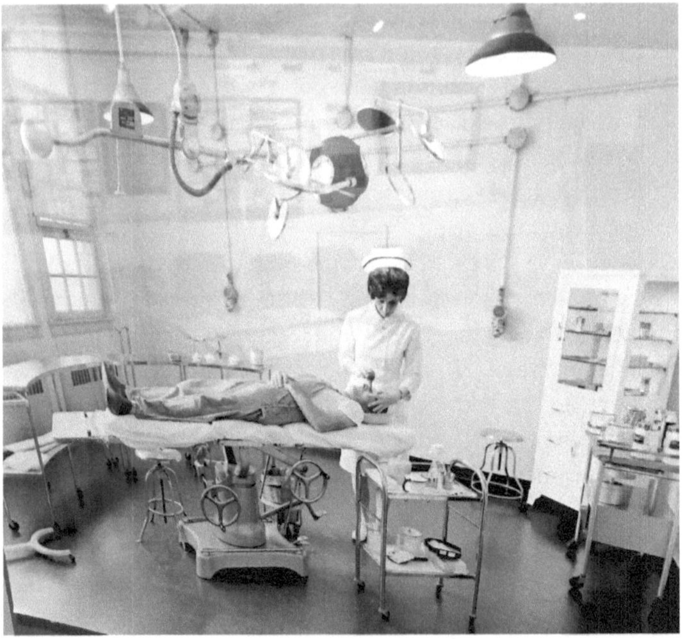

Badger's onsite hospital was a fully staffed medical facility. During World War II, the hospital could handle most of the health and injury needs of plant employees and families living in Badger Village. By the Vietnam operation, the hospital service had changed to that of a doctor's office and urgent care for employees. More severe and life-threatening injuries were sent to an offsite hospital. The plant ambulance was available for emergencies. *Image:* Badger History Group, Inc.

Road Runner (1968-1969)

It is summer 1968. David remains on D shift. Our work hours match a few days every three weeks. Badger and shiftwork do not stop, not even for Thanksgiving or Christmas. I go to family gatherings alone. We miss attending birthday and holiday parties as a couple. Connecting with friends is impossible. When we are together at home, one of us is sleeping. We buy a beat-up, white Volkswagen Beetle for Dave to drive to work. I use the Fairlane. Donna Two rides with me.

It is a tremendous relief when David starts the straight day shift. Within a month, Norma and Mary, two other lab techs, join our carpool. Conversation ensues while my husband maneuvers the seven miles of heavy traffic through the Baraboo Bluffs.

"It's disturbing how reporters announce the daily body count of our soldiers," Mary says. Her son serves. She's on edge because she is never sure of his location.

"I wonder how long it'll last?" Donna Two speculates. "I hate the war. But when it ends, everyone will be looking for work. Going back to old wages won't be easy. I just hope I can find a job." She and her husband have three young children.

Everyone in the area knows from experience what happens when a war ends—people are unemployed. David scours newspapers for job opportunities. He keeps his eyes and ears open. Miraculously, United Parcel Service posts a mechanic position in Baraboo.

"It must be a mistake," he says. "There's no UPS center here."

When he calls the out-of-area number, the man tells him to submit his resume.

He noses around local car shops for gossip.

"I'll never get the job," he reports. "Every mechanic in the area is applying. They all have more experience than me."

Area mechanics call my husband Davy, as in Crockett. They took him under their wing when he finished technical school because they know Harold, his dad. I am known to these guys as Davy's girl.

"I'll be Asshole instead of Davy if I get the UPS job," he laments. He respects these seasoned mechanics and hopes to keep the feeling mutual.

The call comes two weeks later. "The job is yours unless a former UPS mechanic takes it."

Dave tells me, "The mechanic, Kenny, was at the Milwaukee shop until he left UPS to work at a dealership in the city. He initially turned down the Baraboo position because his wife didn't want to leave Milwaukee. That's when the job posted. Now, Kenny's having second thoughts. He has until the end of next week to decide."

We sell the Beetle and look for a better second car. Dave finds a used black Ford Ranchero. It's his first truck. It is like a two-door station wagon with a cab and cargo bed.

When he gets the call, my husband is told, "Kenny took the job. We'll keep your resume. UPS plans to expand in Baraboo. We'll let you know when the next position opens."

The news is a combination of disappointment and relief.

Ten months later, the UPS ad reappears. David doesn't want to call UPS because they told him they would retain his resume. "I don't want to wear out my welcome. They'll let me know," he says.

I am not so sure.

Before I voice my opinion, his mother calls. She saw the ad, too. "Did you contact UPS?" Jean doesn't have the same confidence in the company as her son. "Call them again," she prods. She is not authoritative or demanding. But her son respects her and takes her advice.

"Can you believe they lost my resume? They said they would keep it. I'd be considered first when a new job posted. I don't have much confidence in these people."

I think David's rant is directed at himself for not following up on his own.

I also think big companies don't operate like the small businesses in town that my husband usually deals with.

A week later, he is hired. He starts on second shift, straight four to midnight.

"How long before you get on days?" I remember the nightmare of shift work.

"They said a year. No more than two."

DRAT.

He's not happy with shiftwork either. Fortunately, his hours will not rotate every week. And UPS does not work weekends. The pay and benefits are comparable to Badger's, which is a big plus.

Highway traffic is awful when I take over the carpool. My husband intuitively maneuvered the red Fairlane through the bluffs. I keep up to speed. But it's not my nature to dart from lane to lane. I avoid aggressive drivers like the plague.

The chaos starts in the parking lot. Every eight hours, a sea of cars randomly stream to one of the three exits. Chevys, Fords, Pontiacs, and an orange Road Runner scream through the mess like they are driving the Daytona 500.

These guys dodge in and out of traffic through the curves up the bluff. They blow their horns at vehicles without enough horsepower to make the climb at breakneck speed.

Some are inclined to get even with a stunt Dave pulled back in the day. Those guys probably think my husband is driving the Fairlane, not me.

The Road Runner sports a tall wing on the back. He does not like to follow anyone. The Runner occasionally roars his engine just to show he can. Bill, the driver, graduated from high school with David.

The chaos heightens at the top of the bluff. It is a short way from there to where the highway changes from four to two lanes. Brakes screech, leaving black tire marks where the two northbound lanes narrow to one.

I crest the bluff one summer afternoon, coasting to a slower speed in the right lane of bumper-to-bumper traffic. I hear him. Road Runner is terrorizing drivers behind me and coming up fast. In my rearview mirror, I see him pull to his right and pass a slow mover hanging in the fast lane. Laying on his horn, he lurches ahead of the slower car.

I maneuver into the left lane, knowing the right lane is ending just ahead.

Road Runner's engine roars again. I see him in my side mirror swerve and speed around another vehicle. I am sure he will be forced into the single lane where the highway narrows before he catches me.

I tuck close to the car ahead. The Runner approaches, attempting to pass me on the right. He runs out of room.

He thinks I am Dave.

Road Runner has no choice but to duck in behind me.

Bill is so close I can see his eyes in my rearview.

What a jerk.

When he does not back off, I manually turn on my taillights.

The Runner lurches sideways with a quick screech.

He backs off.

He must have seen my red lights and thought I stepped on the brakes.

My riders sigh in relief.

I motor on with a smile.

David wakes early one Saturday morning shortly after he starts working for UPS. It's a sunny spring day in 1969.

"How would you like to buy the house?" he asks.

"What house?" I am baffled.

"This house. Derlan and Charlotte want to sell." The couple who owns our duplex have a reputation of moving every few years. We knew that when we rented the apartment.

"I would rather not live in a house with someone else renting part of it." My words are a mild protest.

"I agree. That would be ideal. However, property in town is sky high because Badger's operating. Buying a single-family home is years down the road. If we can buy this house at a reasonable price and pull in extra income by renting our one-bedroom unit, we could manage the payments. We'll need to pool our paychecks and not make any other large purchases for a while."

I mull over my husband's words. If we owned the duplex, we could sell it later and buy a single-family home.

"Can we move into the three-bedroom upstairs?"

"Of course." Dave smiles, then interjects something I had not thought of. "If someone else buys the duplex, we will have new landlords. They could raise our rent. They could even make us leave."

Whether by accident or design, David makes a compelling argument to buy. Paperwork churns. Within days, we sign the documents.

The following day—everything changes.

"There's a problem." Frown lines cross my husband's brow.

"What?" Is someone sick? David looks worried.

"Derlan told me the deal fell through on the place they were buying. He and Charlotte want to rent the three-bedroom upstairs from us."

I'm angry. I feel like I was talked into buying a house that I can't live in.

However, having already been exposed to the humbling parts of marriage, I say nothing.

Then, being naïve, I ask, "Can we back out of buying?"

"No. I should have known this would not go smoothly," Dave commiserates. I can see he is as disappointed as I am.

"One good thing," he says. "We'll be getting larger rent payments than we expected."

I smile, but it seems like we've won the consolation prize.

It will be a year before we move upstairs.

Larry's Bar (1969)

The Vietnam War creates increasing unrest. The creeping wave of divide sweeping the country makes my familiar, safe feeling of living on the farm in North Freedom a memory. It began with the antiwar demonstration in downtown La Crosse while I was a college student.

Coworkers talk about protests on State Street and by the university in Madison. I first shopped in the exclusive stores by the state capitol the year before our wedding: Manchester's, Yost's, Carmen's. I crave what I saw, merchandise and activities I never knew existed, sophistication at my farmgirl fingertips. Now that wonderland is tarnished. Not safe. Out of reach.

By the late 1960s and into the 1970s, protests throughout the country become violent. National Guard units assist with crowd control. Natalie's husband is now a lieutenant colonel in the Air National Guard at Truax Field in Madison. Weekend after weekend, local law enforcement calls his unit for support in dealing with demonstrations around the campus. She fusses with concern for his safety as he deals with the mess.

Protesters appear in front of the main gate at Badger, sitting, marching, waving signs. Supervisors alert us of their arrival and tell us when they leave. When protesters linger by the main gate at the end of our day, buses take us to an alternate gate and back to the parking lot. At least one lab supervisor is trained as a guard for extra support should demonstrations escalate.

One eerie event happens that's not a protest. Wednesday, September 10, 1969, traffic slows to a crawl at the top of the bluff. It stops. Start and stop. Start and stop. We inch past Ski-Hi Apple Orchard, Chuck Naidl's Snake Farm, the outcropping of granite studied by geology students, and along the straight stretch between the flat cornfields of Heatherstone Farms.

A feeling of dread penetrates. It must be a terrible crash. The women who ride with me pray no one we know is involved.

Coming down the gentle slope toward Baraboo, a sea of flashing red lights involves the entire crossroad. Police officers man the intersection of SR 12 and CR W. Closer still, other officers talk to people in cars stopped in the middle of the road. There are no crashed vehicles.

"What's your name?" the policeman asks.

"Carolyn Dallmann. Is something wrong?"

"Where're you going?" His voice is strained.

I hesitate.

Why does he want to know? Why hold up traffic from Badger?

"We're headed home from the ammunition plant. We work there." The ladies bob their heads up and down in agreement.

"Show me your driver's license."

I grab my purse. The car ahead of us is undergoing the same procedure. Two policemen are pawing through their trunk.

"Roll up your windows and proceed." The officer motions me straight north.

"I want to turn into Baraboo."

"Go straight ahead," he curtly orders.

The ladies are shaken. So am I.

What in the world is happening?

Are we under attack?

Why did the policeman say I should roll up my car windows? It's 80 degrees.

We leave the windows down but peer all around as we proceed "straight ahead."

The news rolls across the county like wildfire. Out-of-towners walked into Larry's Bar at LaRue. The thugs shot Wanda and Larry and stole money. It happened a little over an hour ago.

My world crumbles as I absorb the information. Thoughts reel my mind. Wanda and Larry and their boys are friends. Memories of Dad and me stopping at their bar after we checked our young stock flood through me.

During summer, my family pastures cows on the Forty, 40 acres high in the bluffs about three-and-a-half miles south of our farm. We haul water to the corral tank at least once a week because drilling a well through the granite bluff would be too expensive.

Larry's Bar is halfway between the Forty and our place. Dad capitalizes on an opportunity to stop in for a beer and cigarette. I picture my father's short dark hair curling from under his straw hat as he sits on a bar stool in his striped, bibbed overalls. He enjoys exchanging local news and gossip with Larry and the other patrons.

When I was a kid, Larry gave me coins to play songs on the jukebox as I munched a vanilla Bun candy bar—Dad liked maple nut. Wanda would pop out of the kitchen off the bar and say, "Hello." She patted my curls.

LaRue was a thriving mining town in the early 1900s. These days, the surrounding agricultural community supports the establishment. The large hall off the bar hosts weekly Euchre and Sheepshead card parties, private celebrations, and dances.

When events run late, Wanda tucks sleepy youngsters under a blanket on the cot in a room off the bar. A couple of times in the 1950s, I fell asleep in that heap of children.

During high school, Mom called me to fill in at LaRue's card parties.

Wanda and Larry raised their six rough-and-tumble boys in the accommodations on the second level. Their youngest son, Gary, is a year older than I am. They are now grown men.

Dave and I joined couples from our local dance club when The Illusive Sounds played at Larry's Bar a few months ago.

How could this happen?

LaRue is a mile south of the Dallmann family farm.

Are Harold and Jean in harm's way?

Their daughter Cheri, Dave's sister, just graduated high school.

Where's Dave's sister?

Where's Dave?

My husband, driving a package car out of the UPS parking lot seven miles north of Baraboo, pulls into endless traffic on ST RD 12. Shortly, a deputized civilian, carrying a shotgun, stops his vehicle. Although they know each other, David must answer the same questions I was asked. The guy cautiously rummages through the truck. Finding nothing, he says, "Move on," before stopping the next vehicle.

The crooks cased Larry's yesterday.

Today, Wanda was alone behind the bar when they entered.

The strange man told her to "Hand over the money."

"You've got to be kidding," she replied. When she rejected the demand, the assailant knocked her down with the butt of his rifle.

Larry rushed from the back of the building when he heard the ruckus. He grabbed a bar stool to protect his wife and property and attacked the man. The perpetrator fired two shots, hitting Larry, who escaped out a side door where he heard more gunfire.

Wanda died of a gunshot wound to the head. Larry was shot in the chest and is in the hospital.

The paper quotes Sheriff Hearn, "The county was sealed off and aircraft was used extensively in the search for a white car believed to have been used by the assailant." Locals breathe easier when two suspects are in custody within 24 hours.

Many feel the crooks are lucky the police caught them before the Klingenmeyer boys tracked them down. That scenario could have been much worse for everyone.

This sudden violence in my small community signals an end to an age of innocence. The war is one thing, but this assault on a family close to mine is personal.

Vanguard of the Revolution (1969-1970)

The UW-Madison campus is a hotbed of antiwar activities in 1969. Late in the year, an isolated incident perpetrated by one member of a trio of young radicals foreshadows an incident with national implications.

Karleton Armstrong was born in 1946 in Madison. By the winter of 1969, he is already implicated in several antiwar crimes. On December 28, he leaves his fraternity room on the UW-Madison campus with a brown paper grocery bag containing two gallon-sized glass jugs of gasoline. Karleton walks to a Quonset hut on the west end of the campus. The US Air Force trains officers in the building. He pulls a hammer from his pocket and breaks a window in the unoccupied structure. Tossing the gasoline through the broken glass, followed by a match, the young man escapes in the predawn darkness.

This is not the first action staged by the "Vanguard of the Revolution," comprised of Karleton, his younger brother, Dwight, and his girlfriend, Lynn Schultz. The Vanguard is compelled to create antiwar sentiment.

Empowered by previous successes and watching the continuing turmoil ravage the country, Karleton hatches an unconventional plan. He will drop a bomb on Badger Army Ammunition Plant.

Karleton implements his plan by purchasing ammonium nitrate from the Baraboo Cooperative. He explains to employees that he works for an area farmer who wants to use it as fertilizer, which is not unusual. The young man procures three discarded commercial mayonnaise jars from the pizza joint he delivers for in Madison. The jars and an ashtray purloined from his fraternity house will hold his explosive mixture of ammonium nitrate and kerosene. There is no detonator, so the bombs will not explode on impact. However, Karleton hopes to drop them on a strategic target, like down one of the smokestacks of the massive powerhouse at Badger. If the bombs knock out power to the facility, the ammunition plant will shut down.

Karleton coerces his reluctant younger brother's help. Dwight Armstrong, age 19, dropped out of high school in the tenth grade. He worked at Morey Airport in Middleton, a suburb of Madison, during the first part of 1969 as a line boy, fueling and moving planes and other vehicles. He gained informal flying instructions in a Cessna 150.

The older brother sees Dwight's experience as a resource and pulls him into his plot. Security at the ammunition plant is formidable. A ground attack is out of the question. But Karleton believes he knows Badger's weakness. The Vanguard will demonstrate the facility's vulnerability from the air.

New Year's Eve 1969 is a snowy night. After midnight, the brothers break into Morey Airport and steal a Cessna 150. But plans do not go smoothly. Dwight finds the ignition key in its usual hiding place, under the engine cowling. The engine starts. However, he cannot turn on the instrument panel lights. He does not know how. He never flew at night.

Karleton awkwardly settles into the passenger seat with the mayonnaise jars under his arms.

Dwight steers the Cessna down the runway. Fortunately, Karleton carries a flashlight. He swings its beam back and forth across the instrument panel, enabling Dwight to read the gauges. His actions are not smooth. They jerk light around the cabin because he must maintain a hold on his weapons.

The passenger door unexpectedly pops open. In the excitement, Karleton failed to latch the door before takeoff. He cannot secure it while controlling the flashlight and maintaining his hold on the slippery jars full of explosive material. Snowflakes swirl inside the cold cabin. The temperature on the ground is below 20 degrees.

Visibility is not good as Dwight gets the small plane airborne. Karleton manages to secure the door as his brother announces, "We're lost. I forgot to set the gyrocompass."

Panicked, Dwight instinctively drops below the clouds, looking for landmarks. Relieved no hills or radio towers lay ahead, the boys locate the lights of Cross Plains due west of the airport. Dwight banks the plane. He backtracks toward Middleton until the brothers see car lights on SR 12.

They fly above the highway to Sauk City, eight miles south of Badger. They recognize Karleton's girlfriend exiting her car at the intersection west of the Wisconsin River Bridge at Water Street and Phillips Avenue below.

Karleton had persuaded Lynn Schultz, a 19-year-old from Wisconsin Dells, to provide a vehicle and transportation. After she drops the young men at the Morey airport, her boyfriend directs her to Sauk City, where she is to call an anonymous bomb threat to the ammunition plant. After the call, she is to proceed to the Sauk Prairie Airport to pick up the brothers. They will land the plane on the small runway after they drop the bombs.

Schultz is having problems, too. The first phone booth she tries is occupied. After repeated, unsuccessful attempts to persuade the person to end their call, she gives up and drives to a different booth. That phone is out of order. She returns to the first phone. as the plane flies above her. She does not hear it.

When her dime drops into the slot, nothing happens. Fearing she will be late for the pickup, she foregoes the phone call and hurries to the Sauk Prairie Airport.

Overhead, the Armstrongs head due north. The lights of Badger are visible as they skirt the plant. Having located their target, Dwight passes it by and continues toward Baraboo. He banks the plane south, approaching the massive facility from over the bluffs and Devils Lake.

Karleton directs his brother toward what he believes are fuel tanks but are chemical tanks in the acid manufacturing area. Dwight wants to maintain a 1,500-foot altitude to avoid the potential blast area. The older brother directs him to 750 feet.

At the lower altitude, Karleton opens the door and kicks out the ashtray bomb. It falls into an open field, away from buildings and chemical tanks.

Dwight banks the plane for another low pass over the smokeless production area. The brothers fly through plumes of powerhouse smoke as the storm rages across the prairie. Karleton throws the mayonnaise jars out the door without thinking where they might land. The bombs fall to the ground in the chilly night air in the early hours of January 1, 1970.

On the ground, guards at the main gate hear what sounds like a small airplane's engine above the storm's wind and traffic noise. The sound fades but returns, then disappears. Planes are not to fly over Badger.

"That poor sap is lost. The storm probably blew him off course," one guard speculates. They take no action other than putting a note about the airplane in their shift report. In their defense, the guard's reaction may have been different if it was a clear, warm summer evening.

The Armstrong boys continue south over the plant for six miles to the Sauk Prairie Airport. Dwight plans to land on the snow-covered runway with the help of two flickering flares Schultz stuck in the snow. However, the storm's tailwind pushes the Cessna too hard and fast on the first approach. Dwight banks and comes around again, dropping to a near-perfect landing.

The young men hustle out of the plane and into the waiting car as planned. The trio arrives in Madison in less than an hour. They will be known as The New Year's Eve Gang.

January 1, 1970, falls on a Thursday. New Year's is like any other day in the lab at the powder plant. Donna is busting at the seams as she reports, "Some crazy guy landed a Cessna 150 in the storm last night. He left it sit on the runway." Her husband manages the Sauk Prairie Airport.

"Milt says he must have been some pilot. He brought the plane down, going in the wrong direction in that wind." Discussion is cut short. Samples are incoming.

In Madison, the Vanguard waits, anticipating headlines. But their extraordinary feat gets no recognition.

"Why don't we hear something?" they wonder.

A couple of days pass. Impatience overwhelms Karleton. Emboldened, he places an anonymous phone call to the Kaleidoscope, an underground newspaper out of Milwaukee.

"Somebody dropped a bomb on that ammunition plant in Baraboo. No one's talking about it." He issues his statement and hangs up.

The Kaleidoscope people know nothing about a bombing. Neither do their sources.

"Was there a bombing?" they wonder.

The Kaleidoscope calls the FBI.

On January 5, the FBI contacts Lt. Colonel Russell Enoch at Badger concerning the bomb. They tell him the Kaleidoscope is historically accurate. Also, there were three firebombs in Madison during the past few days. A bomb lurking inside the plant is a possibility.

Enoch alerts Olin Corporation, the operating contractor at Badger. An Army bomb squad, 259th Ordnance Detachment, is dispatched from the Savannah, Illinois, Army Depot.

Badger initiates an internal investigation. All departments receive alerts. Communication flows through the main switchboard. Security locates the guard report concerning a small aircraft heard at 0213 on New Year's morning. Rumors spread like honey on a warm summer day.

Word reaches the powder lab in record time. I am working with Ruth in the instrument room when I hear. David gets the message at the main garage.

Many laugh. "It's a fabrication. A figment of a warped mind. It's only been four months since the incident at Larry's bar."

A bombing? At Badger?

Impossible.

Bomb (1970)

The FBI investigation concerning a potential bomb at Badger extends to the grain cooperative in Baraboo. Agents ask questions and walk from the co-op along the railroad tracks to the train depot. Employees and the farming community pass along stories of a bombing.

Lt. Colonel Enoch, the FBI, and Olin's security chief organize a search team. Rumors become reality at Badger on January 6 when grid searches commence in the northwest part of the facility. Ordnance people, civilian federal officers, plant firefighters, and safety personnel slog through ankle-deep snow in high-topped boots and long overcoats.

They find the bomb.

Broken. Shattered. The men scoop the material from underneath and transfer it to a 24-inch square, white enamel pan with a blue edge.

Ecstatic, they seek the nearest resource to continue the investigation. With the remains of the bomb in hand, they head directly to—the powder lab.

A dozen men trudge into Room 3 where Ruth and I work. Snow slides from their boots. White blobs collect on the dark floor. They gingerly place the pan on the tray by the spectrophotometer like it is their trophy prize.

Startled by the intrusion, Ruth and I exit. Only four people are allowed in Room 3. The men are shoulder to shoulder gazing at the debris.

Helen's eyebrows rise upon hearing the commotion. The secretary alerts her boss when she sees Ruth and me in the hall peering at our workstations through panes of glass in the door.

Bob Theide's professional demeanor is on alert as he marches toward us. "Why are you ladies out here?" His voice is calm but has an air of authority. He sees the men as he speaks.

We hear the boss's stern voice as the door closes behind him. "This room is overloaded. My people work here. Move your business to the hall. We'll talk out there." Boots shuffle, leaving melted puddles in their wake.

Theide motions Ruth and me back to work. "I'll straighten this out. Let Helen know if more than two try to enter," he tells us. Agitated voices overlap in the hall.

"How many—What is it—How long—Only four?"

Two men enter Room 3. They poke the material in the pan with a short glass rod. Ruth and I stay away.

The bomb stinks.

The strangers leave. Two more enter.

Theide's voice comes from the hall. "Yes, we can. But it'll take time to set up." Voices become muffled as the meeting moves to the boss's office.

Most coworkers are unaware of our visitors. They do not know the bomb is close by. Theide likely wants to keep it that way.

Men rotate in and out of Room 3 two at a time. The strangers are a distraction. Their presence makes it difficult to concentrate.

The bomb, the center of attention, has made its grand appearance, like the leading actor in a Broadway play. Its character is a mystery begging to be solved. Puzzle parts are there.

Can we put the pieces together?

Why does a bomb sit ten feet from me?

Can 'I' find the critical formula to unravel the plot?

I cannot.

Neither can the FBI.

My fantasy evaporates when Don Peterson enters. The three of us finally see the bomb. The snow has melted. The residue in the pan is ammonium nitrate. Jagged chunks of glass poke out at odd angles. The sickening smell of kerosene permeates the air. Sophisticated testing is not needed.

The FBI whisks the pan from the room when they depart.

The unsuccessful, crudely executed bombing may have gone unnoticed if the bomber had not called it to the media's attention. The probability of the bombs hitting a critical target and causing significant damage—extremely low.

More troubling is the real possibility of the small plane crashing into buildings. A 19-year-old novice who was not licensed was at the controls. He never before flew at night or in bad weather. Innocent people doing their job, working with acids, accelerants, and explosive material on the ground, would have had no chance. The results? Catastrophic for them. Catastrophic for the Armstrongs, too.

Schultz's warning phone call five minutes before the bombing would have been meaningless. It takes longer than a few minutes to shut down Badger's manufacturing operations. Employees would have had the choice of leaving or staying at their workstations.

Where could they go on such short notice?

Additionally, processes, like blending, mixing, or pressing explosive material, left unattended could be significantly more dangerous than a mayonnaise jar of ammonium nitrate and kerosene with no detonator.

It is not something to brag about, but on January 1, 1970, the Armstrong brothers accomplished the first bombing of a continental U.S. military installation since the attack on Pearl Harbor in 1941. The sad event happened at Badger Army Ammunition Plant.

The powder lab, like all of Badger, is busy and returns to regular operation. As winter settles in, the drama of the bombing fades to a memory.

Unfortunately, authorities do not capture the perpetrators.

Over the summer, David Fine and Leo Burt join the Armstrong brothers. The foursome concocts a devastating plan.

They blow up Sterling Hall on the UW-Madison campus at quarter to four in the morning on August 24, 1970, eight months after bombing Badger.

Physicist Robert Fassnacht, a 33-year-old researcher, is killed in the blast. An unintentional target. He is a husband and father of a three-year-old son and twin daughters less than a month old. Three others are injured.

The Physics Department was more affected than the targeted Army Mathematics Research Center. Surrounding buildings are severely damaged. Data is lost.

The four men celebrate at a truck stop as their car radio announces the results of their work. A news bulletin interrupts the broadcast saying someone was killed in the explosion.

The men thought the building was empty. This is the first they heard about a death. They panic and head out of town.

Dane County puts out an all-points bulletin concerning a light-colored Chevy Corvair observed close to the scene of the explosion. A similar car with four men inside was seen leaving Madison, headed north at a high rate of speed. Sauk County forwards the alert to Officer Danny Hiller, who is on patrol. Danny proceeds south on SR 12 out of Baraboo. He sees a Corvair across the median headed north as he descends the bluff toward Badger.

Did the Armstrong brothers think about the bombs they dropped on Badger eight months earlier as they passed the facility?

Danny makes a U-turn, follows the Corvair, and alerts Sheriff Hearn. The four men make the first possible turn to the right off the state highway toward Devils Lake. Danny follows.

Off-duty officer Bob Frank is in the sheriff's office when Hiller's call comes in. Frank has a shotgun. Hearn sends him toward Danny's location. He tells Danny, "Stop the car. Hold the men. Bob Frank is on his way."

Hiller turns on the lights and stops the Corvair on South Shore Road at the bottom of the hill of switchbacks before it makes the long, flat curve around the southern end of Devils Lake.

Danny approaches. He does not recognize the four young men. But his gut says, "These guys blew up the campus building."

After brief questions, Danny tells the men to stay in their car, returns to his vehicle, and calls Hearn.

"I got'm," Hiller tells the sheriff. "Those guys that blew up that building last night."

"How can you know? There's been no description of the bombers. We need to wind this up." Hearn is not a patient man. He lacks authority to hold the men without cause. He has added pressure because of the fast-approaching shift change. The county has only four cars, and Danny's is needed back at the office.

"No—No, sir. These are the guys." Danny is adamant.

"What makes you so sure?" Hearn questions.

"My gut." His officer holds firm. "My gut tells me these are the guys."

Hiller is insistent. Hearn relents.

"Hold'm," he tells Danny. "I'll call Madison." Hearn knows there is little he can do unless the subjects are named.

Danny's fingers fidget while he waits. He glances nonchalantly at the car. It has not moved. Bob Frank has not arrived.

Hearn's voice crackles through the radio. "No warrants have been issued. We have no authority to hold them. Let'm go."

Bob Frank pulls up thirty feet behind Danny. They both know what they must do.

Danny repeats his story over the years. It never changes.

He knew he had the bombers. He had to let them go.

"Laws about holding suspects were changed after that incident," Danny adds when I talked to him recently.

The Armstrongs, Fine, and Burt are eventually on a list of suspects. They elude the law for years.

Karleton is taken into custody near Toronto, Canada, in 1972 and extradited for trial.

His brother Dwight is arrested in 1977 in Toronto.

Bomber David Fine obtained his law degree and is a practicing attorney. He is charged in 1976 in San Rafael, California.

Leo Burt is never found. He is later presumed dead. In August 2023, the FBI releases age-processed photographs of Burt, who has evaded authorities for 53 years. He is referred to as "Wisconsin's state ghost."

Karleton is questioned about the Sterling Hall bombing. Interrogators press him on why he was compelled to inflict such carnage. Why kill someone, injure others? Why destroy years of research the university did for the Army?

Worn down, Karleton answers, "My uncle was killed at that ammunition plant."

WHAT?

Karleton implicates himself with his answer.

The question was about the bombing of Sterling Hall on the UW campus, not the bombing at Badger.

Authorities take advantage of Armstrong's error.

"What uncle?" they ask.

"My mother's brother," comes the reply.

Who was Karleton Armstong's uncle?

His name was Ellsworth Goff. He was one of four men killed on Thursday, July 19, 1945, when the nitroglycerin storehouse blew up.

Mom told me about that explosion the day before I started school.

Ellsworth Goff's son is Edwin Goff.

I know Edwin as my classmate, Eddy Goff.

The aftermath of the New Year's Eve bombing at Badger unfolds as unceremoniously as the bombing that happened months earlier.

Moments of initial disbelief flash almost as fast as the events. A sad realization that something terrible happened follows. No good can come from it.

Robert Fassnacht, his widow, children, and family suffered the most. No words or punishment of the bombers can replace or repair what happened to them.

Karleton and Dwight Armstrong and David Fine are convicted, serve short prison sentences, and go on with their lives.

Both the bombing and the prosecutions leave me empty. The feeling does not go away. It lingers still.

Parties (1968-1974)

A sleeping giant during peacetime, Badger becomes a behemoth of moving machines and material during war. Its surface ebbs and flows like an undulating ocean pushed by swells of employees. At shift change, a potential tsunami issues waves as the masses migrate back and forth between work and their homes.

Under the surface, workers intermingle like puddles that coalesce into one body. They are a homogenous force knitted together for a finite period that will expire when the war ends.

Departments overlap in various ways. Some couples are on the same shift but work in different departments. Other couples work opposite shifts to cover childcare. The Army employs a substantial staff; they blend with Olin's employees. Multiple generations of one family are common at Badger. Carpools meld individuals.

Our rural community turns topsy-turvy.

Businesses stay open beyond their usual hours to cater to the crowd. Many people want to start their day when their shift ends, at midnight or sunrise. Grocery stores, gas stations, banks, restaurants, and bars maximize their hours. They struggle to find employees. It takes months to get an appointment with your doctor or dentist. Beauty shops book weeks ahead.

Shift workers miss Friday fish fries, Saturday night dances, Sunday church services, and family gatherings. Coworkers become their quasi-family.

A cross-section of Badger employees attends local dances, picnics, and parades. If a band, food and drink, or a celebration is happening in Sauk County, a group of Badger employees will be there.

Management organizes a variety of special events like picnics and dances. The Army introduced this practice during the WWII operation because there were few opportunities to socialize. Tires and gasoline were rationed in the early 1940s because of the war. Travel was limited, if not impossible.

It's a win-win. People want to socialize. The Army retains employees.

We enjoy company-wide lunches in huge meeting rooms during work hours when we meet Army goals, like completing a specific number of work hours without a time loss accident. Supervisors rotate technicians to these lunches. Lab operations, like the rest of Badger, never stop. Large boxes of doughnuts or cakes arrive at the lab for a department achievement or a holiday.

The onsite Conservation Club draws crowds for chili dinners and chicken barbeques. Dave and I attend some of the first scheduled Con Club parties when our hours match, which is not often. I do not go alone.

Management provides food and hires bands. Rows of picnic tables are set in the shade by the building. Dancing starts inside but spills outside. The building is not large enough to accommodate everyone.

David and I stick together and hang with lab people during dinner. They are more social than the guys he works with. When mosquitoes become unbearable, we squeeze shoulder-to-shoulder between other couples on the dance floor. But it is impossible to move about without getting stepped on.

Offsite parties are planned. But even the biggest venues, like the Lodi Bowling Alley, Dorf Haus at Roxbury, Baraboo Elks Club, Rathskeller in Sauk City, and Herman's Supper Club in Baraboo, were not built to hold the hundreds of people showing up at Badger events.

That does not stop employees and their families from attending. Offsite parties spill into parking lots and along sidewalks. Some of the overflow crowd patronize businesses close to the main event. They pay extra to avoid the crush of people.

My husband and I join the fun. It's different from the card parties, potlucks, and other activities in the village of North Freedom because employees come from places far outside our local area. It's not like college because of the wide age range. People old enough to be my parents or grandparents are suddenly on my level and vice versa. The old become young, and the young grow up fast.

Once we know the lab crew better, I occasionally attend parties without Dave. Natalie and Roger take me under their wing.

Like other departments, the lab is a mixed group. Most are glad to have their job and eager to participate in the festivities. We make more money than we did before coming to the ammunition plant. The entertainment is free. We make the most of it while we can. Because, when the war ends, Badger will close.

Many technicians are homemakers whose children no longer need round-the-clock care. A few grandparents are in the mix. A dozen high school classmates were hired into various labs before the 21-year-old age limit became effective. Some women have husbands, fiancés, or sons who enlisted or were drafted.

Individual shifts plan special social events because their days off fall in the middle of the week, and their hours change constantly. Dave and I score tickets with a group of D-shift people to hear the Ink Spots perform at Behnke's Supper Club in Rock Springs. Hosting these well-known musicians is a significant event in this village of 400. The Ink Spots play multiple gigs over several days to meet demand.

In my sheltered life, I never imagined the variety of landscapes and things available in Wisconsin. My world expands as I enjoy adventures with coworkers.

Several times each summer, a group of us, anywhere from six to 20, drive to Door County, the thumb of Wisconsin. David and I have never been there. I have seldom been outside of Sauk County before working at Badger.

We never make reservations because *the Door* has residents who alert each other to folks like us. We stop by a restaurant or bar in one of the villages the afternoon we arrive, tell them what we need for accommodations, and leave. They split us up amongst their network of homes. Before nightfall, we pick up a list of addresses, determine where we will sleep, negotiate costs with our hosts, and designate a morning rendezvous.

When I first saw it, I thought Lake Michigan was the ocean because I couldn't see across the expanse. We get drenched standing at the top of the cliffs at Cave Point County Park. Waves rhythmically thunder against the worn rock below our feet, throwing clouds of water above our heads. Am I still in Wisconsin?

A mile south at Whitefish Bay State Park, rolling dunes offer a stark contrast in terrain. Would I ever travel to this exotic place if not working at Badger?

Small churches put on fish boils. Huge pots containing wire baskets are filled with water and hung over fires in makeshift lawn pits. Potatoes, carrots, and onions simmer until tender, then chunks of white fish are dumped into the pots to cook fast. Finally, an accelerant is added to the fire, causing a vigorous boilover that drowns the flames with the hiss and steam of an angry dragon. Men lug the baskets from the boiling water to serving tables on poles. Door County's famous cherry pie tops off the meal.

We climb the tower overlooking Green Bay at Peninsula State Park on the west side of the thumb. Some of us take in an outdoor performance by the Peninsula Players.

By 1969, snowmobiling has become a popular winter recreation. Natalie, Roger, their son Brad, George and his parents, and employees we meet through shiftwork and ridesharing have sleds by the winter of 1970. David buys a yellow Ski-Doo. I ride behind him that winter. The following season, I drive a yellow Nordic. Mine is a wide-track, stable machine with heated handlebars. We alternate planning rides on the various trails that have sprung up across our rural area.

Dave and I take our turn at hosting. Twenty snowmobiles, all Badger people, leave our home high on a hill south of the river on the outer edge of Baraboo. We travel west along CR W to North Freedom, where we have arranged a pit stop at my family's farm. Mom serves our homemade summer sausage, cheese, hot sandwiches, and cookies. Dad hands out drinks. My brother David joins us with his sled.

Group rides are organized in northern Wisconsin well before resorts in this tundra have winterized accommodations. David wakes one morning to snow accumulated on his pillow. Like children, we peer through the crack in the log wall at the head of the bed and see Roger already fueling sleds.

I learn to drink shots of blackberry brandy, not beer, to minimize how much liquid I consume. Dropping a one-piece snowmobile suit to pee in a snowdrift is not easy or comfortable. Worse, one lady thought it was leaves blowing across the crust of snow while she relieved herself. It was not. She had disrupted a mouse nest.

Cookout (1971)

Sharing social time with coworkers is the new normal.

Loyalty to your first shift remains strong. D shift plans weekend parties when they work days so spouses and friends can attend. One cookout in 1970 represents many other parties. Lab folk know each other well by this time.

David and I join a short happy hour at Herman's Supper Club in Baraboo. George, the solutions guy, has already left to light the charcoal. Others take a list to Pierce's grocery store. The women head to the meat counter. The guys spread out.

When Milt, the meat cutter, holds up the first naked chicken body for our inspection, it tickles Natalie. Her giggles trigger a chain reaction. Each chicken Milt displays becomes funnier than the last until we are hysterical and can only shake our heads yes or no. I unsuccessfully stifle laughter and hope Milt doesn't recognize me. I shop here weekly as a reserved young woman who graduated from high school with his son.

Note to self—buy groceries before happy hour.

David does not drink alcohol when he drives. "My job at UPS depends on it," he says to those who raze him.

We follow the others to Wisconsin Dells and pull into a gravel parking lot on the west side of the Wisconsin River close to the bridge going into downtown. A small, nondescript trailer sits on the far side. Cute Jack, with his twinkling dark eyes, bunks there with Jim, the accountant who went to help in the aftermath of the explosion of the Hardening House in 1966. Jim will become plant manager after the war. Several circular metal grills glow under shade trees beyond the trailer. Jack is not around. And we do not see the accountant. Do they know the party is at their place?

The usual mix of young people and several married couples old enough to be our parents have assembled. We hang with the couples who have set their chairs in the shade away from the grills.

Dave and I park our bottle of Korbel brandy on the tiny kitchen table and mix two Old Fashioneds. Maraschino cherries and orange slices for garnishes are on the counter. A small window air conditioner barely controls the summer sun's heat hitting the side windows of the trailer. As we step outside into the fresh air and festivities, more people arrive.

Employee banter spills into the festivities, putting the oldsters and young adults on the same playing field. Spouses and guests have become used to this casual teasing.

Bernie, one of the parent types, fusses about washing the chicken before it goes on the grill. She knows about preparing food. She and her husband Bud raised four children. The young people are teasing her about being too persnickety, just like they tease her at work.

"I never wash chicken before I grill it. Heat from the charcoal kills germs."

These comments only fuel Bernie's persistence. She makes a production of returning to the trailer and washing two pieces of chicken for herself and Bud.

"If you people get sick, don't say I didn't warn you," she sputters while bustling the clean chicken halves back to the grill.

Bernie stops in her tracks. All the grates are full.

With an about-face, she huffs back to the trailer.

"I'll wait. I'm not mixing my chicken with any that's not washed."

The young people snicker, knowing they bested Bernie.

Having made their point, some look to mend the wound. Sandy and others try to convince George, the grill master, to make room for two more pieces of chicken so Bernie and Bud can eat with the rest of us. George holds his ground for several minutes but relents.

Sandy heads to the trailer to convey the news.

But Bernie has her own surprise. She steps out with a wide smile and her two chicken halves on a plate. Each has a maraschino cherry tucked under its naked white wing.

George's face sags as Bernie proudly places her dinner on the grill without saying a word. She turns and struts back to join us with a satisfied look.

"I may be older, but I'm also smarter," she quips.

The young people go quiet.

"Something's going on over there." Natalie's eyes shift to the grills. We stifle giggles in anticipation of more antics to come.

"Nah," Bernie exclaims with confidence. "They're just not used to being outsmarted by us wiser types."

"I don't know, Bernie. There's something in the works." Natalie snickers behind her cupped hand.

Bud hands his wife a fresh Old Fashioned as the rest of us casually peer toward the grills.

Roger stands and flamboyantly asks Natalie, "Would you like another Old Fashioned, My Dear?"

"Why yes, I would, Sweetheart," Natalie replies with equal fervor.

Roger responds with a low bow, to everyone's delight.

"How about anyone else? I'll be bartender." Roger takes drink orders and heads to the trailer.

Natalie pokes my arm, nods toward the grills, and rolls her eyes toward Bernie. I don't know what the young people are doing. But mischief is happening.

"They wouldn't put anything on Bernie's chicken to make her sick, would they?" I whisper to Natalie.

Nat shakes her head. "I don't think so, but you watch. We'll warn Bernie if they do."

The screen door rattles. David jumps up to hold it for Roger, who balances a cake pan of drinks.

"I couldn't find cherries for the Old Fashioneds," Roger apologizes. "There are only slices of orange. We'll have to make do."

Bernie stops talking midsentence. Her eyebrows arch upward. She jumps out of her chair.

"Cherries? You stinkers better not have taken my cherries," Bernie yells as she marches toward the grills.

"We didn't touch your cherries, Bernie. Honest. We're just turning the racks so the meat doesn't burn." George gives one a quick spin.

"Not so fast. I don't want my dinner on the ground." Bernie is fired up.

"Why? What did you do? Why, you. Come back here. Which one is mine?"

George takes off like the Road Runner. Bernie, like Wile E. Coyote, sprints after him in hot pursuit. They head toward the bridge. I'm surprised at how fast she can run.

Natalie and I can't bear the suspense. We chuck our drinks and hurry to the grills. Tears of laughter spill down our cheeks as we watch the chicken halves circling above the charcoal.

The plant photographer took this photo for Badger World, the in-house newspaper, because the powder lab received a significant safety award. We assembled in the lunchroom. Carolyn Dallmann front row, second from left. *Image:* Badger History Group, Inc.

Every piece has a bright red cherry tucked under its wing.

The confusion ends when George and Bernie return. They sort the chicken to Bernie's satisfaction.

At work Monday morning, we hear Bernie holler, "Yikes!"

Someone put a rubber chicken on the counter by her workstation.

"Yikes!" Bernie yells again when she opens her locker to grab lunch. Someone has taped a long piece of paper with the word Chicken in red letters inside.

The fun continues until D shift goes off days in the middle of the week.

Sadness, Confusion, and Water (1970-1971)

It is March 1970. I'm 23. David and I have been married four years when Dr. Pearson confirms I am three months pregnant. The baby is due in September. We receive a round of congratulations for our happy news. Many classmates and friends have young children. They will share maternity clothes and baby equipment.

I have experience caring for babies. Mom needed help with my little brother, Randy. I was nine when he was born. Families I babysat for added more children while I worked for them.

This child will be ours.

However, I feel a gnawing threat of losing the new freedom David and I enjoy. A baby will create significant change.

My husband continues working night shifts at UPS. The long-ago promise of working days has not yet happened.

Those thoughts make me feel guilty. I push them away.

Badger will require me to go on maternity leave when I reach six months.

In May, I'm admitted to St. Clare's Hospital during the night with stabbing pains in my abdomen. Cramps continue until injections end the contractions. The bleeding does not stop.

Dr. Pearson enters my room late that evening. Blood pressure is dropping. Surgery. Days in the hospital. I am no longer pregnant.

I am tired.

Dr. Pearson gives me the clinical details. He advises a blood transfusion.

"Is it necessary?" I ask.

"No," he says. "However, it will give you more energy and make you feel less tired."

I resist saying, "I'd rather not."

Pearson does not push me. He adds lifting restrictions on my return-to-work papers for next week.

UPS does not grant David time off for my medical situation.

The hospital relaxes their strict visitation hours for us during my stay. My husband spends time with me. However, the continual stream of staff in and out of my room interrupts our conversations. We feel like they are spying on us.

My best school friend is getting married in two weeks. I'm a bridesmaid. She offers sympathy when I talk with her from my hospital room. Dr. Pearson approves of me being in the wedding.

Focusing on the event is a relief, something to look forward to. I no longer worry about fitting into the long pink satin and organdy gown. I don't feel guilty about my excitement.

Should I?

I feel. I don't know how I feel.

I do not cry. Crying is not my nature.

Should I feel guilty because I do not cry?

I don't know anyone who's had a miscarriage.

Should I ask?

Would they tell me? Would they talk about it?

When I return home, David and I communicate via notes during the week. We have done this since we started working opposite hours. I feel him watching me on weekends, assessing my health. He worries about my physical condition. We focus on the future when we are together. What happened is seldom discussed.

My husband is afraid of a second pregnancy. So am I.

Some people extend words of sympathy for our loss. Others avoid us, not knowing what to say. Despair creeps inside me—a deep, dark cavern.

I am tired.

My job requires concentration and provides needed space for me to heal. Intentionally or unintentionally, I bury myself and the miscarriage in work.

Weeks later, the overwhelming, tired feeling dissipates. Dave and I rejoin family events and parties with friends and coworkers.

Before the miscarriage, Don Peterson, my supervisor, explained he would oversee new testing that has nothing to do with gunpowder. "The government has established rules to assure the public has clean water. They take effect in 1972," he tells us. "Norma will start setting up physical tests."

We ask why we are starting this project now when the rules will not be effective for two more years.

Don explains, "The Clean Water Act of 1972 has two parts: sewage treatment and industrial discharge. Both parts affect Badger. The government has funded water testing for facilities like Badger. Results will show if our systems comply or need updating before the deadline. If we start testing now, there'll be time for adjustments or to obtain additional funding if necessary. Additionally, the results will establish a baseline."

My training under Norma started a week before the miscarriage.

Like Natalie, Norma is a mom. She and Wally have five daughters. Rita, the oldest, is about my age. She and Natalie have different personalities, but they best understand my complicated situation when I return to work. They handle me with kid gloves, like mother hens, until they see my old self return.

I have been back to work for a month when Norma ventures, "Can I ask how you're feeling?" She is usually less direct with her concerns. But her question does not surprise me.

"I slept almost ten hours Friday night," I respond. "It seems I need a lot of rest."

"Did you tell your doctor?" she asks.

"Yes. He says I should expect that."

I add, "I don't like to sleep that much on weekends because Dave and I have so little time together. I managed with eight hours on Saturday and Sunday."

Norma does not probe deeper.

One late summer morning, Don tells me to ride with Norma when she collects weekly water samples. I was hoping this would happen. I want to know more about Badger. Opportunities like this will disappear when the war ends and the plant closes.

Ball powder production buildings sit close to the road that runs south of the lab. We pass where the 1966 explosion happened.

An open prairie lays beyond ball powder except for a three-story screen house sitting to the east and rows of poles supporting various pipes. No evidence remains to indicate how this area looked before the government built the plant.

We enter a grove of woods—no buildings, poles, or pipes. A heavy canopy of mature trees creates a dark green arch as the road bends and twists. I wish I could hear the stories these trees could tell.

The temperature drops in the sun's absence, a subtle suggestion of the coming season. Crumbled foundations that were once homes and farm buildings are reminders of what families lost in the early 1940s.

"The Army left these old roads," Norma explains. "We'll take a different route back to the lab. You'll see."

I gawk with wonder.

Norma explains our mission as she drives. "Most sample points are not easily accessed. Some are reservoirs. Others are small waterfalls. Few are within reach."

The collection contraption lies in the back of the truck. It's a long pole with a metal container attached to one end. A quart-sized glass jar fits in the container. Holes in the metal drain excess water.

When we arrive at the wastewater facility, Norma says, "Let me collect the samples. You watch." Is she questioning my stamina? Or is she afraid I will take this job away from her?

"I'd like the hands-on experience," I offer. "Why don't you demonstrate? Then let me try."

"You seem to be back to your old self," Norma smiles knowingly.

"I'm fine." I appreciate her concern but object to patronizing.

Norma struggles with the first heavy sample pulled from an outfall. She hands the pole to me.

I cut Norma slack. The job is more taxing than I expected.

After that day, Norma and I alternate taking the three-mile trip to the wastewater treatment plant and sewage disposal facility.

I venture on various worn country roads that existed years before the government claimed this land. Old stone foundations conjure ghosts of families who once lived here.

Where was the Shimniok farm located? I do not know.

A glass quart jar of water in a metal container at the end of a long pole is heavy and challenging to control. If the sample point is a waterfall, the difficulty increases with the distance I must reach and the force of the falling water. Some sample points require squatting or otherwise lowering or twisting your body.

It takes both my hands to steady the long pole. The force of water from outfalls can easily knock the entire apparatus from my grasp.

Weather changes the pleasant experience of these outings. Late summer air becomes stifling. Insects buzz my ears as the sun beats on my green lab coat. Controlling the beastly pole makes my hands quiver. My arms ache.

Some days, I question why I ever wanted to collect samples.

It's worse in winter. The heavy coat I wear over my lab coat offers protection from the cold, but the wind across the prairie is brutal. The Army provides tall rubber boots. However, the grated metal bridges over some of the collection points are slippery with ice. The steel covering my toes negates the warmth provided by my footwear.

I use the metal railings to steady myself, but the wide-spaced rails would do little to keep me from slipping into the icy water below.

Lightweight gloves worn inside the required plastic or latex offer minimal insulation from the cold. Gloves make handling the glass containers a challenge. They occasionally slide from my fingers. Some break, and I must start over.

The worst condition is when it is so cold that water freezes in the grooves of jars or bottles before I can turn on the lids. In those situations, I maneuver the container close to my body without touching it to me. With my back to the wind, I wipe as much water as possible from the grooves. The last resort is to return to the truck with each sample, thaw the ice, and screw on the cover.

Red and numb fingers slip into my heavy, warm mittens for the drive back to the lab. On those days, I think back to farm chores. When temperatures dipped to unbearable, my brothers and I warmed cold hands and feet in the lower level of the pig barn. A huge metal cauldron of water heated by the wood fire wrapped in flexible metal sheathing beneath it provided heat.

Pigs do not generate heat like cows and need extra warmth. The shelter of the pig barn was a godsend for my brothers and me on cold winter days.

Sample collection is an integral part of testing. If a sample is not appropriately collected, preserved, and transported to a laboratory, test results are compromised no matter how sophisticated the testing equipment.

Water work expands. The war rages on. Norma and I split our time between working with water and gunpowder.

We implement sulfate and chloride water testing using the UV/VIS spectrophotometer and initiate biological testing. Each new activity becomes a resource that significantly affects my future.

The Safe Drinking Water Act of 1974 and the Resource Conservation and Recovery Act, RCRA, of 1976 will expand rules to include testing drinking water and groundwater. Those regulations change my life.

Testing gunpowder and water samples generates many numbers. Most of these require calculation. Lab staff share one 9-line calculator located in the lab office. Numbers are handwritten. There are no computers. And even if someone owns a calculator, the Army does not allow us to bring private property to work.

It is in everyone's best interest to calculate their work incrementally during their shift and not wait until the end of the day. Technicians stand in line with workbooks in hand waiting their turn at the 9-line beast. Supervisors get after anyone hogging the machine just before shift change. Additionally, missing your bus to the clock alleys or loitering until the next shift arrives may result in a reprimand report placed in your permanent file.

The plant photographer took the following pictures for *Badger World*, the in-house newspaper at Badger. The associated article explained the new water testing at the powder laboratory for the Clean Water Act of 1972.

* * *

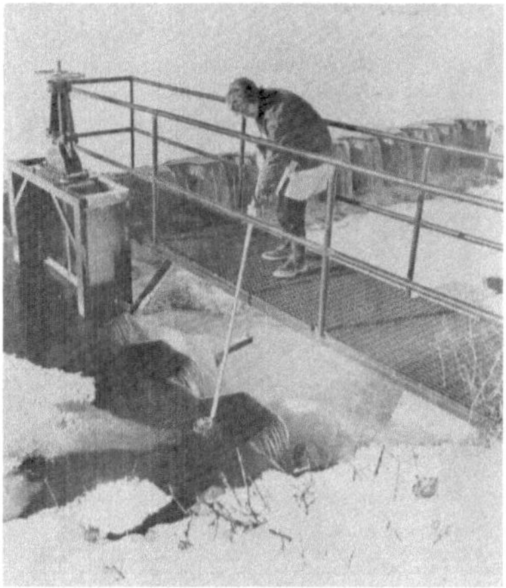

(l) Norma Clavadatscher collects a water sample from an outfall location; (r) Norma places samples in an autoclave. *Images:* Badger History Group, Inc.

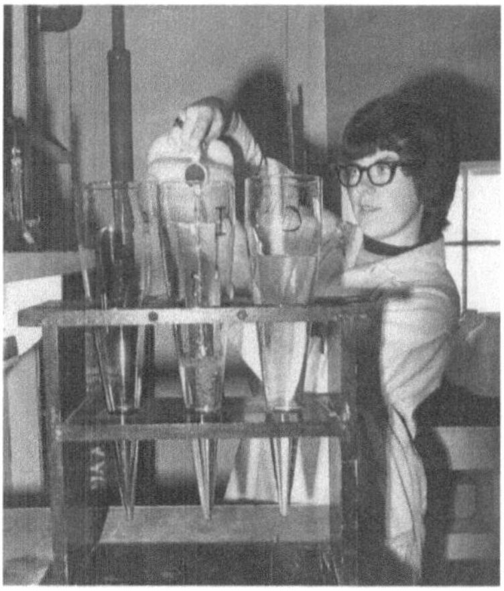

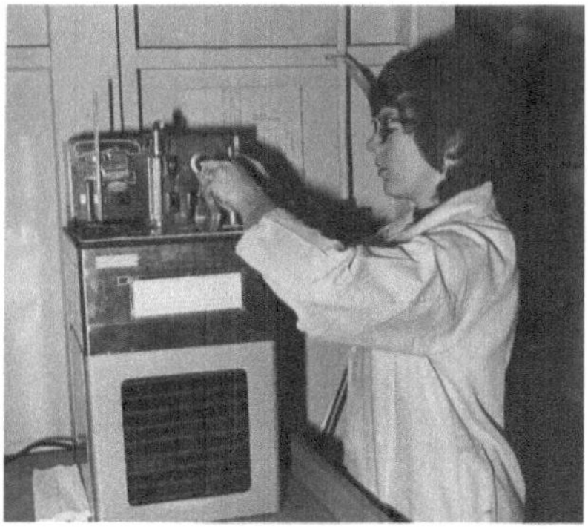

(l) Carolyn Dallmann measures settleable solids; (r) Carolyn places samples in a water bath for a fecal coliform test. *Images:* Badger History Group, Inc.

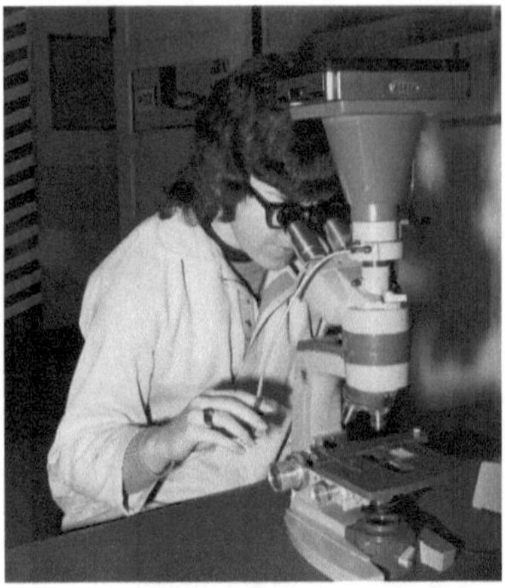

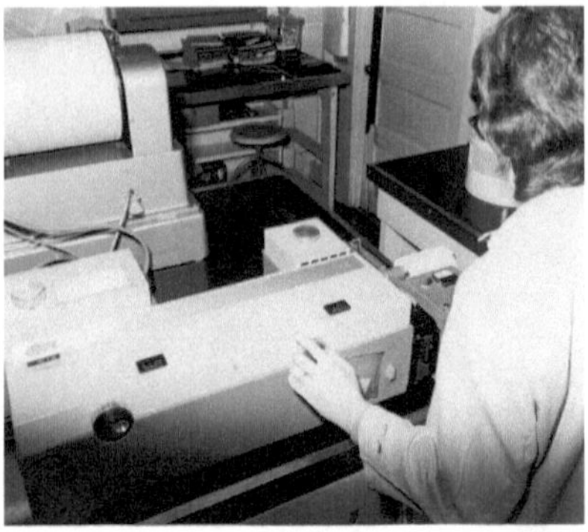

(l) Carolyn Dallmann counts colonies on a water sample after incubation; (r) Carolyn tests water samples for nitrates and sulphates using the UV/VIS spectrophotometer. *Images:* Badger History Group, Inc.

Don Turkowski, Gary Kramer, and Verna Hackett work at the supervisor's desk in the powder lab office during the Vietnam War. Clipboards hold data relating to individual batches of gunpowder. The 9-line calculator sits on a table across the room from this desk. Propellant was not allowed in the office, which makes the room appear different from testing rooms. Notice the conventional outlets and clock. The in-house telephone by Verna's shoulder could not be used to make or receive offsite calls. . *Image:* Badger History Group, Inc.

Escapes from War (1970-1974)

The war shows no signs of slowdown.

Line supervisors scream for test results. Supervisors move their people around to maximize sample flow. Lab technicians perform hundreds of tests and measurements daily.

Antiwar protests continue throughout the country. Riots break out on city streets and campuses. On May 4, 1970, the Ohio National Guard opens fire on students at Kent State University, killing four and injuring nine. The students were protesting our military forces being used to expand the war into Cambodia and the presence of the National Guard on their campus.

Will the carnage ever stop?

Coworkers avoid talking about the war both on and off the clock. We seek escape from news broadcasts blaring gruesome details and statistics.

David and I are part of one of the Badger cliques. We also have a different circle of friends, classmates from high school and locals. These friends belong to two community organizations: the men are Jaycees, and the women Jaycettes. Most communities throughout the state have chapters. Members must be under the age of 36. The men meet on Mondays, work on projects on Wednesdays. The women meet on Tuesdays, work on projects on Thursdays. This arrangement allows one parent to be home with children, which eliminates the cost of a babysitter. The Baraboo chapter grows as Badger employees join.

Dave and I party with four of these couples at least one weekend every month. All are high school classmates. One of the husbands is in the food industry, another is in the asphalt business, one is a court reporter, and the other is an electrician. All the wives are stay-at-home moms. Their children range from newborns to early teenagers.

With the children in tow, we utilize local campgrounds, play minigolf, and ride go-carts. The court reporter has a foldout camper. The food couple has a motorhome. The asphalt people camp in an old school bus painted light blue with makeshift bunk beds in the back. We and the electrician couple have tents. Theirs is a newer model with a floor and a zipper door. Ours is an old Army officer's tent with a hole on the side to accommodate a wood stove. The Dallmann family uses it when they hunt deer in northern Wisconsin.

Crowds assemble to watch us set up our unique tent. Children point and laugh out loud when a gust of wind lifts the heavy canvas away from the stabilizing center steel pole. We look like pirates setting sail in a brisk gale.

With Badger booming, supper clubs and halls sponsor Saturday night dances. Impromptu parties depend on Casey Kasem's Top 40 to provide the music. Retired Jaycee couples form a dance club by splitting expenses for private parties. When hiring bands becomes too expensive, they invite us younger couples to join to defray costs.

To cover expenses for community projects, we become proficient fundraisers. Brat stands, bake sales, and raffles are typical. I crochet afghans with my name label attached. Years later, people tell me, "I won your afghan."

We sponsor a 26-mile Walk for Cystic Fibrosis. One couple has two young boys diagnosed with the disease, which causes breathing issues. They move to a larger city with a medical facility better equipped to treat their sons. Learning about the devastating illness creates awareness. I co-chair the event and participate.

Our route begins at the Baraboo Senior High School and heads west out of town on country roads along the Hogsback Bluff on the north side of the Baraboo River Valley. A direct turn south descends to Rock Springs, a small village with a few bars that serve food. It continues south toward LaRue, then shifts east up Brilliott's Hill on CR W through the bluffs south of the river and back to Baraboo. Members who are not walking will monitor hydrating stations. A number of Badger employees walk or volunteer.

I partner with Paulette. She and her husband rent what was our one-bedroom apartment below our three-bedroom. Paulette is an attractive, petite brunette. If she didn't joke about her glass eye, no one would ever know.

We walk a mile or two daily during the weeks before the event to prepare for the challenge. Our pact is to pace ourselves, support each other, and finish. But we are naïve about what a long walk entails.

My tennis shoes are old, so I chose to wear comfortable Hush Puppies—a big mistake.

Four of us women take off at a steady pace at eight in the morning. Groups of men charge ahead of the pack. The walk lasts ten hours. Anyone on the 26-mile course at six in the evening will be hauled back to town.

Two of our four ladies give up at the first hydrating station on the Hogsback. Refreshed with water, Paulette and I head to Rock Springs.

Descending off the Hogsback to the village, the aroma of burgers and fries pulls us toward one of the bars. We have completed the first ten miles.

"Let's eat and have a beer," Paulette says. I agree. My stomach is growling.

Approaching an establishment, the door swings open as we are about to enter. Half a dozen guys pour out.

"I'm done. They can pick me up and haul me home. I don't care," one says.

"If you quit, I will too. Let's have another beer." The guy pulls his buddy back into the bar.

I stop Paulette. "Let's not go in. We'll end up like those two if we have a greasy burger and alcohol."

"My feet hurt," my partner admits. "I didn't want to say anything and let you down."

"We need a rest. Let's grab water and a snack at the hydrating station," I suggest. My feet and legs are tired, but I say nothing to Paulette.

Workers at the station tell us many men dropped out after eating. We smile.

"I told you those guys who took off like racers would wear themselves out by the halfway mark," Paulette whispers. Her exuberance has returned.

We decide to slow our pace, conserve energy, hydrate, and rest briefly at every station. The stops are closer together on the last part of the route. It's twelve-thirty when we head south.

The bottoms of my feet feel warm, an unusual sensation. I say nothing. My legs are stiff when I stand after resting at the LaRue station. One volunteer encourages us to stretch. "Ouch," we simultaneously holler when we bend.

At three-thirty, we haul our aching bodies upright at the bottom of Brilliott's Hill. It looms a quarter mile straight up at a stiff pitch. We're leaving the Baraboo River Valley.

Stopping on the bridge at the bottom of the hill, Paulette starts to sob. "I can't do it. I hurt all over," she moans.

"Let's try it slow. Like a turtle," I encourage. "If we can make the hill, it'll get easier." I don't say it, but every part of me screams "STOP."

Paulette dries her tears but shakes her head no. She turns. We are six miles from finishing the route. I'm relieved she's calling it quits.

But she does not quit. Instead, she takes a first step backward up the hill. Then another. "It doesn't hurt as much when I walk backward."

I give it a try but walk facing her as we inch along the incline. We're both in agony at the top, but continuing on level ground is less painful. Cars roll through the bluffs monitoring our progress. We hide our pain with smiles and do not give in when they beckon us to ride.

WE—CAN—DO—THIS.

Going up a short rise out of a swale, it hits me. EXHAUSTION.

I get weepy when Paulette puts her hands on my shoulders. "We'll ride into town when the next car goes by," she comforts.

I shake my head. "No. I'll make it. We'll see Baraboo in a mile."

We cross the finish line at 6:03. Pain muffles the applause we receive for our effort.

The project raises over $10,000 for cystic fibrosis research and support.

The following day, five large blisters shine on the bottoms of my feet. They squish when I walk. It's Family Day at UW-Stevens Point, the college Dave's sister attends. My husband and his grandmother sandwich me in the backseat. His parents are upfront. We drive 90 miles north.

My hips ache.
My feet throb.

David and I learned hard work and responsibility as farm kids. The Jaycee and Jaycette organizations teach teamwork and leadership skills. Working together towards common goals builds precious, invaluable friendships.

The two organizations depend on support from local businesses. One offers a unique suggestion to support us.

George and Ruth Culver own and operate the Farm Kitchen Restaurant south of town by Devils Lake. They also own the A&W Root Beer stand in Sauk City. George had been a production line supervisor at Badger. Their son, Craig, is three years younger than me.

They offer us a monetary reward if our members manage the buffet, serve as hostesses, and bus tables at one of their famous Sunday morning breakfasts at the Farm Kitchen. The restaurant holds 150. People often wait in a line outside the front door for a seat.

The event was a win-win. Some lab people and other Badger employees were part of the attending crowd. It was their first visit to the Farm Kitchen. They will return. The money earned by the organizations goes toward community projects.

Years later, George, Ruth, and Craig build the first Culver's Restaurant on the site of their old root beer stand in Sauk City. Crowds will flock to savor FROZEN CUSTARD and BUTTER BURGERS at their many locations in the future.

When Will It End? (1973-1974)

Coworkers speculate about the war. "How long will it last? Should I look for another job? I hear the plastic factories are hiring." Badger has never continuously operated for this long.

I reflect on the Vietnam War. I remember President Kennedy's assassination and President Lyndon Johnson's swearing-in on the airplane. Naïvely, when I was hired, I did not associate Johnson's "Operation Rolling Thunder" with my job at Badger.

I remember President Richard Nixon taking office in 1970.

The Watergate scandal, 1972-1974, adds to the madness of the war. Although the mess does not directly affect Badger, everyone has an opinion. Break-ins, investigations, finger-pointing, coverups, litigation, impeachment proceedings, and the resignation and pardoning of President Nixon push war statistics to the back burner.

The constant barrage of disturbing news wears on everyone.

There are no plant-wide announcements that Badger is closing. However, those with experience know when funding ends, operations stop. The result is abrupt. Talk of moving on undulates the workforce like quiet waves escalating to a tsunami.

On September 28, 1971, President Nixon signed legislation to end conscription. On January 27, 1973, Secretary of Defense Melvin Laird announces, "The draft has ended."

The 1973 Paris Peace Accords are signed, and US forces are withdrawn. But those rules are broken almost immediately.

What will it take to end the war?

The now not-so-young chemists are job hunting.

The in-house newspaper, *Badger World*, posts an article in 1973 thanking nitrocellulose workers for a job well done. The NC lines shut down.

Lab technicians scan the want ads in local and Madison newspapers, looking for opportunities. Businesses post job openings on cork boards in grocery stores in town.

Sandy lands a job in one of the Baraboo plastic factories. Donna Two goes to Industrial Coils, also in town. Some of the youngsters enroll in college. Karen buys a bar in Poynette, where Natalie and Roger live. Donna One and her husband build a motel across from the Sauk Prairie airport.

Options run through my mind and tangle. I could return to college. Where? UW-La Crosse, my alma mater, is 100 miles northwest. UW-Madison is 50 miles southeast. The two-year Wisconsin System campus in Baraboo is the logical choice. I have money saved toward tuition. But our lifestyle will change if we rely solely on my husband's income. I could work part-time and attend classes.

In late August 1973, Helen calls me to the office for a personal call.

Now what?

It's David. He has never called me at work. I suspect the worst.

"Remember that small motorhome on the trailer lot north of town?" he asks.

I remember. It is the same model as the food guy's but shorter. A for sale sign of $10,000 has been posted on the vehicle all summer—out of our price range.

"I stopped in to look at it today. The unit has less than 7,000 miles on it. A couple drove it to Arizona and back one time before he got cancer. They traded it for a trailer home. That's why it's on the lot. I offered the guy $6,000." My husband sounds nervous. "He said it was mine if I had the money tomorrow."

I am silent, knowing a good deal. Everything we own is paid for except the mortgage on our home. But $6,000 is a lot of money if I don't have a job and return to college.

"Call the bank. Ask if we can get a loan so we do not have to deplete our savings." Now my voice is trembling.

We have camped in the Army tent for seven years and have been looking at foldout campers. The little motorhome is a good buy. BUT.

When I get home, Dave tells me he conditionally put money down on the vehicle. We can drive it and let the man know in the morning if we will take it. We cruise across town to meet the food guy.

The men are like boys with a new toy. They check the engine and inspect each external storage compartment. One contains the batteries that operate the electric system in the cabin. Another is labeled generator. When the door pops open, it's empty. That means no air conditioning. DRAT.

Food guy suggests we drive the unit to his RV dealer in Madison. The salesman he sends us to is from Baraboo and will wait for our arrival in an hour.

My husband inspects gauges and dials on the dashboard as he drives. "Look over the interior. Check the drawers and cushions. We need to know if anything is broken," he tells me.

The inside of the motorhome is in perfect condition. The carpet, upholstery, and stove are bright red. The driver's and double passenger front seats are black faux leather. The cabinets and walls are light wood. A map of the United States covers the Formica table. It drops down to become a bed. There is a closet and a small bathroom. The sofa in the back converts to a double bed. It is like driving a house.

"I wish it had air conditioning," I lament.

"We can add a generator later if we need air conditioning." I am glad my husband is familiar with such things.

The RV man performs a thorough, professional inspection. "If you don't buy, call me. I'll take it."

David does the paperwork in the morning. The motorhome is ours.

Knowing the camping season will end soon, we eke out several trips to state parks.

"Natalie said we should go to Disney World. They went when it first opened. She gave me her brochures." I lay the papers on the table. We have explored much of Wisconsin but rarely travel out of state.

My husband hesitates. "The price of gas is going up." His discomfort crawls around the room and up the walls.

I say nothing.

"We bought it to use it," he says, wrestling with himself.

"If gas becomes an issue, we should be able to get our money out of it," I venture.

We head for Orlando in October 1973 in high spirits. Disney World is our first weeklong escape from work. Our mood dampens when we drive through Chicago. Gas is an unheard-of 55 cents a gallon.

Disney World is everything we expected and more. We spend two nights in their recently developed campground. Before leaving Florida, we take turns driving on the sand of Dayton Beach and explore Castillo de San Marcos, the old fort in historic St. Augustine.

We plan to repay the new loan in a year. I can return to college when Badger closes if we manage our savings judiciously.

Buying the motorhome was timely. Camping weekends with friends are a big part of our social life. The motorhome allows me to drive and meet our friends at a campsite on Fridays while Dave works. I quickly master leveling the unit using ramps of propped slab wood. David joins us around the campfire or stretches out for a long snooze when he gets off work.

I see the lab with new eyes when we return from Florida. Everything is in flux.

George, the solution guy, takes a job with a laboratory up north near Tomahawk. It is an ideal location for him because he likes to hunt and fish. He will manage that lab one day.

Jim, the chemist and quasi-guard, married Sue, one of the technicians, in the late 1960s. With degrees from UW-La Crosse in chemistry and accounting, he successfully writes the CPA exam and works for a private firm in Baraboo. Jim will become a partner in that business in the future. He is our tax guy.

Don Peterson goes to one of the plastics plants in Portage. Gary, another chemist, does too. They will retire from their respective companies. Dave, a relatively new, young chemist in the instrument group, lands a job at Caterpillar in Illinois, where he has a long and successful career.

By early 1974, the sample flow dwindles to a trickle. There is talk of moving the acid-nitrocellulose lab into the powder and government lab buildings. We feel the pinch, the beginning of the end.

Management addresses the inevitable. Employees are offered voluntary layoff with severance pay.

Natalie is selective in her job search.

"I sent my application to be a dispatch operator for Madison Gas and Electric," she announces one morning.

"What does a dispatch operator do?" I ask.

"People call MG&E when they need a hookup, Diggers Hotline, or if they smell gas. I will be one of the people answering those calls." Natalie laughs. "I like variety. It shouldn't get boring."

She is ecstatic when she gets the job.

"Don't look so sad," her arms wrap around me. "We'll still see each other."

I manage a smile. "I don't want to come to work if you're not here."

"Things change, Carolyn. Don't idealize situations. Adapt." Nat's words bolster my outlook.

The slowdown is demoralizing. Everyone is looking for their next job. Departing employees are grouped for farewell celebrations. Festivities with doughnuts and cake do not disguise the stark reality of Badger's looming closure.

I hold on until spring when we find out I am pregnant. David and I agree I should take the layoff. The pregnancy is a surprise. The baby is due at the end of October. We do not want to compromise this child or my health. The severance pay will help me transition to being a stay-at-home mom.

I continue with the instrument group, but sample flow incrementally slows. I thought I would be one of the last to leave the powder lab because of my high seniority and even hoped I would be retained for water testing.

The pregnancy changes all of that. Natalie is already gone when I make the announcement at work. However, I tell her the happy news first. She is already talking about a baby shower in the fall. My outlook changes. Badger is ending. I must adapt.

Two other techs retire with me. Our names are spelled out in blue frosting on the sheet cake. After so many departures, it does not seem special. A numb feeling runs through me. Badger and the powder lab can never be what they were unless there is another war.

I let it go.

We have a baby on the way.

I walk across the parking lot for the last time at the end of May 1974, eight years from when I first walked into Badger. I am proud of my accomplishments at this strange place. A soft "goodbye" escapes my lips. My career, like the powder lab and Badger, ends.

Little do I know what lies ahead.

3

THE IN-BETWEEN YEARS

1974–1988

Daughters and Sewing

Unexpected energy replaces the overwhelming exhaustion of the first three months of pregnancy. We transition the small bedroom to baby's room. I crochet a reversible baby blanket; mint green and white do up nicely. I love this child I have yet to meet.

David leaves for work early in the evening. He is a light sleeper and wakes at the slightest noise. I sleep soundly and seldom hear him return home in the wee hours of the morning. I stick to quiet tasks until he wakes.

Jaycette projects keep me involved with friends. We have fewer members because Badger is winding down. Church membership is also dwindling.

A Jaycette, whose husband's family owns McGann's Furniture Store, asks if I am interested in repairing draperies from out-of-state sewing shops. She is aware of my crochet and embroidery skills.

I decline, saying, "I have little experience with drapes."

Pat persists, "You wouldn't have to make them. Shortening or lengthening and small projects are the main tasks."

How hard can it be? The extra income would be nice.

Soon small sewing projects are strewn about the guest bedroom.

The baby is due October 26. I have followed my doctor's directions: no alcohol, a diet of fruits and vegetables, minimal fats, sweets, and salt. Medical people recommend a woman gain no more than 20 pounds during pregnancy. I have stayed at 14 with only a week to go. David and I have attended the new birthing classes at the hospital.

October 26 comes and goes. October changes to November. Early on November 2, I go into labor. The nurses in the maternity ward treat me like a star pupil. They unwisely tell me my labor will be short. They expect a six- or seven-pound baby. Our daughter is born at ten-thirty that night, weighing nine pounds, twelve ounces. I am exhausted.

Baby.

My life changes in a blink when I see her. I feel love—responsibility. I have new respect for my mother.

David takes us home from the hospital a week later. He delights in caring for our daughter when he is home. She sleeps eight hours at night within a few weeks and is perfect in every way.

As my strength returns, I resume sewing. The small income restores the sense of independence I felt for eight years. It will also help with Christmas gifts.

By 1975, we are squished into our duplex's three-bedroom upper half. We start looking at single-family homes. Prices are down because the powder plant is closing. A split-level three-bedroom on the hill above the Second Ward Park on the east side of Baraboo fits our needs. It is yellow with white trim. The adjacent lot to the west is vacant. Six weeping willows sweep fronds above the gently sloping lawn.

David and I meet with the bank president about a loan. We are naïve when it comes to real estate. Mr. Kent discourages us from buying until the duplex sells.

"A baby doesn't need much room." Kent's words are a subtle warning. Charts and numbers lay across his desk. The five percent interest rates of 1966 have now crept to nine.

We try selling the duplex on our own. One party commits, then backs out hours before signing. DRAT.

We list the duplex with a realtor, buy the house we love, and continue to rent the lower apartment to cover the extra house payment. After several months of skimping, we lower our asking price. The sale finalizes eight months later.

It's a good thing we bought in 1975. Interest rates continue upward until a 30-year fixed-rate loan peaks at over 16 percent in the early 1980s.

Our daughter sleeps on the table bed in the motorhome when we camp. My mother watches her on the rare occasions we go out of town snowmobiling.

I work sewing projects while tuning in to *Happy Days* and *Laverne & Shirley*. David misses evening television because of work. The book Jaws terrifies me. News programs feature the Patty Hearst kidnapping and Watergate convictions. Hank Aaron returns to Milwaukee to play for the Brewers, and Paul Harvey's *Rest of the Story* premieres on radio.

In 1975, Betty, an accomplished seamstress, approaches the furniture store about a job. Her husband is recently discharged from the Army. Pat shows me a sample of Betty's custom drapery work.

"It looks good. Better than what's been coming in from the workshops," I tell Pat.

Betty gets a job. McGann's starts advertising hand-sewn draperies. When Betty becomes overwhelmed with work in 1976, Pat asks me to do full orders.

I'm scared. "What if I mess up?" I ask.

"I'd like you to try. Work with Betty," Pat encourages.

"I want to talk with my husband before I commit." I am reluctant to take on more work because of the baby. But learning a new skill is enticing.

"What's in it for you? How do they pay Betty?" my husband asks.

I look around the house. Our existing drapes look sad and faded.

I ask Pat to quote me a price for my favorite material. If Betty helps me fabricate window treatments for our home and depending on how the drapes look when finished—I will try sewing for the store.

This is a big ask. Our home has an open design, a mid-century modern look, with many windows in the main living area.

Pat agrees.

Betty teaches me the math to calculate how much fabric to order. When the heavy bolt arrives, she drills me on how to inspect every inch before making the first cut. I work slowly, fearful of making a mistake.

David helps hang the drapes. They look fabulous and update our home. I am soon sewing complete residential and commercial orders.

Betty and I cannot keep up with demand. We look for someone to train. Most people who sew use patterns to make clothes. Draperies are different; there are no patterns. With Pat's help, we pool our resources, find, and train another seamstress, then another.

Our daughter is a tiny Artist. First using crayons, then colored pencils, she draws scenes and figures by age three. She is independent, not cuddly, and prefers indoors to nature.

A second baby is on the way, due October 15, 1978. The Artist is almost four years old and not happy about having a brother or sister. A month before the baby is due, she finally says we may bring the baby home if we call her Linda. Boys are out of the question.

Where did that come from?

In the wee hours of the fifteenth, I go into labor. A baby girl arrives on her due date, weighing nine pounds, six-and-a-half ounces. I gained less than ten pounds with the pregnancy. My arms are skin and bones. David takes us home a week later because the baby has an allergic reaction, a rash, and I am fighting a nasty virus and sinus infection.

This baby cuddles but does not sleep as well as her sister.

Keeping the house quiet during the day is a challenge. We tell the girls they can only cry in the family room in the southwest corner of the house. Daddy sleeps on the upper level in our northeast corner bedroom.

We invest in a baby monitor to relay sound between the sewing room in the basement and the girls' bedrooms on the upper level. I begin sewing when they go to bed and during naps—burning the candle at both ends.

The baby sings. By age two, she knows the words and melodies for songs her sister brings home from school. At age three, she knows multiple verses of familiar hymns. Otherwise shy around people, she belts out random songs to entertain. She performs silly tricks to garner more attention. Her favorite is to pull her sister's stocking cap over her eyes, put her arms straight out, and walk until she bumps into something. She is our tiny Actress.

McGann's business picks up when school starts because moms have extra time to focus on their homes. Fabric warehouses offer wholesale discounts, which stores like McGann's pass on to customers.

Betty and her husband move two years after she first walked into the store. But not before we train other seamstresses to sew handmade drapes for McGann's. We stitch all side and bottom seams with a needle and thread.

Sewing is piecework. The faster I sew, the more money I make. I inspect and cut fabric, stitch widths together, insert buckram, tack pleats, and press and pin hems in my basement workroom before I haul the panels to the family room to tackle handwork.

We pick up a small black and white television for my workroom. This luxury brings me *The Tonight Show* with Johnny Carson. Time flies during the program.

I follow news stories. Jimmy Carter defeats Gerald Ford. Pope John Paul visits New York City and meets President Carter at the White House. NASA space launches are commonplace and remind me of Neil Armstrong's first walk on the moon in 1969.

Headlines announce trouble in the Middle East. Ayatollah Khomeini returns to Iran and regains power. Saddam Hussein becomes President of Iraq. There are mass murders. On November 4, 1979, 500 Iranian students loyal to Ayatollah Khomeini seize the US Embassy in Tehran, taking 90 hostages. This marks the beginning of the Iran Hostage Crisis.

Only days later, there is a false alarm of a Soviet ballistic missile attack by the US NORAD system after a technician fails to code a message properly. The country is on edge.

Jimmy Carter announces a halt to Iranian oil imports and freezes Iranian assets. Days later, Iran cancels all contracts with US oil companies.

Crowds attack US Embassies in Pakistan and Libya.

The grand finale happens on Christmas Day 1979 when the Soviet Union invades Afghanistan. The following day they take the presidential palace in Kabul. On December 27, the Soviets pull off a coup, killing President Hafizullah Armin.

The constant barrage of bad news reminds me of the daily Vietnam War reports while I worked at Badger.

Locals stop asking me about the powder plant as they realize I am sewing. Lab work fades from my mind. However, when the news reports chaos in the world, I think about Badger.

Will we be pulled into another situation like Vietnam? Will the powder plant operate again?

I remember the 10-Year Modernization Plan introduced in 1970 by David Fordham, Plant Engineer for the Army at Badger. The Army funded 27 projects over ten years to completely overhaul Badger at a cost of 385 million dollars. Manufacturing areas would be centralized and updated with the latest equipment.

Frank Wolf is the Chief Modernization Engineer.

Although I worked in the powder lab at the time, the details did not concern me. Now I wonder, "Is the Modernization Plan ongoing?"

I ask past employees about the plant. They assure me that modernization is ongoing. In late 1979, I sign up at the local employment agency, specifying my interest in a job at Badger.

I do not want to work outside of our home now because the girls are so young. However, I do not want to miss a future opportunity to return to lab work.

Over the next few years, I hear that the first of the 27 modernization projects are complete. Others are in progress or design. Then the Army expands their original plan to include environmental and other work, making a total of 55 projects at a cost of 626 million dollars and extends the program to 1994. Frank Wolf will serve as Chief Modernization Engineer through 1998.

A new acid facility, built in the central part of Badger, went through prove out. I can see the 150-foot building from SR 12. The manufacture of sulfuric and nitric acid, and oleum are combined in an automated, computerized operation. The old 32-inch piece of platinum gauze in the reaction vessel of the old facility was small compared to the six-foot platinum gauze in the new facility.

A Biazzi continuous production nitroglycerin facility was built over the site of the old facility and went through prove out. No NG was made, only water, because there are no customers for the large volume of product the unit can produce. It would take the pharmaceutical industry a year to use what the facility could produce in a couple of hours. The continuous process is unlike the old, more dangerous batch procedure, which yields a large amount of NG made on demand. The Biazzi facility makes a much smaller amount and stores the NG in underground steel-reinforced concrete tanks that hold 12,000 pounds of product.

Paul, the chemist with the handlebar mustache, and Doris, one of the lab techs, continue water testing in the powder lab. A few engineers, property and accounting people, and tradesmen maintain the facility in readiness should another war require a return to operation.

In early 1980, I receive a call from Badger asking if I am interested in a position funded for 18 months working with water.

My days in the powder lab flood back—a lot of fun with great people. But the girls are young. David still works nights for UPS. The thought of resuming sewing after being off for 18 months is overwhelming.

I decline the offer.

Badger remains a sleeping giant throughout the Afghanistan and Middle East situations.

1980s—The Bead

As the 1970s melt into the next decade, news first turns to politics. In a landslide election in 1980, Ronald Reagan wins with 489 electoral votes to Jimmy Carter's 49. Minutes after his inauguration on January 20, 1981, Iran releases the remaining 53 hostages, ending the 444-day crisis.

On March 30, 1981, 69 days after taking office, President Reagan is shot by a would-be assassin. Reagan quickly recovers and returns to the White House.

Tension between our country and the Soviet Union escalates. The threat of a large-scale nuclear war ebbs and flows. Badger remains on standby even though propellant is not needed for a nuclear war.

Interest rates for a 30-year mortgage drop from 16 to ten percent. This is an improvement, but still high.

In the fall of 1981, Mom and Dad auction the family farm. The event is deeply personal. My youngest brother Randy ran it until he married and moved to Oklahoma. My parents retire to a new two-bedroom home in North Freedom near the village park.

Dave's parents continue farming. However, they require more and more of their son's help with animals and repairing or updating tractors, equipment, and buildings.

Hundreds, then thousands of yards of fabric move in and out of our house. The installers come to our home to pick up orders.

My husband mentions that my sewing is taking over our home.

I consider starting my own business. But that would require moving it out of our house. Renting commercial property, marketing, dealing with the public and suppliers, installation, and the nuances of running a business become mind-boggling. Plus, competing with McGann's in our small town is intimidating. I am stuck.

Working at Badger was much more fun.

UW-Baraboo/Sauk County, the local two-year college affectionately known as BOO-U, offers computer programming courses. In the mid-1980s, I sign up for a summer class, hoping to track my business finances electronically. Our friends lend me their son's old computer for assignments—he needs to upgrade for university in the fall.

The first time I walk into a classroom of college kids, I want to turn around and run. But my comfort level grows when I find other nontraditional students in the mix. I get an A and register for a more advanced course.

We enjoy group camping with our friends and their children. I drive the motorhome to the chosen destinations, register, and use driving skills I learned on the farm to level the unit. The other couples watch the girls until the motorhome is stable. David comes to the campground after work and joins the fun.

One day, as the mother of young children, represents the many predicaments I routinely faced.

It's the summer of 1981. I am 34 years old and finishing work so we can meet our friends at Yogi Bear Campgrounds, a big treat for the children. But first, I must finish a sewing job and pick up the girls' studio photographs at JCPenney.

Twenty yards of sheer fabric drape across my lap and cascade to the floor. My needle glides through the material.

Footsteps clamber down the six carpeted stairs from our bedrooms to the living area. A scuffle through the kitchen follows. The girls bound into the family room where I work.

The Actress, three years old, is a drama queen. The Artist is an opinionated seven-year-old. Their hands clamp tightly over their mouths, keeping sobs and cries buried deep inside. Tears stream down their faces.

Rules are: No crying on the bedroom level where Daddy sleeps. Crying is allowed only in the family room on the opposite corner of the house.

"She shoved—they spilled— lost—picked up—she pushed," blurt out simultaneously.

"I'm glad you waited until you got downstairs to cry." I let them spill the loud part of what happened, "Beads—it was an accident—she wouldn't share."

"I need your help," I tell them. We quietly go up the stairs, tiptoe past the northeast bedroom, and sort their problem so we can concentrate on camping.

Bead drama replays while I finalize my purchase at JCPenney. I tell the girls to "shape up." The Artist's smug smile indicates a small victory. The Actress continues jabbering about beads on our way to the motorhome in the municipal parking lot two blocks away.

"What's she saying?" I ask.

"She has a bead in her nose." The Artist is nonchalant.

"What does that mean?" I ask, ignoring the obvious.

"She has a bead in her nose," comes the reply.

The photo package shifts to my oldest daughter. I hoist the youngest above my head. Her tears fall to my face. A shiny orb far back in the kid's nostril reflects daylight.

DRAT.

She tries to blow it out to no avail. Her cries become a howl. I cannot extract the bead even if I take her home. This dilemma will not improve at the campgrounds. It is Friday afternoon. The bank clock says it is almost five.

I jaywalk the girls across the street to Dr. Hansel's office. His receptionist leaves as we enter.

Two nuns sit in the waiting room. The girls are wide-eyed when they see the sisters in their habits. Crying stops.

St. Clare's Hospital, on the north side of town, is a division of a Catholic order. It is not unusual to see nuns at the hospital. But this close encounter is something the girls have never experienced. We are Lutheran.

Hansel excuses himself to the women, then invites the girls and me to an exam room. A bright light directed at the Actress's nostril reveals the problem. The Artist and I observe the doctor's maneuvers to remove the bead. It will not budge.

"I need something to get a grip," Hansel explains. "Have her lay still." I rephrase his orders to the Actress, who wants no part of the procedure. When she sees the long tweezers, she puts up a big fuss.

"My nurse is gone for the day," the doctor explains.

He points at me. "You. Hold her tight."

The Actress squirms. I cannot contain her powerful pushes and twists.

"I have an idea." Hansel leaves the room. He returns with the nuns in tow.

"They're trained to assist," he explains.

The Actress quiets as the sisters sandwich her between them. Habits frame their smiling faces above her watchful eyes. Their hands grip her tiny shoulders and arms. I hold her feet.

The Artist sits in the corner, her face ashen with fear.

With Hansel's hand on my daughter's forehead, the tweezers go in and slightly twist. He extracts a pink bead. It shines at the end of the instrument.

"That's my favorite bead. That's why she hid it in her nose," the Artist hollers. "I want it back."

"Let me wash it first," says Hansel. He moves to the basin and holds the bead under the stream.

Plink—Plink—Plink.

The bead comes loose and bounces around the white enamel. The doctor grabs, but he's not fast enough. The bead disappears down the drain under the Artist's horrified gaze.

"It's lost. I'll never get my bead back." Her wails bounce off the walls.

The nuns do not even attempt to hide their amusement.

The Actress grins from her perch on the exam table.

In August 1988, I meet Paul, a chemist I worked with at Badger, in front of the dime store. This was not the fussbudget guy that harassed poor Gordie. This is Paul with the handlebar mustache, yellow shirts, and brown pants.

"Did you apply for the job?" Paul asks.

"What job?" My name is at the local employment center specifically requesting a job at Badger.

"Doris is retiring. We have a college intern who is leaving for the fall semester."

"Where is it posted? Can I still apply?" My mind swirls with possibilities.

I call. The lady tells me, "Resumes will be accepted until Friday."

Two days.

I pull out my portable Royal typewriter with the Pica font.

4

RETURN TO BADGER

1988–1998

Assistant Chemist (1988)

It is 1988. I am 41 years old when I pull the assistant chemist job posting from the top of the refrigerator. The girls are in bed. Two hours later, many rejected drafts scatter across the floor. But I have a solid, single-page resume. A sheet of carbon paper from days gone by allows me to create a duplicate copy for myself.

The annual salary ranges between $18,500 to $23,500. I think big. The top of the range is a large sum compared to my sewing income, less than $10,000. Duties include laboratory tasks, collecting water samples, and technical writing. I have that skill set.

It also says candidates should have a bachelor's degree. Someone else without a degree would not apply. Hopefully, eight years of lab experience will compensate for the requirement. I must try.

On Friday morning, the guards record my personal information at the main gate and point me to the parking lot. I have never been inside the imposing, two-story administration building. A receptionist in the nondescript, tiny lobby smiles and takes my manila envelope.

That was easy.

Waiting is hard.

I worry. It's been over two weeks. Do they think my application is too audacious? Did it get lost?

Finally, I get the call. The lady schedules me for an interview in three days.

When I hang up, I wonder if what I heard was in my imagination.

I jump up and down, then stop. David is a light sleeper. I want to share my news, but he needs rest.

Nervous energy makes my hands shake when I try threading the needle. Fabric slides from my lap when I stand and dance like a little kid.

Settle down. You don't have the job yet.

My husband gets sideswiped when he wakes.

"That's wonderful." He asks for details, but I know little. We are calm by the time the girls arrive from school. The Artist is 14 years old. The Actress is ten. They take my news in stride and start homework.

My feet barely touch the ground the rest of the day. David leaves for work after supper. The girls settle for the night.

The interview—I panic.

What will they ask? What do I say? What are my strengths, my weaknesses? How many candidates applied?

I don't have a college degree.

I'll never get the job.

To calm my fears, I rehearse by listing anticipated questions. Sitting on a straight-back chair in front of the full-length mirror in our bedroom, I pretend and observe.

My hands and legs look awkward. Assuming a comfortable position, I concentrate on not moving my body while responding to the made-up questions. My answers reflect strengths. Examples support my claims.

If pressed on my lack of a degree, I will point out my year at UW-La Crosse. My success with the recent programming courses at BOO-U will be a resource.

It's 40 minutes before my interview when I approach the entrance to the main gate.

I drive past. I am too early.

The first right to the west of Badger lets me circle along quiet country roads. Cornfields are ripening for harvest. I relax and arrive for my appointment a few minutes ahead of schedule.

A lady escorts me to the second floor. Worn grooves on the stairs shine from shoes, going up and down during three wars. We twist around the landing and take a right at the top then down the hall to a small office. I am surprised to see an expansive courtyard in the center of the building through an unexpected interior window.

The lady introduces me to George. He looks vaguely familiar, albeit older. Strands of gray curl through his black hair. His olive complexion shows little age. An open smile allows me a pause of relief.

Don't get comfortable and blow this.

I remember him. Although, our paths did not often cross. He was a chemist in the acid and nitroglycerin lab. Our preliminary discussion recalls those days. He has an accent.

George explains that I will work for Olin. They are still the operating contractor at Badger. The Department of Army has three civilians onsite, no military uniforms. They are our only customer.

The lab has access to the entire facility, unlike during the war. However, with around 100 employees, management keeps close tabs on individuals. No gunpowder is being produced.

His questions closely match those I rehearsed. If I do not get the job, it will not be because of this interview. George goes on to describe the position.

"Part of the job is in the field. Riggers pump the wells. There are over 80. The lab collects samples." George glosses over a few testing activities. "Paul will explain when we get to the lab."

"I can follow a map," I offer. "I drove to the NG lab and the water treatment facility during the war. We were preparing for the Clean Water Act of 1972. I helped set up some of the first tests."

He wants to talk and glosses over my comment.

"Good," he manages. "You won't need a map. Just follow the riggers.

"I need standard operating procedures, SOPs. Currently, we send groundwater samples offsite for testing. We're gonna stop that. We're gonna do that testing here. In our lab." His excitement makes his accent more pronounced. One grammar faux pas is especially noticeable.

"What tests?" I ask.

"All kind'a tests. You'll see." His confidence grows. "The government is starting to regulate labs. Wisconsin passed a rule a year ago. Paul ran the test samples. We passed. Ours is one of the first environmental labs to receive the certification."

"So, now we can do the testing?"

"Yes, for wastewater. We're gonna do testing for other labs, too. Not just ours." George has my full attention. "An important part of this job is technical writing," he continues. "We prepared a bid for federal work. The first thing the client wanted was a copy of our SOPs."

I hear frustration as George explains. "Our test procedures are appropriate, but they're in books and manuals. You'll need to format and rewrite them into a single document to meet the new government requirement."

"I'm familiar with the wastewater tests. Standardizing those procedures into a different format shouldn't be complicated."

I can do this.

One final question catches me off guard.

"What is your weakness?"

I have no rehearsed response.

No college degree? Don't say that. But what?

"I'm becoming my mother." The words pop out of my mouth from nowhere.

George's quizzical look unnerves me. It indicates I must explain myself.

"Mom does everything perfectly." A smile flashes across his face.

That's not how I meant it.

"She won't let anything go until she gets it right." My foot is shoving into my mouth.

George knows B*** S*** when he hears it but says nothing.

"I'm gonna introduce you to my boss, Frank Wolf. He's an engineer. The lab is part of the engineering department." We walk farther down the hall. "Don't be nervous. Just keep doing what you're doing."

What does that mean?

The men quietly converse in the hall before Frank closes the door and sits behind his desk. He explains that his team is preparing several proposals to produce propellant, rocket and single base, in response to government contracts. Obtaining the work would have a significant impact on Badger. The assistant chemist position and my application are acknowledged but little discussed.

Walking into the lab is like stepping back 14 years in time, except only five rooms and the men's restroom are open. Makeshift boards seal off the east and south wings. The spectrophotometer housing is stained and worn. But the cuvettes sparkle as they did during the war.

Paul acknowledges his boss with a nod. His fingers pull the ends of his handle-bar mustache as he speaks.

"You just missed the other George. The guy who prepared titration solutions during the war. Remember him?" Paul asks. We both smile, recalling the old days.

A week later, I get the call. "You were selected for the job. Your title will be laboratory operator. Your salary is $18,000."

What?

I am speechless. Search for words.

"I don't understand. The posting was for an assistant chemist. The salary range was much higher, up to $23,500."

"You don't have a college degree. Take it or leave it. Over 20 applied. We can call someone else."

Caution and Suspicion (1988)

I get the job. But I am humiliated.

The best person is not worth the salary. What kind of company does that?

Anger replaces frustration. "They can keep their job," I rage at my husband. "McGann's wants me to reconsider." David consoles and sympathizes.

"I should have put my foot down when I heard the offer. The salary would have increased."

My husband encourages me to reassess. He asks two questions. "Do you want to continue sewing? Would you rather work in the lab?"

He fusses about how my sewing is all-consuming during the busy spring and fall seasons, which parallel those at UPS. We have considered how my full-time work will relieve the busy season but create a different, continuous stress. We have also discussed what the additional steady income will do for us, not to mention the benefits, especially if something happens to him or his job.

I want to blame someone. "That George guy seemed so nice. I'll never trust him again."

Were he and Frank discussing my pay in the hall? Laughing at me?

My husband sees things differently. "You set yourself up to fail if you start a new job with a bad attitude. George might not have been the person who decided to lower your pay. Frank, either." My husband has learned a few things about how large companies operate. Like UPS telling him he would be on days within two years—a lie.

His words sink into me.

An outward positive attitude can be a façade to conceal caution and suspicion.

I will not quickly forgive and forget.

David is free on Mondays during the day and will drive the girls to school. Badger works four ten-hour days. I will take them on Fridays. The Actress walks four blocks to St. John's parochial in good weather. The high schools are two miles across town. A bus picks up east-side kids a couple of blocks from our home.

The Artist plays the guilt card. "I'm not riding that bus," she wails. "Those kids are mean."

"How do you know?" I ask. "You've never ridden the bus."

Her father tries to de-escalate the conflict. "I'll take you to school when I'm up."

The Artist and I shake our heads, knowing that will seldom happen. He cannot compromise his sleep without putting his job in jeopardy.

"Consider what the extra income will mean for our family." I try to accentuate the positive, but the impact is diluted. Our daughter grudgingly rides the bus. Later, she learns to drive our standard shift Ford Escort wagon and passes her driver's test in record time.

Am I a bad parent?

I could turn down the job. But I've already accepted the offer.

At the foot of the wide staircase the next day, George seems genuinely pleased to see me. I return a cautious smile. "You'll go through orientation this morning," he explains. "I'll take you to the lab when you're finished." He introduces me to the lady whose voice I remember from the devastating phone call. She's younger than me. My shoulders straighten as we make eye contact.

Three hours later, she escorts me to the rear of the administration building. "We'll call Paul to drive you to the lab. George is busy." Her voice is buttery.

As minutes tick by, I survey the monstrous brick powerhouse with the five large smokestacks. It produced the steam to manufacture over a billion pounds of gunpowder for three wars.

Farther north, tall ether stills poke skyward. The stills reclaimed production material for reuse. Long escape chutes hang off the sides of these structures. The chutes, sometimes called slides, provided emergency exits should the volatile solvent become dangerous to people inside.

The rolling Baraboo Bluffs beyond the ether stills are rich green velvet that will soon erupt into a spectacle of color.

A small Dodge pickup truck rounds the old hospital building.

"I just got the call about you," Paul explains. "I was in the field with Arnie and Wayne."

"Who are they?" I ask.

"Riggers. You'll work with them. We're starting the third quarter of groundwater sample collection."

"Will they try to lose me?" I ask. Paul is the only person I can reasonably trust.

"No," he replies. I think my question caught him off guard.

"Some guys would've delighted in stranding a woman in the field during the war."

"I don't think you need to worry about that." Paul sounds convincing.

I question everything.

We head to stores to pick up my lab coats, shoes, tall rubber boots, hard hat, and safety glasses. The same painful footwear is in stock. Thankfully, there's nothing in my size. I order steel-toed, Thinsulate work boots and Converse tennis shoes.

Arnie and Wayne are ready to head out when we arrive at the lab. I wash down my sandwich and banana with tap water while standing beside Paul's desk. He sits, munching a handful of Oreos. His is a working desk in a testing room. I am curious because food was prohibited in testing rooms during the war. I say nothing.

After a quick lesson on using the pH and conductivity meters, the chemist explains the types of samples to be collected. There are 20 bottles of various sizes for each well. They require different preservations depending on which tests are needed. He handwrote the specific labels for the day before the threesome headed out this morning.

There must be a better way than handwriting. I think of the computer classes I took at BOO-U.

Paul hands the chain-of-custody forms to me while I chew. He demonstrates how to take a sample for volatile organic compounds, VOCs, at the faucet while I gulp the last of my lunch. The unique small vials already contain the preservative. To minimize introducing air, they must be slowly overfilled and capped with zero headspace. Air would strip VOCs from the water sample; test results would be meaningless. His motions are flawless. He turns the bottle upside down and taps the side. No air bubbles float upward.

Paul empties the vial and hands it to me. I overfill it, tip the cap and screw it down tightly. But when I turn the vial upside down, two tiny bubbles appear before I get a chance to tap. I try again—and again. Thankfully, my fourth attempt is successful.

"Time to go. We have six samples on the list this afternoon." Arnie heads to the door. The chemist nonchalantly tosses me the truck keys. I dash after the men, not wanting to get lost on my first day.

My VOC technique improves in the field under the watchful eyes of my companions.

Arnie is an average-looking guy about my age. He drives the truck with the blaring generator on the bed, consults his map, and calculates purge times. Wayne is a block of a man, over six feet tall and older, an aging wrestler.

"You two won't try to lose me out here, will you?" I ask when we stop at the first well.

Their glance says the thought never crossed their mind.

I laugh. "I'd like to be more familiar with this place. I grew up on a farm in North Freedom. Worked here eight years during the war. Badger's been a mystery since I was a kid." Two broad smiles tell me I have opened a door.

Arnie shows me the location of this well on his map. Wayne points his big paw in various directions as Arnie speaks. They operate together like one person.

Powerhouse #1 sat along SR 12 close to the main gate. An identical building, Powerhouse #2, a backup should weather, sabotage, or attack disable Powerhouse #1, was in the center of the plant. This photo was taken as powerhouse #1 one was being demolished by a company the Army subcontracted. *Image:* Carolyn Dallmann, 2006.

The Ether stills reclaimed solvent for reuse in the manufacturing process. The buildings and escape slides in the photo are in various stages of dismantling. *Image:* Carolyn Dallmann, 2006.

Badger Ordnance Works, circa 1990s. *Image:* Carolyn Dallmann, 2006.

Spaceship (1988)

I follow the riggers to the first well in the September sunshine. Wayne lowers the pump into the casing. The roar of the generator drowns conversation. Arnie taps me on the shoulder, pointing to a 22-minute purge. I settle in the truck and reflect on recent events.

So far, so good, but did I make the best decision—to work at Badger?

The racket stops when the purge ends. The pulley at the top of the well creaks and shivers against the woven rope attached to the vessel full of water below. The men hoist it to the top of the casing and heft the heavy load to Wayne's ham of a shoulder. He opens the release at the bottom and controls the flow with his meaty fingers. I catch the samples.

Arnie pulls on latex gloves to collect VOCs. He takes over from Wayne. His fingering technique drains the water slowly, minimizing the introduction of unwanted air into the small bottles I hold.

The morning samples are ready to go when we return to the lab. Paul fills my coolers with ice and seals them. Each contains the sample from one well. We release custody at the shipping office. The samples will arrive tomorrow at the MetaTrace lab in St. Louis, one of eight federally approved laboratories to test groundwater.

George is waiting for us when we return to the lab. "Where were you?"

"Dropping off samples," Paul explains.

George looks at the chemist while pointing at me. "Is she ready to go out tomorrow?"

"Yes. She went out this afternoon while I worked with the wastewater samples."

Momentarily lost for words, George asks, "Where's her desk?" My boss's sharp tone indicates something is wrong.

"She can use the intern's," Paul says.

I have a desk? Why don't I know this?

George motions me to the adjacent room. Paul is not invited. A dust-covered desk has replaced the large lunchroom table used during the war. George clears scattered papers into the drab dark-green metal wastebasket, making room for two hardcover maroon and gray binders.

"How did sampling go?" he asks. His manner is now formal.

"Fine. I didn't get lost." He disregards my comment and pushes the thickest book toward me.

"These are the federal rules for testing groundwater." The smaller book follows. "This one's for sample collection.

"I need you to keep an eye on everything in the field. If we're gonna expand the lab, sampling must be appropriate. Test results are meaningless if we don't follow protocol in the field. I want to know what you see out there." The determination I heard during the interview has returned to his voice. "We don't collect samples on Thursdays because there's not enough turnaround time for the contract lab, MetaTrace. I'll stop by that morning. We'll talk."

What does he expect from me? What's my job? Am I a spy?

I open the testing book and look at the table of contents.

"There aren't any tests listed."

"It explains how we are to use our test procedures." George is impatient.

My eyes land on familiar words. "The federal format for SOPs is in the first chapter," I tell him. "I'll review those sections and the sample collection book by Thursday."

Standing to leave, George says, "The Army procured those books. They're the only copies we have. Don't lose them."

"These books won't hold up in the field. I'd rather use a copy."

He takes the manuals. "Stop at my office in the morning."

I nod and smile.

Good attitude. Be cautious.

On the morning of day two, George talks with a familiar face at the bottom of the wide stairs at the front of the administration building. He introduces me to Jim, the program manager. I am pretty sure Jim does not remember me. He's the accountant who bunked with cute Jack in the trailer in Wisconsin Dells during the war—the trailer where we grilled chickens for a D Shift picnic. Recalling that event makes me smile. George's dark eyes flash at the stairs.

He wants me out of here.

With a quick acknowledgment to Jim, I step between them and run up the steps. I collect the two stacks of looseleaf paper sitting on the desk and race back down. The men are gone.

Paul is waiting at the back door. "The riggers won't wait for you," he says, peeling the truck toward the lab.

Thankfully, he wrote labels yesterday while I was in the field with the riggers.

I frantically look for binders or clips at the lab. The loose papers will fly around in the truck if not secured. A half dozen rubber bands are in a corner of Paul's bottom desk drawer, along with a stack of narrow sticky notes and a coffee-stained legal tablet. The first rubber band breaks when I try to secure the stacks of paper. The others will have to do.

How can people work with no supplies?

I gingerly place everything in the cab as the riggers pull alongside the pickup. "You ready?" Arnie calls.

In the quiet morning sunlight, thousands of garden spiders hang like Christmas ornaments from dewy webs spun through tall, late-summer prairie grass.

We have a 40-minute purge after the blare of the generator begins at the first well. I attach labels to bottles, jump into the cab, and grab the sampling rules.

A dozen sticky notes poke out of the papers by lunch break—guides for later reference.

I jabber with Arnie and Wayne during the afternoon.

"How do you know purge times?" I ask.

Arnie explains the well depth and water level calculations. I take notes.

"What happens when it rains? Or when the temperature is subzero?"

"We collect the quarterly samples," Arnie laughs. "You'd best pick up a raincoat and pants. Those earflaps that fit inside your hard hat, too. Do you have an insulated winter jacket or snowmobile suit for under your lab coat? The things they provide aren't the best." Arnie does not mince words or warnings.

He continues, "It's barely dawn when we go out in December. We collect the last samples after dark. A strong wind is the worst." I cringe at the thought.

On Wednesday, day three, the rolling terrain at the bottom of the bluffs makes driving off the perimeter road circling the plant precarious. The first well is in tall grass 200 feet off that road. Our trucks perch toward the top of a steep ravine.

The powerful noise of the generator takes on a deep rumble as I concentrate on the rules manual. After ten minutes the sound deepens—then deepens again.

Sunshine turns abruptly dark.

I sink from the encompassing pressure around me—bow to it.

Something black is on top of the truck.

I'm being overpowered.

Metal. Lots of heavy black metal.

A spaceship?

Aliens?

We are being attacked!

Arnie and Wayne look skyward.

A Blackhawk helicopter is feet above our trucks.

The thing pauses, turns, and lifts higher—straight up—pulls away from the ravine and heads southwest.

"The National Guard practices here. Does maneuvers," Wayne explains when the generator stops.

"No one told us they'd be at Badger today," Arnie shakes his head. "The Guard people out of Madison let the Army know when they're coming. The Army tells Olin management. But those guys forget to tell us fieldworkers."

Sweet Jesus, I thought I was going to die.

Steam Engines (1988)

On Thursday morning, I realize how little I have seen Paul since starting work on Monday. It has been only four days, but it seems like weeks.

"A helicopter," he says and chuckles as I recall my experience from yesterday.

"George is coming out to the lab this morning," I tell him. I wonder about the chemist's mindset concerning our boss but do not ask.

Paul is a pleasant man but not one to start or jump into a conversation. Intelligent to the point of being eccentric—an inventor who designed several timesaving pieces of equipment that streamlined mundane tasks during the war, like what we called the "Ferris wheel."

Before the Ferris wheel, some lab techs spent endless eight-hour shifts cleaning total volatile tubes until the tubes became skinny globes of glass that sparkled like Christmas ornaments. Clean tubes were covered with special cloth to prevent particles of dust from accumulating. The added weight of dust particles would skew test results.

The test is precise because volatiles, which evaporate in an instant, must be measured. Techs wore soft, white cloth gloves when weighing and handling the tubes because fingerprints would also add weight and skew results.

The unique test tubes are closed on both ends with a nipple opening in the middle. The nipple attaches to a vacuum hose inside an oven during the 24-hour procedure. At the end of the test, the thick, sticky, dissolved propellant clings inside the tubes and must be removed.

Teams of technicians manually filled dirty volatile tubes with solvent and ball bearings, plugged the nipple, and started a tipping motion. The action causes the ball bearings to roll over the inside glass surface to release the goo.

Shake, empty, add fresh solvent, shake, and repeat.

Paul's design was a long, rotating contraption constructed of flat steel fabricated like a small Ferris wheel. It was about four-feet tall and four-feet long. Grabbers secured over two dozen tubes to the Ferris wheel. Once implemented, the technicians had only to switch out the solvent incrementally. After six months of shaking, they were thrilled to be assigned to other duties.

Dave and I saw Paul, a confirmed bachelor, at the handmade ice cream stand at the local Steam and Gas Show in August. The annual event at the county fairgrounds draws over 10,000 enthusiasts to our town. Paul was explaining to spectators his design of the triple churning mechanism that makes the ice cream. It operates with jack shafts and belts, doing multiple tasks with a single hit-and-miss gasoline engine.

The steam show is the highlight of Paul's year. He often mentions that he communicates best with people under age seven and those over seventy.

"How did the club do this year?" I pick a topic not related to work.

The chemist's eyes brighten. His demeanor changes from stoic to animated. "Good. But we've outgrown the fairgrounds. We turned exhibitors away and can't set up more demonstrations."

"Dave had two helpings of your ice cream."

"We've fine-tuned the vanilla recipe." The chemist straightens in his chair, taking credit. "We're modifying the chocolate."

"How many engines do you have now?" I ask, meaning to draw him into conversation.

Paul twirls his handlebar mustache, contemplating before he speaks. "About 200 last count."

"200? Engines? Like those big ones?" I am astounded.

"Some are big. Others are small."

"Where do you keep them?" I ask.

"That's a problem I'm running into. My garage is full. The Steam and Gas Club lets me store some in their buildings." Paul glances toward the hall door, which is behind me.

"Good morning." I turn and face my boss. Distracted, I did not hear George enter the lab. He acknowledges Paul before turning to me. The chemist's face indicates his mind remains on engines. I am on full alert.

"We'll talk." I follow George to my desk.

"How was collecting samples?" My boss doesn't notice my desk is clean and organized.

"I wrote a few notes if you want to look." He puts his hand out for the legal pad I hold.

"If I had a computer and printer, it'd be faster," I suggest. "Even a typewriter would help."

"Computers are hard to procure under this contract. There must be a typewriter." George turns in his chair, looking around the room like he can conjure one out of thin air.

"Paul said he didn't need a typewriter and turned them all into *office supply.*"

George shakes his head with a grimace. "We'll take care of that."

His irritation dissipates when he glances at my short list of bullet items. "Tell me what you saw." I'm surprised at his interest in fieldwork.

"First, Arnie and Wayne have been professional. They don't appear to hold anything back from me. Arnie showed me how he calculates purge time. His calculations match those in the federal manual. Actual purges match the calculated times."

Looking for the best words, I continue. "You might be questioning if one man could do the job rather than two." George nods.

"I'm not the person to make that call," I venture. "However, in my opinion, one person could do the job alone. But it would take longer. Although probably not twice as long."

"Like me, the men spend part of their time driving and waiting during the purge. The other part is labor-intensive. A few well casings are high off the ground. It takes two guys to lift the pump up and into them."

Have I overstepped my boundary?

George urges me to continue.

What's he looking for?

"Hauling the sample up from 15 feet is doable for one man. Hauling that vessel up from greater depths all day could be a stretch, even with the aid of the pulley. Then, there's holding it while releasing the sample for collection. It's awkward and heavy."

"Go on." He is an impatient man.

"The weather has been ideal the last three days. The guys suggest I pick up gear for rain and winter."

"We'll get that for you."

Watching my boss scribble on the legal pad, I see a man of average height and stature in his late forties. He has two personalities, one from before he lowered my salary, the other after—accommodating and personable the former, driven and approaching rude the latter. I am relieved his office is upfront, in 200, not in the lab.

When he catches me watching him, I quickly turn to my notes.

"Go on," he prods.

Not wanting to get the riggers in trouble, I chose my words.

"There's one concern—collecting VOC samples. Wayne manages the collection vessel on his shoulder. We fill the large bottles first.

"Arnie pulls on latex gloves for VOCs before taking on the vessel's weight. His fingers push the release ball aside to regulate the flow. That's satisfactory while the weather is good. But it'll be challenging to manage when the temperature drops below freezing.

"I asked the guys if there was a special release gizmo for the VOCs. Arnie said they searched and found nothing."

"Explain your thinking about the release thing." George is curious.

"A narrow delivery system with a stopcock that controls the flow would be ideal. It would reduce air getting into the sample and minimize the chance of contamination. It'd be easier for the guys to handle, too."

I do not say that the federal manual says to collect VOC samples first to minimize air stripping. That is because VOCs quickly transfer from water into the air. The sooner the sample is transferred to the collection vial, the better.

My thought is to solve the first issue to correct the second.

"Come up with something. Draw a picture. Don't mention it to anyone."

George stands. "Let's get you that gear. I'll introduce you to Tom. He's the person who manages how standard procedures are formatted here at Badger. His office is close to *stores*."

I follow George into the crisp fall air and slide into the passenger seat. The personable boss has returned. He elaborates as he drives. "The lab's gonna grow. We're hiring another person."

I didn't see this coming. "How will it grow?" I am curious.

"We are certified by the State to test wastewater for sulfates, nitrates, and chloride. If we test the same groundwater samples as

MetaTrace for those components and our results are comparable to theirs, we're gonna bring that work in-house. It would be a considerable saving for our customer, the Army. HR is currently scheduling interviews." George's accent is again more noticeable.

"Why do we send samples to a lab in Missouri, if we can test them here? The shipping costs must be exorbitant. Those coolers each weigh a ton." My husband works at UPS. I have insight into this expense.

"It's a federal regulation. We must have samples tested by one of their eight labs because of potential contamination caused by making gunpowder at Badger," George explains. "MetaTrace laboratory was awarded the contract to do the work. The other seven federal labs are scattered throughout the country."

My boss's campaign to expand the lab is good for my future.

But why am I privy to this information? When will the next surprise smack me?

George continues, "I want to hire recent college graduates. Most certified labs train laypeople to do testing and rely on only a few chemists to review their work. A lab with degreed chemists at the bench is stronger and more reliable. I also don't want older employees with baggage from prior employment. Chemists trained in our lab will have a common goal."

Hearing this, I'm curious why he hired me. I don't have a degree.

And just like that—he explains. "I'm a concept person. I needed someone to cover details and writing. Chemists, especially seasoned chemists like Paul, shy away from details and writing. You seem to gravitate to both. Additionally, you were the person Paul wanted to work with."

Really?

"I appreciate you telling me."

Keep a good attitude, I remind myself.

When we stop, George waves to Tom, who is just exiting stores. "Got a minute?"

"Sure." Tom's friendly reply sounds encouraging. "I already pulled our SOP requirements and some examples." After introductions, Tom shows me Badger's format. It looks nothing like the one in the federal testing manual. I open our book and show him the lab requirements.

"Can't do it." Tom shakes his head. "Others have tried. The Army won't allow anything but this."

In the truck, George tells me to create a template incorporating the lab requirements into the Army's operations format. He will campaign for an SOP variance but doesn't think that will happen.

He relates the bad news the following day.

No variance.

I struggle to fit analytical chemistry testing into the static template used for manufacturing gunpowder.

The following Thursday, I assume we will discuss my draft SOP template. But George wants me to accompany him to Timco, a local plastics business. He has my drawing of a water delivery tool in hand.

When we start the next quarterly round of sample collection, I show Arnie and Wayne the federal rule to collect VOC samples first. Arnie nods and smiles as he attaches Timco's prototype to the delivery vessel. It looks exactly like the picture I drew.

Timco adds this piece of equipment to their product line when they hear it supports new lab certification requirements.

Falsified Records, Fraudulent Activity (1989-1990)

It is 1989. I am 42. I continue working for Olin Corporation, the operating contractor. Badger remains under the Army's ready to operate, standby status. Standby requires continual equipment, building, and infrastructure maintenance and upgrades. Additionally, Badger must meet all government regulations, including OSHA and the everchanging EPA codes.

The lab grows. George appropriates two computers rejected by the engineers—we never get a typewriter. My boss correctly intuits he will lose leverage to gain computers if we have a typewriter.

In late spring and between quarterly sample collection, George directs me to classify old production chemicals for disposal. Paul has gathered them from testing rooms and stacked them on the racks of four rolling carts staged in the unheated southern part of the lab.

The rooms off the south hall are cold well into summer. Wearing my winter jacket, I quickly sort familiar chemicals. Less familiar chemicals require research, so I make a list and use books and manuals in the lab to classify them while sitting at my desk in a heated room.

When quarterly sample collection resumes, wait time in the field flies while I write SOPs into my template. At the end of each shift, I slide my day's work into a mail envelope and place it in an inbox at the Administration Building, 200. In the morning, I pick up finished copies of my earlier writing for my review.

Various administrative staff in 200 type for me. These women are assigned to engineers or managers. I seldom interact with them. My boss warns me that employees caught lingering under watchful eyes in 200 may be considered expendable by Olin or Army management.

I finish the initial draft of the new 990 page, four-volume SOP document in late summer. Eight Olin and Army higher-ups must review and sign off on each volume before it becomes official.

Our lab's test results for samples run parallel with MetaTrace's, the contract lab's, match.

We hire Darrin and Brent, both recent college graduates with degrees in Chemistry. Darrin finds an apartment at Bluffview, the renovated Badger Village, across from the main gate. Brent is a local from Sauk Prairie.

I'm surprised George has me, not Paul, train them. I understand when my boss explains. "They know chemistry but need to learn associated regulatory requirements as well as the tests. You know those rules best."

The young men, like Paul, are bachelors. When we talk, I often feel like I am in a foreign country. Conversation, however, is limited because we are busy at scattered workstations or in the field.

Food is our shared enjoyment. We frequently bring treats for our 15-minute break or something to share during our half-hour lunch. Brent does chips and sodas. Paul is big on packages of cookies, especially Oreos. Darrin is more creative with hotdogs and brats, or chili. I make a casserole large enough for our family and the guys. Everyone's eyes light up when I bring lasagna.

Olin management makes it clear that we may only do work funded by our customer, the Army. If funding runs out or is cut off, work stops abruptly. For example, that's why the old chemicals remain in the lab. When the war ended, the Army did not spend tax dollars to remove them—they may be needed in the future.

Another example is when George initiates orders to open rooms in the south and east wings of the building. The lab is expanding because of the heavy workload. The old flooring in the south hall deteriorated and crumbled over the years. George's campaign to have it replaced meets partial approval. In-stock tiles may be used. No funding is available for new.

The shop guys start the project, but their supervisor complains there are not enough tan tiles to finish it. George smiles and says, "Put down everything you have."

When the tile runs out halfway down the hall, the flooring crews leave. My boss invites his buddy Jim, the plant manager, to see the new floor.

"This looks like hell," Jim explodes.

"They used all the tile they had. We'll make do," George replies nonchalantly.

I never hear the details, but the shop guys finish the floor—tan tiles meet brown at an off-set line at the hall's midpoint.

The riggers clean offices in the east wing. They have been boarded shut since the war. Painters haul in light green and creamy white to finish the update. George eventually occupies the northeast corner. He's not one to micromanage subordinates. The political arena of 200 is more to his liking. He briefly appears in the lab each morning before returning to his other office upfront.

Our boss's mindset is growth. "If you're not moving forward, you're in reverse." He repeats this at our weekly lab meetings—whether to remind us or himself is hard to determine.

Curious about George's accent, I ask Paul.

"He's from Haifa," the chemist replies and abruptly drops the subject. My geography is not good enough to know where Haifa is located, and Paul is suddenly too busy to explain. At home that evening, a map in our World Book Encyclopedia shows Haifa is in Israel.

In the morning, I ask again, "What nationality is George?"

"He's Palestinian." The chemist offers no further information. Being raised in rural south-central Wisconsin, my boss is the first Palestinian I have ever met.

I've worked at Badger over a year when George hands me an annual performance review form to fill out. He explains that he will complete the same form. Then we will meet. The past year floats in my mind like a movie. I have no time for this at work. I take the paperwork home.

That evening, the Actress and the Artist are watching Doogie Howser, M.D. I am drifting away from them. It is an uncomfortable, lonely feeling.

Joining them on the sectional sofa, I ask about school during a commercial. I am an annoying intrusion into their world. They are anxious to hear more from Doogie. The Actress leans against me when the program resumes, warm and snuggly. The Artist keeps to herself.

Is she still upset about riding the bus?

The phone rings. I anticipate my husband's evening calls home. No call means he is out on the road with a UPS truck that has broken down. When that happens, David takes his tools, and with a center manager, they drive a good vehicle to the one that broke down and reload packages. The driver and supervisor leave. Dave is left to fix or limp the bad vehicle back to the center or procure a wrecker to haul it. Sometimes, he must walk until he locates a phone. Breakdowns often happen in the worst weather, snow or icy conditions. Many occur after the sun goes down. Hearing his voice settles me.

When the girls are in bed, I open the form. The questions are unnerving. How do I evaluate myself? —my supervisor? —why? How can I improve? It's easier to work than to fill out this report.

I do not sleep well.

George is relaxed as we compare our comments. I am not. He explains my raise by telling me Olin follows the ranking of government jobs. He has limits on how much he can increase my salary within my assigned range. "You deserve more, but this is as high as I can go."

So why did you lowball me in the first place?

Looking at the number, I smile. "If my annual raises are the same, I'll reach the highest posted salary in five years." The unintentional comment pops out of my mouth.

George says nothing, but a strange look crosses his face—one I have never seen before. His words come slowly like steam starting to push from a pressure cooker. "What salary were you hired at?"

"$18,000," I whisper. My anger is gone. I am only embarrassed to say I accepted the number.

"Who told you that?" His voice goes up a notch.

"The lady at orientation. When she called and offered me the job, I explained to her the posted salary was $18,500 to $23,500. And it was an assistant chemist position.

She told me, "Over 20 people applied. You can take it or leave it." When I hesitated, she said, "We can call someone else."

George shoots out of his chair. The pressure cooker blows its top.

"It's him. This is his doing. That cheap—" His voice disappears with him down the hall.

I never hear what happened. But George is not the person who cut my starting salary. He wasn't even aware someone lowered it. Additionally, I am quite sure Frank was not involved in the decision.

He gives me no further explanation. My starting pay does not change. The raise he showed me is what I get. But in the future, this episode will work in my favor.

Did someone receive a cost reduction perk for lowering my starting salary? I wonder.

The coincidence of my return to the lab in 1988 and the promulgation of the new State Laboratory Certification Code in 1986 is a significant advantage for me. I have an affinity for legalese that many scientific types find unappealing. Writing procedures and classifying old chemicals were chemistry lessons more advantageous to me than some college classes.

A month later, George stops by the lab. "Something for you," he says, setting four volumes of official SOPs on the counter. "Now the lab can grow." My boss radiates confidence.

"A man from the federal certification office will stop by in the morning. You'll sit in when we meet," George tells me. "Take notes. We're gonna get federal certification."

I am speechless.

Is this my next job?

The following morning, George ushers the stranger through our lab. When they head to his office, he asks me to join them.

"When can we start?" George asks.

The man shakes his head and points at the computer on a side table, one my boss procured. "These are too small to load our software," he explains. "Upgrade them, and we'll talk.

Recovering quickly from the blow, George asks for specifics about what we must do.

Several months after that meeting, things take an unexpected turn.

In early 1990, a disaster at MetaTrace compels the first in-house groundwater testing. Headlines and newspaper articles between February and June of 1990 tell the story.

> METATRACE LABORATORY—ALLEGED IRREGULARITIES IN TESTING and RECORD-KEEPING—DRY LABBING.

Two years of expensive groundwater data—gone.

Badger is in turmoil after we hear about the MetaTrace lab. Headlines of their unethical operations are unrelenting. Madison television stations feature the story. It makes national news. The Army tasks Olin with writing responses to the stories. These official reports come from the Army and appear as editorials or opinions in newspapers or on television. As employees, we are warned not to respond to questions from outsiders.

The general public is confused. Many think I work for MetaTrace, the unscrupulous lab. I do not.

"I work for Olin at Badger," I explain. Not being able to say more is frustrating.

A couple of months later, the certification man pays a visit. He explains federal auditors discovered MetaTrace was dry labbing, reporting *created* results without testing the samples. He tells us they worked hard to cheat.

In a follow-up 1996 article, the St. Louis Post-Dispatch reports, "Two former executive vice presidents [from MetaTrace] eventually pleaded guilty; one was sentenced to five years in prison."

Badger quickly subcontracts a different federal lab, A. D. Little.

George ramps up his campaign. "Bring the testing in-house. Why spend good money on shipping samples across the county and testing when we have a certified lab with equal, possibly better, qualifications onsite? We're under the watchful eye of the Wisconsin certification program."

Our lab incrementally performs more parallel testing with A. D. Little.

George's efforts pay off. He convinces management to procure new instruments and to test more parameters. He hires more chemists, young college graduates with degrees in Chemistry who have never worked in a lab and have no experience with regulatory requirements. I hand each a copy of the lab's SOPs, introduce them to their work area, explain regulations, and help with equipment and supplies.

Both the state and federal programs require an internal quality control component. George assigns me. One task is reviewing data packages of test results before passing them on to him for final approval.

My distrust of George is long gone. He is my mentor. I need him.

He needs me, too. Like the other chemists, legalese and regulations are obstacles he must deal with. I guide him through the mess as professionally and efficiently as possible. His focus is managing a growing staff, procuring sophisticated instruments, and calculating budgets.

Audit (1990-1992)

The spring of 1990, the laboratory receives notice of a second State audit, my first. The MetaTrace mess is barely behind us. George tells me I am the contact person. He expects the auditor to schedule it in eight weeks. He feels my temperament is a better fit than his regarding the event. I concur but do not express my opinion.

George hands me a copy of the newly revised State rule, NR 149. It arrived with the audit notice. "Read and understand this."

The previous code was two pages. The new one is 12. The revision makes the state code equal to or more robust than the federal code.

My boss says, "Go through the lab. Make a list of deficiencies for me. I want them mitigated. Noncompliance issues will happen because of these new rules. But if we can't comply with a line item before the audit, we need to prepare an explanation as to how we are addressing it."

I page through the document and ask, "Why is the State scheduling audits before labs like ours can review how their changes affect us? They know we'll have deficiencies."

"You shouldn't be surprised," George says. "We are probably first on their list. Our lab is in the spotlight because we test for contamination caused by the Army when they produced propellant here at Badger. The debacle with the MetaTrace lab put the federal regulatory agency on the hook because of their delay in catching that situation. The State is going to be thorough. They don't want the same thing to happen to them. That's a good thing. We'll come out of the audit a stronger lab."

"What will they look at?" I ask.

"Everything. Sample receiving, chain-of-custody, all testing stations, each chemist at work, hold times, equipment, instruments, calibrations, your reviews, my signoff. They miss nothing."

I am baffled. "How long will it take?"

"Hopefully, only a day."

He continues, "You are not to leave the auditor alone while they are in the lab. Take notes. I'll stay in my office. Plan how you will communicate with me so I'm not surprised at the end of the day."

George hands copies of the new certification code to staff at our weekly meeting and announces the agency will visit us. "Read this and bring questions or deficiencies to our next meeting. The auditor will interview everyone. Carolyn will schedule a pre-audit with each of you during the next two weeks." Eyebrows raise, including mine.

How do I do audits?

The following day, George pulls up a chair in my office. I speak first. "You surprised me at the meeting." I am defensive. He should have warned me. "Is there something I can read so I know how to do an audit?"

He tenses. "This visit from the State could make or break our lab. We need to be a cohesive, proactive department. No one person is better than another."

His words hit hard and fast, like a nuggie on my head that leaves a lasting impression.

OUCH.

My boss offers a pragmatic approach. "I don't know of any material you can read. Consider using the Standard Operating Procedures you wrote and go through the steps with each person as they work."

I should have thought of that.

Most of us have experienced George's reprimands. He does not always strike as quickly as he did with me. I think that's because he realizes his temper might get the best of him if he reacts too soon.

He usually saves the nuggie until the poor offender least expects it. Then, WHAP. A NUGGIE. The good part is that George drops the issue after making his point. His actions are quick and effective.

He continues, "The staff will be nervous with a stranger watching them. Going through a mock process will help put them at ease. Think of it as a learning tool for yourself as well.

"Some advice," George tells me. "To gain people's respect, remember one thing. Your opinion is not important. It has no place in your position. You'll lose credibility unless you quote a state or federal rule. Regulatory requirements are all that matter."

Then he warns, "Don't be the reason for a deficiency because *you* didn't catch something. Everyone must rely on procedures, not on *you* watching them work."

I design checklists for each test and schedule the first internal audit. My nerves are as jangled as those of the chemist I interview. I eat lunch with her every day. However, as my questions continue, we both relax. We know we are in this together. Our boss told us.

Three weeks later, two chemists asked me to repeat my internal audit of their work. I recall George's warning and talk with them about how they did during their first review before encouraging them to self-audit against their SOPs.

Quarterly sample collection continues while we prepare for the audit. The new chemists take turns in the field with Arnie and Wayne. I miss fieldwork, but not the bad weather, grasshoppers jumping into the truck and attaching their sticky feet to me, or the mosquitoes.

Paul collects samples from five farms south of Badger. The aquifer moves in that direction, away from the facility toward the Wisconsin River. My boss tells me I will start collecting those offsite samples because he wants Paul in the lab with the new chemists.

Riggers move my desk to the office next to my boss. "You should be separated from the staff because of your review work," George explains.

Should I be concerned?

In the meantime, the old powder lab incrementally becomes a state-of-the-art environmental laboratory. George initiates procurement of a uniquely designed heating, ventilation, and air conditioning, HVAC, system to create a clean room for sample receipt and positive-pressure rooms for low-level volatile testing. The system will provide the constant temperature required for some of the new mass spec instruments capable of measuring down to parts per billion. Installation is at least a year out.

In 1988, the lab was part of the engineering group. By the early 1990s, we have grown in the number of employees to the size of the entire engineering group. We have significantly increased our capabilities. At a weekly lab meeting, George compliments us on our achievements. He is stingy with praise. Today, he explains that he wants the lab to be an independent department like the engineers.

Addressing our blank stares, he says, "This will benefit each of you—your paycheck." We need no further explanation. "I can't promise it will happen. But I want you to know I'm fighting for you," he adds.

The day after the meeting, George calls me into his office. Before I get a chance to sit, he says, "There's good news and some not-so-good news."

I am on alert. Why is he saying this to me?

"The lab is reclassified." He pauses. "That's the good news." He searches for words and then spits them out. "Everyone except you." I have the feeling it is hard for him to say this.

A wash of emotion wraps around me. I just stand there.

"Did I do something wrong?" I ask.

"Without complicating things, the classification requires a bachelor's degree. You don't have one." He's direct—does not mince words. That is one thing I like about him.

But this stings.

"I trained them. I know the instruments and the procedures. I wrote them." I try to justify my case without knowing how to attack the situation. The more I say, the more I feel my foot stuffing my mouth. I don't need to tell him. He already knows.

George puts up his hand. "I did the best I could. They're following requirements."

Red prickles up my neck and stings my cheeks. It's humiliating. NOT FAIR.

Then, a different emotion grabs me. I am ANGRY. FURIOUS. Not just for myself but for all the men and women who have been in this position. I know there are many. George talks while I process.

"...choices...hire someone...money..." I snap back to what he is saying.

"Could you repeat that?" I ask.

"I want you to continue doing the same work. Regulations will force me to hire someone with a college degree to cover the quality position. That person's salary will be higher than yours. You'll retain your current responsibilities because you know the lab and understand this quality thing. You have a decision to make."

George pauses to let that sink in. He continues.

"There's another option. You can enroll in a program and get a degree." He pauses again. "I have no idea how you can do that. I don't know what degree programs are available. I can't promise, but you have my support if you pursue a degree. You'll pay for classes upfront but will be reimbursed as you submit passing grades."

What's he saying? I'm 45 and work full-time. Our daughters are in junior high and high school. My husband works nights and puts in long hours at UPS. Quitting work and going to school is not an option. By the time I get a degree, my job will be gone. Obstacles bounce in my head.

"I'm not sure how?" He stops me.

"Think about it and let me know your decision. You don't have to give me an answer now."

My head spins. Concentrating on test results is impossible.

I have little time to contemplate college while preparing for the audit.

The day arrives with little fanfare. Chemists take turns monitoring the hall. They stroll by me slowly enough to read or grab notes I have written for George. This is how we communicate what happens on the floor to our boss.

"Document thermometer traces to certification," my note says. We calibrate our thermometers against certified equipment. However, in the eyes of the auditor, if we did not document that calibration, it was not done.

"Equipment not in use," says another note. The auditor wants to know the function of every item. Explaining that something in a drawer or cupboard is left over from production days and no longer needed is unacceptable.

The person who carries the message flashes it to staff, who check their work areas for similar issues. George is anxious when he greets the auditor at the end of the day.

The exit interview does not happen. Instead, the auditor explains she will return the following day—all day.

UFF. Exhausted, I debrief with George.

The following day is a repeat.

The exit interview is grueling. There are deficiencies. Most relate to documentation, an expanded regulation in the revised code. Our testing procedures and instruments are appropriate. Associated documenting and tracing are lacking.

George uses the audit report as leverage to procure an integrated computer system for lab work.

The old powder laboratory was updated to a state-of-the-art environmental lab. The metal tubes and vents on the north end of the building are part of the uniquely designed HVAC system that created a clean room for sample receipt, positive pressure rooms for low-level testing, and controlled temperature rooms where required. *Image:* Carolyn Dallmann, 2011.

Offsite Contamination (1990)

The process of coordinating response reports for audit closure drones on. George controls the reins encouraging, sometimes forcing, us to work in groups. This is the first time we have undergone such scrutinization. In the end, I, as well as the entire staff, gain confidence and energy from a job well done.

In the spring of 1990 and during this busy time, George's phone call summons me to the plant manager, Jim's office.

Now what?

Their conversation stops abruptly as a lady ushers me into the room.

What were they saying?

Jim begins, "George has been telling me about your work."

Then, he is silent, as if he does not know how to talk to me.

My boss takes over following Jim's nod. "One of the offsite wells tested positive for a volatile organic, a low-level hit. I need Paul in the lab. We feel you're the best person to represent Badger offsite."

Does Jim not know my boss has already told me I will replace Paul in the field?

The plant manager jumps in, "We expect the Army will want samples from other locations, not just five farms."

Why me? The only one without a degree. Am I your scapegoat for this delicate situation?

I remind myself to keep a positive attitude.

"Who knows about this?" I ask for I have heard nothing.

"The Army is issuing a press release," Jim explains. "You cannot say anything about what you just heard. The Army is responsible for communications."

He continues, "George tells me your family has a farm in North Freedom. Much of the property around Badger is agricultural, except for some small parcels on Lake Wisconsin. Your father-in-law is Freedom Town Board Chairman, so your name is local and recognized."

Jim certainly knows a lot about me.

"How do I?" I stammer.

George stops me. "We'll go over details in the morning. The press release should be out by then." He walks me to the door but does not follow.

They didn't give me a chance to decline.

This responsibility is a new challenge—dealing with the public in a sticky situation.

Nerves claw like an angry tiger in my gut.

I collect my first onsite sample at the farm with the hit. Grandma, an exceptionally sweet woman, is home alone when I call. Both of us are nervous. After removing her spotless apron, she leads me to the sampling point in the basement. Chosen because it is closest to their well. After the purge, I put on latex gloves to draw the VOC samples.

"Oh no," Grandma's hands cover her mouth. "I didn't know the poison was that bad."

Momentarily startled, I smile out loud. "The gloves? They're not to protect me. They're to protect your sample." Grandma looks relieved but curious. "I wear gloves because anything on my hands could potentially contaminate your sample."

"My goodness. You had me scared."

"Your well had a low-level result for one volatile organic compound. VOCs are in many common products and substances. You can ask the Army if you want more information."

Test results by both the A. D. Little lab and the Badger lab of the sample I took confirm the initial low-level result.

Headlines hit the newspapers in April 1990.

Between the audit, the MetaTrace mess, and now a hit in an offsite sample, turmoil sweeps through Badger. The lab is in the thick of it.

A flurry of excitement swirls in Sauk County and beyond as word spreads about contamination migrating off and away from the Badger property.

The day after hearing confirmation news, I follow George into a narrow room in the administration building. A long table fills the space. Twenty tall-backed, padded chairs swivel an invitation. I have never been here before. Jim is at the head of the table closest to the door. The Commander's Representative is at the far end. He is the top civilian employed by the Army at Badger.

George points me to a chair next to Jim. He sits on my other side. "It's okay," he says. He seems caught off guard as the room fills.

What does he mean, "It's okay?"

I recognize the Olin people and the three Army men as they enter. They separate like oil and water toward their respective leaders. I am the only woman. The chairs are almost all in use when an administrative assistant closes the door. Disarming quiet fills the space.

Again, Jim appears uncomfortable with me in the room. Does he not trust me? Or is he doubting himself?

Undaunted, Jim begins, "The Army talked with a few landowners who live around Badger and explained the offsite hit. Those people are now expecting a call from you." Jim nods my way. "You'll schedule picking up a water sample from the tap closest to their well. From now on, you'll be the sole point of contact for everyone on the list."

One of the Army guys jumps in, "We want field operations to go smoothly."

George frowns at him and looks at Jim, who draws the meeting back to Olin's end of the table.

"We've worked out guidelines with our friends over there," Jim speaks to me and nods toward the Army people. "We expect the public will ask you questions. Don't answer them. Rather, write down their questions and tell them the Army will call with an explanation."

Part of me wants to run out of the room and never look back. But curiosity overcomes that thought.

George takes over. "We'll work out details later. We have a new logbook dedicated to offsite sample collection. You'll document everything: scheduling, collection, and conversations." He directs the comment to me, but it is clearly meant to reassure the Army.

"We want a copy of that logbook," the Commander's Representative says.

"Of course," Jim replies.

"I have a question." Jim turns pale when I speak up. George's eyes are wide, likely fearing what will tumble from my mouth.

"What if someone who is not on the list asks me to collect a sample from their property?" I ask. "All of this news is creating quite a stir."

The Commander's Representative answers. "Tell them to call Badger and ask for the Army. We'll respond."

Jim is compelled to add, "Go only to places on the Army's list."

I nod. My boss breathes relief.

Driving back to the lab, George explains that Jim assured him our meeting would be small, not an entourage of management trying to impress each other.

The first list of 20 landowners grows to over 200 in three months. Local activists fuel speculation. Letters to the editors fill local newspapers.

Words from the meeting with the Army stick with me when I deal with the public.

Most people are congenial. Some are not. One uppity, 40-ish lady living on Lake Wisconsin yells at me as I exit the truck.

"Hey there, girlie, wear your gloves."

I calmly explain the importance of waiting with gloves until just before the VOC sample is collected. Putting them on earlier could contaminate the gloves and the sample. She crosses her arms and frowns. Her body language says she does not believe me. I make a note in the logbook.

Another home is set 100 feet beyond where the long driveway ends. A half dozen vicious dogs stretch chains staked in bare red ground on either side of a makeshift path to the house. Their ferocious barks and growls make the hair on my arms stand on end but do not deter me. To access the house, I walk back and forth on the path, to avoid the creatures. The confidence I portray belies my fear.

Do they leap to defend their master or beg me to release them from the stench of their dwelling?

The owner, a scraggly man in filthy overalls, emits a low snarl through yellow teeth. His voice is as intimidating as his canines.

The place is in a swale close to the river below the dam. It reeks of excrement. My note in the log reads, "Do not return unless accompanied. NOT SAFE."

George assures me I will not be asked to go back.

I emphasize my point. "No one should ever be allowed on those premises without backup."

"That will not happen." His voice is confident. He adds, "Don't put yourself in that kind of situation. Leave and report it."

At a different location, the owner and I talk while a small dog yaps constantly from the garage. When the man steps into the house, the nasty pooch runs out and bites me three times in the back of the leg before scampering back to his presumed shelter. The mutt growls his outrage because he cannot do more damage. My jeans prevent the bites from drawing blood. The owner does not return from the house.

I explain what happened to George, who writes an incident report. A triple set of bruises appear on the back of my leg the following day.

In retrospect, I should not have ventured past the fierce dogs. If anything went astray, I could have been injured, and the police could have been involved, which would have made matters worse.

If the little mutt's owner had returned to talk with me, I would have shown him the bites on my leg. The man might have said the bites were from a different dog, not his precious pooch. But I would have addressed the injury with him.

But in both instances, I chose the path that created the least disruption at the moment.

Upon returning to the plant each day, I copy pages from the logbook at 200 before debriefing with George. We don't have a copy machine at the lab. George submits the copies to his boss before Olin sends them to the Army.

After a week of collecting samples offsite, the Commander's Representative casually strolls past the copy room while I am there.

He asks how the day went.

I feel obliged to tell him what happened in the field. He is our only customer, and we employees are frequently reminded of the importance of a satisfied customer.

Several days later, George and Jim stand at the copy machine when I return. "Have you been talking with the Army?" They speak in unison.

"No," I reply. The men look confused.

"Sometimes, the Army man is in the copy room when I return from offsite. He asks questions," I confess. "Did I do something wrong?"

"I'll take care of this," George mutters to Jim.

Jim says he'll talk to the Army.

My lesson in chain-of-command at Badger: Never talk directly to the Army. Debrief only with your supervisor and let him take the information up the ladder. The person at the top of Olin management is the only person who passes information to the Army.

The Commander's Representative never wanders into the copy room while I am there again.

Local activists stir the public and urge the Army to do more and more testing. Some of those tests are for chemicals unrelated to Badger. The Army complies with reasonable requests.

The Army directs Olin to test groundwater for nitroglycerin, NG, because it was manufactured onsite.

Our lab has the capability. However, an outside lab doing the initial testing takes precedence. This is a problem. Procedures require standard testing material to create linear regression graphs.

Pure-certified NG is not available on the open market. Therefore, no other laboratory has the capability.

Finally, Hazelton Laboratory in Madison says if Badger provides the raw material for making the graphs, they can do the testing. Our lab retains a small amount of NG as standard material for such situations.

George directs Paul to prepare the material for shipment to Hazelton. This means Paul will transfer a small amount of the NG produced at Badger during the Vietnam War, neutralized with stabilizer, to a plastic bottle and cap it with a rubber stopper. It will require special packaging for transfer.

I return from collecting samples, as Paul completes the task. We pack ice into my coolers filled with water samples and attach the chain-of-custodies. He seals them with tape while I change into street shoes.

I find Paul waiting for me in the truck. We must drop the coolers at shipping and take the NG to George before we leave the plant. We assume our boss will deliver it to the Hazelton Lab himself.

I scan the small cab. "Where's the NG?" I ask as we approach the railroad tracks. "Do you have it?" My voice creeps up—insisting. Even under the stabilizer, NG must be handled with care.

Paul is silent. Except his mustache flutters a bit, suppressing a mischievous grin.

"Alright. Where is it?" I play along.

Paul glances down. My eyes follow his.

There, between his legs, is the NG.

"I figure it's the safest place in the truck." He manages a straight face momentarily. Then our guffaws fill the cab.

The Army attempts to quell the public's frenzy. At the end of May 1990, they agree to test the water from Prairie du Sac's municipal well even though geographical maps tracking groundwater flow indicate the public's drinking water is safe. NG was never detected in environmental samples at Badger.

The groundwork for this event requires a special meeting with George, Jim, the Commander's Representative, and me. My only request is that my name not appear in the article. I am already recognized as *The Water Lady* at restaurants and whenever I am out in public. The attention makes me uneasy.

On the big day, I head the pickup to the well site to meet a local newspaper reporter covering the sample collection. As I approach the city, an aggressive driver passes my truck. The speeding vehicle is still visible when its brake lights flash in the distance. It makes a hard right into the parking lot of the municipal building.

Making the corner myself, I see the vehicle has smashed into the chain link fence that secures the facility. I cannot see what happened to the car, but a post and linkage are pulled out of the ground below where the right headlight made contact.

My nerves are already on edge because of the newspaper story. The accident is a further disruption. Taking a deep breath, I grab the logbook and pull the meters and cooler from the back of the pickup. A lady remains sitting in the car.

Inside the building, the city employee I am to meet peers out the window at the vehicle with its headlight stuck in the fencing while I explain what I saw.

"I think the lady getting out of that car is from the newspaper," the man sputters. "I don't like being in the news. Now I have an accident report to deal with."

The urgency of the young woman to get her story baffles me. In retrospect, she was probably thrilled to be the person chosen to cover the event. Her nerves were likely more frayed than mine.

I never see an article about her collision with the fence. However, the story she wrote and the photo she took of my hands taking the sample make the front page of the *Baraboo News Republic.*

In the end, the city well tests negative for contaminants from Badger.

A Professor in a Field (1990-1993)

David and I celebrate our 25th wedding anniversary with three other couples: the asphalt guy, the food guy, the court reporter, and their wives. We plan a Caribbean cruise to five islands, departing in January 1991. Planning commences months in advance.

Taking a week off work is frowned upon at Badger. I do not want anyone to think I am expendable. However, I really want to go on the cruise. George gives me the okay but says not to talk it up with other employees.

Trouble begins brewing in the Middle East in August 1990. Scuttlebutt at work speculates the ammunition produced at Badger might be needed. I recall the production contracts Frank, George's boss, mentioned when I interviewed two years ago. I never heard more about them. Never asked.

The combat phase of Operation Desert Storm begins January 17, 1991, a week and days before our vacation. There is a real possibility the government will cancel all cruises.

When the cruise industry receives the go ahead, we wonder what special safety measures will be in place. One concern is going through customs when we return to the U.S.. None of us carries a passport, and there is no time to apply. We have only our birth certificates.

We fly from Madison to Nashville, Tennessee, to San Juan, Puerto Rico. We spend the evening and the following day exploring the city before boarding the ship.

The first evening on board, David and I watch the war on a 16-inch black and white television in our tiny stateroom. The video shows smart bombs dropped from airplanes on strategic locations to render the enemy defenseless. No ground warfare is televised or reported.

The island of Barbados, our first port, is quiet. Most businesses are closed for a holiday. We spend our time on the white sand beach. The Secret Island is sparsely inhabited. The ship's crew creates a tropical paradise with live music and a colorful luau-style dinner in the shade of a grove of palm trees. The guys snorkel while the wives lounge on the beach and cool off in the crystal-clear water.

On the third day, soldiers bearing automatic rifles and bandoliers heavy with rounds of ammunition greet us in Martinique. They stand guard throughout the island.

The following days on Saint Martin and Saint Thomas progress like a typical Caribbean cruise. In Puerto Rico, we claim our luggage, proceed to the airport, and board our plane. Some passengers make light of our country not letting us return. Their jokes fall flat.

The gate is anything but ordinary at the airport in Miami, Florida. U.S. soldiers hold automatic rifles and carry bandoliers of ammunition over their shoulders. We are kept separate from our luggage. It must pass special searches. Like cattle, the soldiers herd us through narrow turnstiles. I hold on to my birth certificate for dear life. Hours later, we finally get through customs. Our flight is delayed, but we return home just in time for work.

I expect to hear about the contract Frank spoke of when I interviewed, the contract to produce ordnance. Word trickles down. The contract has been scrapped. The Army says future wars will be fought with smart bombs, not with guns on the ground, or mortars fired from helicopters. They will not need smokeless powder to clear beaches or fire from battleships. Smart bombs will be used to fight future wars.

Thoughts of a college degree remain on the back burner because final audit reports and new offsite sample collection consume me. I finally schedule a visit to UW-Baraboo, BOO-U, in late December 1992. They offer an associate degree. I need a bachelor's.

"We just started collaborating with UW-Platteville on a bachelor's degree in business. You would be among the first to enroll." The counselor is exuberant. "You can attend classes right here—online." Her enthusiasm is contagious.

It will take time. But I can do it.

Optimistic, I hand the information to George.

"This is good. Really good." My boss grabs the folder and heads to 200, leaving me standing.

A couple of days later he hands the folder back to me. "There's a problem."

Now what?

He explains, "A degree in business is not technical enough to qualify for support. I'm sorry. I tried."

We share disappointment without words.

I find three private schools that offer nontraditional four-year degrees but only in business.

Another door slams shut. I'll never get a promotion.

The Army continually places new wells on the offsite list. One is a second sampling point at a regular stop, a farm southeast of the plant.

Following the owner's directions to drive beyond the outbuildings, I find a faucet at the top of a pipe standing in an open field. How strange.

A second house, nestled beyond, surprises me. Even though I am familiar with the area, I've never seen it before. The home's eclectic design blends prairie style and greenhouse with plants and foliage strewn about.

I open the faucet to purge the well, set up bottles, and calibrate meters when movement catches my eye. An older gentleman, short in stature, approaches with authority, although his gait is slow.

"Hello," he calls from a distance.

Never knowing what to expect from initial encounters with the locals, I smile and wave but wait to speak. Given his age, he may have hearing issues. I want to explain my mission only once: schedule and collect samples, conduct field tests, and document findings. Do not offer information.

I log residents' comments and debrief with George at the end of the day. The Army responds to questions posed by the public.

After introducing myself, I explain, "The owner told me to collect a water sample here."

"Yes, my daughter. What's that you're doing?" He sounds interested, not confrontational. I explain the simple nuances of field testing. He nods for me to continue while he contemplates the meter readings.

"What kind of training did you have to do this work?" His question surprises me. No one has ever asked. Should his question be referred to the Army? I dismiss the thought.

"The short answer is, I was trained on the job. However, I attended UW-La Crosse, their biology program. During the Vietnam War, I worked for eight years with the instrument group in the industrial lab at Badger, testing gunpowder. I also did initial water testing for the Clean Water Act in the early '70s."

The man absorbs every word.

Did I say too much?

"What instruments did you work with?" He leans in like he is more than politely interested.

Should I tell him more?

"Spectrophotometers—IR and UV/VIS, atomic absorption, and gas chromatograph," I hesitantly respond.

His eyebrows raise. "So why are you out in the field collecting water samples?"

I wince at the relevance of his question before replying. "I've asked myself that same thing recently." A short version of needing a bachelor's degree to get anywhere these days follows.

"Don't quit your day job, young lady. Do not quit your day job." His feet seem to lift off the ground with excitement. "You can get a degree while you work. Go to the university in Baraboo. They can help you."

He sticks out his hand, "Theodore Savides. I was dean at UW-Green Bay before I became the first dean at UW-Baraboo. I developed some of the first nontraditional degree programs early on."

Reluctant to squelch his enthusiasm, I am compelled to continue. "I've been to BOO-U. Took computer programming courses there a couple of years ago. It's a great school, but they only have a bachelor's degree in business. I need a degree in one of the sciences to qualify for a promotion. They're only available at four-year universities. I need to work." My stomach tightens, contradicting him.

"Let me think." The dean is in his own world. "You stay right here. Don't leave." Muttering to himself, he walks away.

I am packing samples in ice when Savides returns. His step quicker.

"You call this lady." He thrusts his business card into my hand with a number written on the back. "Barb Doherty is at UW-Superior, or at least she was. She can help you find the program you need."

He looks me straight in the eye. "Remember now. Don't quit your day job. You call me if you need anything." He holds out his hand with a broad smile. "It was a pleasure meeting you, Carolyn Dallmann."

Holding up the card, I return his smile. "Thank you, Dean Savides. The pleasure is mine. Especially if this works."

Savides' name and achievements are recognized throughout the area.

My eyes lift heavenward. Is this some kind of divine intervention? How did I happen to be in a prairie field at that moment? How did Dean Savides happen by for a chat?

I still ask myself that question.

My exuberance dwindles by Friday. After so many disappointments, what's one more? I dial the number on the back of the dean's card and ask for Barb Doherty. Her "Hello" surprises me.

"I need a bachelor's degree."

"Be specific," she replies, then patiently listens to my story.

"There are extended degree programs in chemistry but not in the UW system. Associated labs require hours outside of the classroom. You said you can be away from work only five hours a week. Chemistry's not possible." Papers shuffle while I wait for bad news. "I'm thinking of a college out east that might work. I'll do some research and let you know."

Out east? That's impossible.

I hang up, thinking I'll never hear from this lady again.

An hour later, the phone rings. Doherty tells me, "Thomas Edison State College, TESC is the school. It's in Trenton, New Jersey."

Trenton, New Jersey?

Doherty continues, "Would a degree in mathematics work for you? TESC offers both an associate's and bachelor's."

UGH.

I shudder, picturing myself at a computer screen listening to a calculus professor. "Mathematics would probably be accepted at work. But I'm not that good at math. If I get stuck, what would I do?"

"It's not like that. TESC and the University of Wisconsin are both accredited by the same institute. You may take classes at UW schools or any universities whose credits they accept. Graduation requirements are the same.

She sounds so sincere. Or is this a sales pitch?

It's the late 1980s. Her information sounds impossible.

"I suggest you call TESC. You're a good candidate for a non-traditional degree, and this school may be one of the few that meets your needs."

MATHEMATICS.
AN IMPOSSIBLE MOUNTAIN.
A GLIMMER OF HOPE.

I want a promotion.

I Will Succeed (1993-1998)

It is 1993. I am 45. It has been over 25 years since I have been in a math classroom.

The student service rep at Thomas Edison State College makes it sound so easy. He explains that TESC is a credit bank school with no brick-and-mortar campus.

A college with no buildings? I've never heard of such a thing.

"We'll assign you an advisor after evaluating your previous academic work," the man says. Following a few quick phone calls, my credits transfer.

The TESC associate's and bachelor's both require three semesters of calculus. The four-year program increases the amount of advanced math.

The elusive promotion floats on the horizon—out of reach.

How will earning a degree in mathematics help me do my job? It won't.

But it will qualify me for a promotion and a raise.

My advisor says I have amassed over half of the 120 credits needed for a bachelor's.

The foothills of the mountain are below me. An overwhelming climb lies ahead.

BOO-U offers the three required semesters of calculus. A grade of C or better in college algebra or trigonometry or an acceptable score on a placement test is needed to get into Math 221, the lowest calculus level. I have none of these.

My BOO-U advisor suggests starting with Basic Mathematics 090.

I laugh. "No. I work and can take only one class at a time. I'd be retired before I got a degree."

"There's nothing we can do. These requirements are meant to help students succeed."

BANG. Another door closed.

"Would you like to talk to one of the math professors?" she asks.

"Yes, I would." My reply is firm. I want to make this happen.

Considering what the advisor said, my exuberance soon dwindles to apprehension.

What if I fail? People at work will know. I can't handle that.

The professor who I will talk with holds a Ph.D. in mathematics. He worked on the space program in California before teaching.

Impending doom looms as I enter the meeting room. He appears tall and lanky as he sits across a table from me. He absent-mindedly flips through my file as I explain my goal.

"I need advice—suggestions," I tell him.

Pushing my papers aside, he says, "I don't know why you're doing this. You'll never succeed."

I am stunned. Of all the things I expected this man to say, this was not one of them.

But the professor knows what he is talking about.

His *degree* gives him *credibility*.

I do not touch the papers spewed between us. He is right. I have humiliated myself.

Suppressing tears, I trudge across the small campus. My insides ball into a tight knot. I am demoralized.

I am guilty of allowing myself to get into this mess. I am furious with a system that forces me into such a despicable situation.

Reaching the parking lot, I reconsider.

Is the professor, the rocket scientist, correct?

He may be right—but he may be wrong.

His words were, "You'll never succeed."

I smile. People like this professor do not realize what happens when they make a comment like his to someone like me.

Maybe he said, "You'll work harder than you've ever worked before. Go, girl."

I will not give up easily.

I drive directly to the high school.

Cliff Anderson is the Artist's math teacher. He was already at the high school when I graduated in 1965.

"You can get the degree," Anderson says. "But it'll be hard work. I suggest you talk with Glen Riggles. He heads up our math department."

I know Riggles as the varsity basketball coach. The team has had several successful seasons under his leadership. A good omen.

Coach says, "Your advisor was right suggesting you start with a low-level course. You'll need to write a placement test. College algebra may be the highest you want to attempt. Pick up one of our algebra textbooks and do it. Get the answer book, too. When you finish, you'll know if you're ready to test in the fall."

He adds, "A student in your daughter's class is a tutor if you need help. You'll need to pay her. But she's outstanding."

I head to the car with the coach's note tucked inside the books he suggested.

Nicky, the young tutor, is a lifesaver as I spend summer evenings and weekends sweating over algebra homework.

I pass the college algebra placement test by the skin of my teeth in August.

As luck would have it, the rocket scientist mathematician is my algebra professor. I pass with flying colors.

Isaac Solomon holds a Ph.D. in mathematics. He is my trigonometry professor. We meet after my first class. He explains the small university rotates its three math instructors through the advanced courses. The person I start calculus with will take me through all three if I take the courses consecutively.

Concerned, I ask, "Does that mean I get the algebra guy?"

My fears subside when Isaac explains, "No. Unless you miss a semester, I'll be your instructor." He has someone in mind to tutor me.

There are 26 students in my first calculus class at BOO-U. One of them is another nontraditional student and my tutor. Hoyt spent almost ten years on a Navy nuclear-powered submarine. He taught math and calculus pertaining to the sub's operations for much of that time. Hoyt is also one of the four students in my third-semester calculus class. The others either transferred to other schools, changed their academic direction, or dropped out.

The instructor-to-student ratio is an advantage at the small campus. A possible disadvantage is that there's no grading curve. You either understand the math, or you fail.

A continuous cycle of course approvals, classes, and work unfolds. To complicate matters, the Artist attends UW-Stevens Point, and the Actress enrolls at BOO-U. Three of us are in college at the same time for an entire year. Juggling finances and schedules is mind-boggling.

My husband is concerned, "You do nothing but work and study. Why do you keep putting yourself through this hell?"

"It's the only way I can get ahead."

David understands because he would do the same.

November 1995, at age 48, I complete my third semester of calculus. I hand George a copy of my associate degree in mathematics. I am surprised when I receive the long-sought-after reclassification. My new job title is *Auditor*. And my salary increases appropriately. Management says nothing about a four-year degree.

Are they tired of dealing with me?

I never again want my career held back because of academics. A bachelor's is within my grasp—it will take another three years. Advanced math classes are only available at UW-Madison. Isaac recommends matrix linear algebra over advanced calculus. "It'll be more useful to you," he says.

"May I continue?" I ask. George shakes his head but smiles.

I must register by telephone at the big university, but I am consistently rejected. Enrolled students are allowed to register before people like me. Courses fill fast. Time is running out. I need paperwork showing I am accepted before I can leave work for class.

On the Friday before the registration deadline, I drive to Madison. It is late August. The many open parking spaces on the Francis Street ramp indicate students have not returned. The usual State Street crowd is sparse. I head up Bascom Hill to Van Vleck Hall, the mathematics building. The impressive structure is adjacent to where Sterling Hall stood before Karlton and Dwight Armstrong, David Fine, and Leo Burt blew it up in August 1970.

Goose bumps prickle my arms as memories of the Vietnam War crash over me.

My steps echo on shiny tile when I enter Van Vleck. The classrooms I am looking for are on the upper floors.

I do not take the elevator because eerie thoughts of Sterling Hall linger. I would not want to be between floors if something catastrophic happened.

Even if nothing bad occurred, what if the door stuck? The campus is empty. It would be days before anyone found me.

My quest to locate a professor does not happen.

CLINK. CLINK. A strange sound resonates in the hall ahead as I make my way toward the stairs to leave. Walking toward the sound, I spot a man with his hands full of glassware. Catching up to him, I ask, "Are you a professor?"

"No. I set up labs and troubleshoot equipment." He keeps walking—wants to lose me.

"I need some help if you have a minute." His glance indicates I'm a bother. But giving up is not my nature. "I need to find a professor who will let an extended degree student into a matrix linear algebra class. I can't register because I'm not enrolled. Do you know a professor?"

"Hmpf." He enters a room, sets the glassware on the counter, pulls a piece of paper from his pocket, and scribbles a name. "I don't know his number, but he might let you in. Not all of them would." He gives me the—you know what I mean— look.

The name on the paper looks difficult to pronounce.

But it's a chance, maybe my only chance.

The unfamiliar last name has three associated numbers in the thick book chained to the shelf below the public telephone in the University Bookstore. One address is close by. I insert coins and dial the number.

"Hello." The man's voice is glum.

"This is Carolyn Dallmann. I want to take a course at the university. Are you a math professor?"

His "Yes" is like winning the lottery.

"I need your matrix linear algebra class. I'm an extended degree student, not enrolled at UW." Breathless, I rush to plead my case before he hangs up.

"You'll be allowed, but it'll take a few weeks." His monotone stops before he adds, "Just show up. Don't say anything."

That's it. I'm in.

But my problems do not end there.

Why must everything be so complicated?

The next glitch is work. I hand my class schedule to George, omitting details.

"Get the paperwork, even if it's the same day your class starts," he says.

Knowing that's not possible, I don't reply.

On the fateful morning, my boss is at 200 in a meeting. I leave a memo in his mailbox.

It is a good thing Badger has an antiquated communication system, or things may have gone differently. I do not lose my job or get reprimanded. Two weeks later, I submit the paperwork for class as usual. No one says a word.

In November 1998, I receive my Bachelor of Mathematics with minors in Chemistry and Computer Science. Reaching my goal feels glorious. It was not easy. But it will prove to be worth my effort in the future. I am proud of my accomplishment but wonder at the personal cost.

Five years of college erased a chunk of my life. I most regret what it took from my husband and daughters, and especially what it stole from me. Time and lost memories cannot be replaced.

Work changes during the years I take classes. The lab staff grows to almost 20. Chemists rotate onsite sample collection duties.

Sophisticated instruments, some capable of measuring down to parts per trillion, grace the rooms like huge, nondescript, tan, metal boxes that conceal intricate, mysterious workings. The new computer system captures data. Minimizes human error.

I continue collecting quarterly offsite samples from resident's wells. Some people await my visit like old friends. Others, I never see. The number has been cut to less than fifty because the underground aquafer has been established. I am consumed with reviewing data, building an internal audit program, managing state and federal accreditation programs, and regulatory audits.

Enjoying a Friday fish fry or Saturday dinner in a restaurant with my family becomes impossible without someone recognizing me as *The Water Lady.* George agrees when I ask to be relieved from offsite sample collection.

I notify everyone on my quarterly route that new chemists will collect their water samples in the future. Kaye, a quiet young professional, is first to accompany me offsite. She is a tiny blonde woman in her twenties. The first two residents are not at home. Kaye's nerves have calmed by the third stop.

The owner of this place is in his seventies. He extends a familiar greeting. I introduce Kaye. He leads the way to the tap on the side of his house. A garden hose on a reel sits next to it. He says he wants to explain about the smell. I glance at Kaye.

"Smell?" we ask, sniffing the air.

"A mama skunk and her youngsters surprised me one morning last week. It's been dry and I think she was looking for water by my tap. My approach must have scared her. She sprayed the entire foundation before she hustled her babies to safety.

"I washed the house for two days. Tried everything: soap, bleach, ammonia. It still smelled like skunk. The odor was creeping inside. I finally asked the druggist in town what he suggested. The guy sold me some Massengill douche solution. It did the job."

A wide smile of pride spreads across the man's face as he revels in his success.

Kaye's cheeks turn bright red.

I chuckle.

Thankfully, Kaye does not ask me to explain.

Some residents appear skeptical when I introduce them to the young chemists. Many wish me well.

My days in the field are over.

For now.

The atomic absorption spectrophotometer, the long tan metal box, was used to test the concentration of metals in water and soil samples. Samples are staged on carts awaiting testing. *Image:* Carolyn Dallmann, 2001.

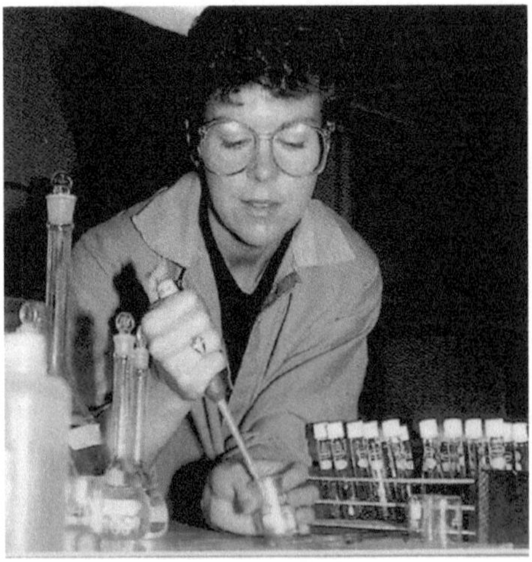

Wet chemistry procedures continue throughout the Vietnam War and beyond. Carolyn Dallmann adds reaction solution to Chemical Oxygen Demand, COD, vials using an Eppendorf pipet. *Image:* Badger History Group, Inc.

5

THE BEGINNING OF THE END

1998–2014

The Critter (1999-2001)

During the late 1990s, George searches for a chemist supervisor. Two potential candidates end up at testing stations. They are fine chemists, but managing people requires a unique skill set. Dave, a tall, young redhead who played college basketball, fills the slot.

Dave is a likable kid with a sense of humor. He gravitates to company politics playing out in the administration building and then speeds through mounds of data packages at the lab, only to return to 200. George takes rare vacation days while mentoring the young man into a leadership role.

Shirley, also a redhead, runs the lab office like a well-oiled machine. She is the same Shirley who was processing new employees the day the hardening house exploded in 1966. Her quiet demeanor counterbalances Dave's exuberance. However, she is not afraid to speak up when files get bogged down in the young man's office.

"When will you get to that data package?" Shirley asks. He has been up front most of the morning.

"Soon," he says. But there's teasing in his voice. "Maybe after lunch."

"Do that one first," Shirley responds. She politely encourages the young man to prioritize.

Dave pokes his head into my office. His broad smile says he knows what will happen next.

Like clockwork, Shirley appears at Dave's door with two lemon bars on a small paper plate. She softly chuckles and says, "I had extras."

"Lemon bars, my favorite," Dave coos his delight.

"You're going to do that data package right after lunch." Shirley's statement hints a plea.

"This afternoon, for sure," comes the reply.

Dave wipes crumbs from his mouth five minutes later when he pauses at my door. "Will she bring brownies tomorrow if I don't get to that package today?" His whispered comment is only half teasing.

Their friendly banter is not new. Shirley never learns that feeding Dave will not get her what she needs. The young man reaps the benefits.

Our offices sit along the north side of the east wing of the lab. Testing rooms require constant temperature because of sophisticated equipment. However, little cool air floats down the long hall to the office area. The cost of incorporating air conditioning into the east wing is not justified.

We open windows when outside temperatures are comfortable but close them against heat and humidity. Ventilation is minimal because there are no windows on the opposite side of the hall. The offset emergency exit door to the south remains closed because prairie critters tend to view it as an invitation to enter the lab when it's open.

"We need more air," Dave exclaims when he returns from upfront one sweltering afternoon. His long arm swings the emergency door open, locking it in place.

Shirley's eyebrows rise.

Minutes later, she hollers. "There's something in here."

"What?" Dave is quick on his feet.

"I don't know. But I saw it." Shirley's voice goes up an octave.

"Are you sure? Like a mouse?" He chuckles as he vigorously pokes a fly swatter behind the filing cabinets close to the secretary's desk.

"It looked bigger than that." Shirley tucks her feet up and off the floor.

A long, brown streak flashes in the hall past my door. "It's headed west—toward your office," I warn. It looked like something I saw as a kid on the farm.

Dave's long legs leap down the corridor.

"Don't chase that thing in here," I yell, closing the door between my office and Dave's.

I stand beside Shirley, who is wide-eyed, her cheeks pink with excitement. Her desk marks the end of the hall—no way out except toward the action. Dave rummages through the narrow storage area between the restrooms. He holds up a piece of wood that looks like a cricket mallet.

"I'll take care of this" He raises the mallet above his head in a dramatic move, shoots us a determined look, steps into his office, and slams the door.

BANG—SLAP—STOMP—THUMP

"Get outta there"—"You little"—"Oh no, you don't." Dave's hollering filters through the thin walls. I think he must be exaggerating his moves just to shock poor Shirley. A final CRASH ends the commotion.

"He's trapped it under the trash container," Shirley cries.

I agree. The noise sounded like the metal wastebasket slammed on the tile floor.

When the door opens, a dead critter slumps over the makeshift weapon. It looks like a ferret but is more likely a juvenile weasel.

Dave smiles triumphantly—a boy with his trophy.

Shirley's nose wrinkles. "What's that smell?"

I get a whiff. "Yuck. That makes my eyes water."

The critter marked everywhere it was cornered.

Dave got the worst of it.

Leaving Dave in charge, George takes an unprecedented two-week vacation to visit his parents and family in Haifa, on the Mediterranean Sea in Israel, around the turn of the century. While out of the country, George ventures to what he calls the Peace Center and meets with Elias Chacour, whom he knows through correspondence.

Chacour is a graduate of the Seminaire du Saint Sulpice in Paris and the first Palestinian to earn a degree from the Hebrew University in Jerusalem. He is instrumental in expanding the Peace Center's work to educate youth in the troubled region. I read Chacour's book, *We Belong to the Land*, about his early work. He accepts George's offer to visit Wisconsin. My boss will one day introduce me to Chacour in Prairie du Sac following their fascinating presentation.

George is contemplating retirement. I think this trip is a trial run. His buddy, Jim, the plant manager, has already left Badger to focus on his water park business in Wisconsin Dells.

Gayle, a woman my age who worked under Jim, is the new plant manager.

In September 2000, the lab organizes a potluck for George. He receives a well-deserved sendoff.

I feel myself treading uncharted water when my mentor leaves, like when Natalie left the powder lab toward the end of the Vietnam War.

Concentrating on a complex data package, I do not hear Jim 2, a master's degree chemist who runs a mass spectrophotometer, step into my office. It is September 11, 2001.

"We've been attacked." Jim is a quiet man with a dry sense of humor.

Irritated with the idea of a presumed joke, I say, "And?" as I turn to face him. His face tells me he is not joking. But I cannot wrap my head around what he might mean.

"What's going on?" I prod.

"An airplane just flew into the World Trade Center in New York City," Jim replies.

I am silent, bewildered.

"You can get to the internet on your computer. Look." Jim does not mince words. Each instrument connects to our internal computer system. However, mine and Dave's are the only computers with internet access.

"I need to finish this data package before I switch to the internet," I say, still questioning what Jim tells me.

"You should look now. They're saying it might be a terrorist attack," Jim insists. He convinces me and peers over my shoulder as I transition to the internet.

Neither of us is prepared for the image on the 14-inch monitor. Black smoke spills from the side of the skyscraper. The reporter repeats that an airplane has flown directly into the building and tries to navigate to makeshift communication centers for more information.

We speculate. The pilot must have had a medical issue. What else could it be?

Jim returns to his workstation but will monitor news reports on the public radio station.

I cannot take my eyes off the screen. It is surreal to watch. But it gets worse—much worse. The monitor shows a second plane fly into the World Trade Center.

Jim and the other chemists float in and out of my office. I leave the internet up.

I consider calling my husband, but UPS, like Badger, frowns on personal phone calls during work hours. Communication must go through the main offices at both companies.

Reports say there are other airplanes in other states, presumably on suicide missions.

We work at an Army installation—surely, we are not a target. *Are we?*

The reporter's voice goes up an octave. "The building's collapsing."

I watch the shift.

The hesitation.

The drop.

Cameras that were rolling through the city's streets trying to get closer to the Trade Center now retreat.

They are not fast enough.

A rolling black cloud rushes toward them like a horrific tornado. The screen turns dark gray.

I call my husband. He has heard but, without an image, cannot comprehend what is happening. He has no internet or television at work. I cannot fully describe the magnitude of the horror. Not wanting to hear more, David says, "I'll see enough on news reports when I get home."

I call the Actress, who lives in Chicago, and the Artist, who lives in the burbs outside the city, and listen to their accounts. They tell me that everyone is looking up.

Chicago is a big city. *Could it be a target?*

Badger goes to code red, danger. Shortly, we drop to code orange, less danger. By early afternoon, management tells us to go home and stay there until further notice.

Shutting down most of the instruments takes time. Some sample runs must be left. Until when? No one knows.

A half dozen Olin and Army managers stay on site.

The rest of us wait at home.

Over a week later, we get the call to return to work.

Badger changed while we waited for the "all clear." Wide, four-foot-tall concrete structures sit alternating down the middle of the drive to the main gate. I serpentine around the barricades to the guard shack. Even though I know each member of the guard crew, one asks my name and the prescribed series of questions. Another guard looks inside my car and runs a mirror along the undercarriage.

Intense inspections ease up after a few weeks. The barricades remain for years.

Because of changing military strategy in the late 1990s, the Army reports they need only two of the over 20 powder plants built to support World War II. They eliminate all except three. Those three are Badger and two others located side-by-side in Radford, Virginia. The Army is reluctant to have its only two ammunition manufacturing resources in an adjacent configuration in case of a disastrous weather event or an enemy attack. Virginia fights to retain the last two. Wisconsin does not.

I am concerned as an employee.

What will happen to me if Badger closes?

As a citizen, I know our country does not learn well from history. Will we again run short of ammunition? One day, will we be in a situation similar to the early 1940s?

And what happens if a tornado hits both facilities in Virginia? Or they're destroyed in an enemy attack? Our country has no other option to manufacture the types of gunpowder we can produce at Badger.

Politicians wrangle from the late 1990s to 2004. State representatives and other political figures speak to us at plant wide employee meetings throughout this time. They tell us they will keep us informed. They will help us find jobs. They do not know when the plant will close.

Some employees leave. Some, close to retirement age, hang on hoping to work a few more years.

The final decision is to retain the Radford plants. The military does not need Badger. They will demolish the buildings, remediate, and restore the land before relinquishing the property.

It's a sock in the gut.

A Fight for Land (2002-2004)

Between 2000 and 2004, Badger wavers in limbo. The wheels of government churn slowly. The powder plant will never again manufacture propellant unless the government drastically changes direction. Our property department reaches out to other military installations that may be able to utilize equipment Badger no longer needs.

Although the Army will not manufacture propellant here in the future, that does not necessarily mean they should remove Badger's massive infrastructure. The powerhouse will continue producing heat and power for other industries to exploit. Likewise, multiple businesses could utilize the industrial electrical service, the water treatment plant, and the sanitation facility. These utilities could support a sizable industrial park on the 7,500 acres.

The Army attempts to industrialize Badger. They have several contracts already in place. Outside companies and organizations rent property from the Army. Dairy Forage, affiliated with UW-Madison and the Department of Agriculture, has raised controlled crops in the southern part of the facility for years. Farm cooperatives rent storage buildings and tanks. A propulsion business operates out of a building at the foot of the bluff. Area farmers pasture herds of cattle during the summer.

Two scientists repurposed the acid and nitrocellulose lab for their research project regarding milk and enzyme production. It's called the Gala Laboratory; Gala is a Greek term relating to milk.

Proposals that did not materialize were, using the filtration ponds to raise fish and building a Superconducting Magnetic Energy Storage system, SMES. Several SMES units operate around the world for power quality control in installations, especially those requiring ultra-clean power, such as microchip fabrication facilities. A string of SMES units deployed in northern Wisconsin enhance grid stability in a distribution loop.

Frank, George's boss and the second person who interviewed me in 1988, is involved in industrialization. Venturing into uncharted business promotion and development does not deter Frank's team.

I idealize the situation. Surrounding communities encroach on farmland to promote business. If those cities pooled their resources and supported one sizeable industrial area already established to fit their needs instead of expanding their own infrastructures, maybe some farmland could be saved. My daydream elicits potential.

I was not privy to the details of seeking new industry to Badger. I do not know if Frank's team approached communities with the idea of a cooperative industrial park. Entering into such an agreement would pose considerable risk. If cities were approached, I suspect there would be reluctance to change *business as usual.* But my daydream offers a ray of sunshine versus a gloomy end to a magnificent structure.

In 2004, the Army announces Badger property will revert to other government agencies. However slow in coming, the beginning of the end hits like a stormy gust.

The fight over who gets the land begins.

Newspapers, radio stations, and television networks announce public hearings. I attend. However, as a Badger employee, I am told not to voice my opinion because someone may think I speak for the Army.

My heart is with the descendants of the farmers. They randomly plead their sad stories at formal meetings. Tension escalates. Lawyers are involved.

The Government Service Administration steps in. Simply put, the GSA is the government's real estate agent. It becomes evident that once the government takes personal property, they seldom return it to the original landowner. Instead, when the agency that took the land no longer needs it, the parcel goes through a pecking order between other government agencies, which must formally request the land and explain its intended use.

Dairy Forage, a research farm that operates through UW-Madison and the Department of Agriculture, does not want to lose the land where they have raised controlled crops for years.

Children and grandchildren of the farmers who lost their property on the prairie so the Army could build the powder plant in 1942 want their family's land back.

The State of Wisconsin wants property to augment Devils Lake State Park, which is adjacent to the north.

The Ho-Chunk Nation wants all the property because it was their home before European immigrants settled on it.

Bluffview, the community across SR 12 in Sumpter Township, formerly known as Badger Village, depends on Badger's sanitary system.

As an observer, I listen to the spokesman for Dairy Forage; he is one of their managers. The farmers' families act as individuals. The State's lawyers have accurate information, but their presentations are not well organized. The Native American lawyers are well-informed, and their presentations are eloquent. Bluffview explains their situation in a document.

The GSA initially said the Department of Interior, representing the Ho-Chunk Nation, would get the central prairie because their intended use is to raise buffalo. But the Ho-Chunk rejected the offer. The Ho-Chunk want the northern bluff. GSA reverses its decision, and the Ho-Chunk Nation gets the northwest part of the property and a piece of the adjoining prairie to the south. The National Parks Department gets the northwest part of the bluff and the central prairie for a park managed by the Wisconsin Department of Natural Resources. The parcel adjoins Devils Lake State Park. The Department of Agriculture retains the southern parcel of land they rented from the Army for Dairy Forage. Sumpter Township gets a narrow strip of land that includes the sanitation treatment station used by Bluffview. Individual farmers receive nothing.

At the end of one meeting, I overhear someone say, "Those farmer people shouldn't complain. Dairy Forage got all of the land they wanted." I want to reply that Dairy Forage is just another government agency to most of those descendants. Their family's land is gone—collateral damage. But I say nothing.

The agitation of it all disrupts my concentration at work and interferes with my family life. I quit attending public meetings, but newspaper articles and television newscasts tell the story.

Work continues. Olin employees manage the powder plant. Collecting and testing groundwater samples consume the laboratory.

Curiosity about what lay inside the fence around the powder plant becomes evident in 1993 when the Army holds an open house and arranges the first public tour. I was one of the guides. Thousands attended. After the event, employees are allowed to schedule family visits.

One sunny day in early September 2001, I drive Dave's parents, Harold and Jean, and his Aunt Shirley and Uncle Donald through the powder plant. The Dallmann brothers share memories of their childhood before Badger was built and point me directly to their farmstead. They trace paths they walked as kids and talk about their home and the outbuildings.

I watch them lean on the tree that shaded their house. They point to where they played on a rope swing strung over its branches. Their conversation drifts to families who had been neighbors, children they knew, where they walked to school and went to church.

Conversations I heard about Badger between my parents, the Shimnioks, and others from the agricultural community were sobering. Hearing the Dallmann brothers talk about their life on the prairie makes what happened to the farmers in the early 1940s personal.

I read a family account about David's great aunt, Annie Kuhnau Groth, and her husband, Harry, a short time after taking Harold and Donald through Badger.

Annie and Harry purchased the farm known as Devil's Mountain in 1918 from Harry's parents. The property was on the west bluff overlooking what would become Badger Ordinance Works.

On December 1, 1941, Annie notices sparks flying above the barn roof and runs to tell Harry. No one is injured. Cattle and horses escape the blaze but roam the night until an old sheep shed shelters the displaced animals. This is about the same time the government starts taking land from the farmers on the Sauk Prairie below the Groth's farm.

In the spring of 1942, when the government auctions off buildings, Annie adds three dollars to Harry's sealed bid of $250 on John Shimniok's barn. She anticipates other bidders will add a dollar, maybe two, above an even number. She does not want to lose the barn by a dollar.

The Groths are the high bidder. Their new barn had belonged to John and Elsie Shimniok, the same couple who own the farm next to my family's place in North Freedom. Although John passed away in 1954, Elsie and her boys still ran the farm when I started work at Badger. A great-grandchild manages the place today.

John and Elsie Shimniok had to leave their barn on the Sauk Prairie when the government condemned 10,500 acres in the early 1940s to build Badger. Relatives of the Dallmann family bought the barn from the Army in March 1942. The Dallmann family captured a photo of the barn while it was being disassembled. In June 1943, they recorded the barn raising on Harry and Annie Groth's farm.

The John Shimniok barn on the Sauk Prairie was sold to Harry Groth, disassembled, and removed from the Sauk Prairie in March 1942. *Image:* Dallmann family album.

The barn dissembled on the prairie in March 1942 was raised on the Harry and Annie Groth farm in June 1943. The photo on the right shows the barn at 2:00 p.m. on the day it was raised. *Image:* Dallmann family album.

The Groth barn at 5:00 p.m. the day it was raised. *Image:* Dallmann family album.

Boom (2003)

In 2003, long after the Vietnam War, I work at my desk when a familiar but distant, menacing sensation comes from the ground up through my body. A slight pressure nudges me all over. A distant, faraway thud or muffled boom follows.

It can't be—there's no gunpowder at Badger.

How could something explode?

Thoughts fly through my head. For a moment, I convince myself I imagined the feeling. But it is too familiar. Maybe something happened offsite.

I almost collide with Shirley when I step into the hall and meet her worried eyes.

"Something blew up," she exclaims. We express concern but are simultaneously relieved that we did not imagine the feeling.

"What's going on?" Dave, the chemist senior, is curious.

"Something blew up," we tell him.

"I didn't hear anything. Nothing blew up." Dave likes to tease. But he is serious when he says he has not heard an explosion. "You two are always talking about the olden days."

Shirley and I agree something happened south of the lab. She has a broad view in that direction from her office and will keep an eye out the window. I head to the testing rooms and inquire up and down the hall, asking the chemists if they heard a strange sound or felt anything unusual.

No one noticed anything out of the ordinary.

When I return to my office, Dave continues to needle Shirley about the old days. She is still concerned.

I pick up the phone to call Gayle, the plant manager, but decide against it. If there has been an explosion, she'll have her hands full. If there has not been an explosion, I'll be embarrassed. I dial the fire station. Bob, the chief, answers.

"This is Carolyn. I felt and heard something like an explosion."

"The decon oven blew up." Bob says Gayle knows. I know Bob cannot give me details. His firefighters may not yet be at the scene.

The decontamination oven is located over a mile directly south of the lab. Shirley and I know its function. We also know it would be unlikely for anyone to be in its vicinity during operation.

Nevertheless, it blew up.

Was anyone hurt?

What happened?

Dave's eyes pop so wide his red crew cut lifts when I tell him and Shirley.

He grabs his hard hat and sprints down the hall.

"We told you so," is left unsaid.

People like Shirley and I do not forget how their minds and bodies feel when they experience a significant explosion. Few people at Badger that day worked there during the Vietnam War or had that experience.

It was not only the chemists who were unaware of the explosion. Engineers, laborers, and other employees in the administration building and the field had not felt the sensation or heard the noise.

But what happened?

I am curious and will find out.

The decontamination oven removes combustibles from equipment that needs repair or is scheduled for reuse or sale. It's a tall metal building with a 16-foot-long basket inside. The basket stabilizes items that have explosives on them.

Heating controls located in a small remote structure increase the temperature inside the oven. The heat ignites and disintegrates dangerous material from the equipment inside the building, making it safe to repair, reuse, or sell.

The day the decon oven blew up, work crews were transporting 16-foot-long sections of old pipes from the smokeless area across the plant for decontamination. During production days, these pipes contained particles, fines, of explosive material suspended in reclaimed liquid. When production ended in 1974, and over time, the liquid in these process pipes evaporated, leaving an accumulation of fine explosive material. Work crews plug the ends of the pipes with rags to prevent the dangerous material inside from spilling out during transport. They remove the rags when they place the pipes into the huge basket. This acceptable procedure is not unusual.

Word is, the day the decon oven blew up, some rags were inadvertently left in the ends of the pipes, creating a long pipe bomb. It exploded when the temperature inside the oven increased.

The force of the blast blew away the walls of the building.

The Army needs the decon oven to remove explosive material from equipment. They eventually replace it—following considerable paperwork prepared by Olin.

Badger manufactured over a billion pounds of propellant. Considering the magnitude of the operation, relatively few explosions occurred. Fortunately, the decon oven incident resulted in no personal injuries because of safety features engineered into its design.

Photos of the decontamination oven following an explosion in the early 2000s. *Image:* Badger History Group, Inc.

Gone (2004-2014)

I feel Badger slipping toward the horizon before the next blow hits. Olin loses the contract in September 2004. SpecPro, LLC becomes the operating contractor the following month. Their task is environmental work: demolition, remediation, restoration, and turnover of the remaining 7,500 acres to other government agencies.

The powder plant is going away.

People go away, too. Shirley receives a well-deserved retirement package from Olin. In 2003, Dave accepted a sales position with Thermo Fisher Scientific, Inc.. The company manufactures sophisticated laboratory instruments. Mike, the new lab manager, guides the lab to the end.

Olin Corporation, established in 1892, is a large, national manufacturing company. Forty-five employees continue working for them at Badger when the transition occurs.

SpecPro is a fledgling environmental company, part of the Bristol Bay Native Corporation out of Alaska.

After being frozen in uncertainty for so long, I expect the worst from my new employer. Either they will eliminate my job or force me to train my replacement. It's an uncertain time for everyone.

To our surprise, SpecPro keeps all 45 of us.

Additionally, they're interested in me because of the quality function in the laboratory. The new contract has a similar requirement for the entire project. SpecPro has no internal auditor or anyone with quality program experience available to fill the position, which requires a bachelor's degree.

I finally realize a reward for all that studying.

Their offer is appealing. First, because of the challenge. Second, because of the higher salary. One disadvantage is that SpecPro offers no pension benefit. I must save my extra income for retirement.

Our family life has settled. The Artist and Actress graduated from college and are now employed in Chicago. David continues to work the night shift at UPS and is involved in the complex issues of his job. We will experience added stress, but he says the decision is mine.

I accept the offer.

While continuing lab work, I find myself on the management team. Most other members are Olin holdovers. Everyone is unsure of everything.

Arriving early for our first meeting, I stand, uncomfortable, in the same long, narrow room where I was assigned to collect offsite water samples. I reluctantly choose one of the highbacked, padded chairs.

Whose chair is it?

When the door closes, others cast a skeptical eye toward me, wondering why I am present. This core group of holdovers, most from the Vietnam War, functioned with little change for years under Jim, the plant manager who retired to spend more time at his water park business. Gayle, his replacement, maintained smooth operations. But Gayle retired when Olin lost the contract.

The Commander's Representative, the top civilian employed by the Army at Badger, addresses our group, explaining the focus of the new contract. He briefly interjects that the quality program is a required component, meant to improve business. He introduces me as an internal auditor and the quality leader.

I cringe. No one *likes* an auditor. But this situation is not a popularity contest. We have work to do.

Suspicious eyes turn toward me.

The lab's quality program is a federal and state requirement. It works smoothly because George was its initial *champion*. He and following lab managers promoted it. They had my back.

When it is my turn to speak, the new plant manager asks me to explain my duties. He doesn't even pretend to understand my job.

I start, "Quality isn't Carolyn Dallmann's program. It's a joint effort by everyone to improve how work gets done." I see eyes roll, glaze over. The CR picks up on these reactions and interrupts.

"I suggest Carolyn meet with each of you. Be prepared to discuss your contributions to this project with her. She'll continue to spend time with you and your subordinates."

Uncomfortable shifting in chairs rustles around the room.

I have a new, and formidable, champion.

I hear rumbles as I leave meetings. "Why is she…stay in the lab…a policeman."

The words hang in the air, a foreboding cloud. I don't fit the mold of other team members. My position doesn't come with a staff. The quality program involves everyone at Badger.

The managers think my position will create more work for them. That may initially happen. However, it is intended to streamline operations and confirm that the work we do adheres to regulations. I take copies of the rules when I meet with the other team members. Outside agencies will likely audit them in the future due to the environmental focus of the contract. The quality program will prepare them for those events.

The dark comments were a turning point. They reminded me of the Rocket Man professor at BOO-U saying, "You will never succeed." But I did succeed. Traditional closed doors did not stop me. When one slammed shut, I constructed a new door. Then I pushed the framework to widen the space for others to follow.

I remember George, my mentor's, words, "Your opinion doesn't matter. Only rules and requirements are important. You'll lose credibility if you don't back your statements with a regulation." His words are my guide.

With a *champion* and regulations to back me, I rise above the dark comments and find a way to make the quality program work. We focus on and document improvements, which boosts morale and satisfies our customer.

Our people spent years caring for buildings and equipment, keeping the powder plant *ready to operate.* The Army's new orders directly contradict what they required from us for over 60 years. Destroying everything we worked to maintain is mind-boggling.

The Army funds hiring 150 additional employees to move the new environmental project forward. Badger is now SpecPro's largest contract.

New, young environmental engineers interview us old-timers about Badger's historical production activities. The young people shake their heads when we explain the daily tasks performed with chemicals and explosives during the wars. We share their reactions to our stories.

"They rolled their eyes."

"She asked me to repeat how much solvent we transported three times."

"They think we're exaggerating or downright lying."

Based on these interviews, the lab receives potentially contaminated soil samples.

Property records show what materials were used to build and maintain structures: siding, insulation, paint, roofing shingles, and mastics. The lab tests these materials, looking for asbestos, lead, and other contaminants of interest before demolition begins. Test results determine the method required to tear down a specific building.

The initial plan is to burn contaminated buildings and sell buildings where no production took place. However, area landowners express concern about air contamination and settling ash. When burning is scrapped, other issues present problems.

Many of the old production buildings are not structurally safe to enter. Removing equipment must wait until a building is deemed safe to enter. Badger hires structure integrity inspectors. Crews reinforce buildings and then tear them down after removing saleable equipment and materials. As many as twenty excavators maneuver the plant like hungry dinosaurs picking and sorting debris into piles of wood, steel, aluminum, and various metals for sale or disposal.

Other crews go through asbestos abatement training before they remove and package asbestos-containing siding and material for geo-positioned disposal in the landfills we build.

Nitrocellulose, like dust, settled in nooks and crannies throughout some of the old buildings. Demo crews are trained on what to look for but cannot always determine whether an accumulation of powdery material is dust or something dangerous.

When workers hit dry NC with a tool and it reacts with a shot of energy knocking two of them backward, work stops and procedures are revised. Fortunately, no one was injured in the mishap.

After that episode, leaders send work crews out early to spray water to saturate the buildings scheduled for demolition that day. Wet NC is relatively harmless.

Hosing down buildings presents a different hazard when temperatures drop. Water freezes on the tarps around buildings, causing slips and falls. Crews cease work early some days because obstacles cannot be overcome.

Chain-of-command allows communication only between the plant manager for SpecPro and Mike, the Commander's Representative for the Army. Other SpecPro employees, myself included, are reminded not to communicate with the Army.

In the fall of 2006, Mike stops me in the parking lot after work. He has attended recent management meetings soliciting us to sign up for an Army funded Project Management Course. He plans to participate and expects the training will improve communication within SpecPro and streamline our environmental work.

Mike, a retired major, is a solid man with broad shoulders, a thick neck, dark hair, and a beard—a force to be reckoned with. He says, "I'd like you to take the management course. The classes will be held here, onsite, after work, so you won't have to travel."

Having already looked at the course material, I explain, "I think there are people who will benefit by participating. However, most classes are repeats of my earlier studies. You funded my education once. You shouldn't pay twice."

I do not say—*I've had it with schoolwork.*

Mike explains his tactic. He wants me to be an example so managers who are dragging their feet sign up—there has been reluctance.

I think this sounds like the men in the early 1940s who wanted one farmer to sign land over to the government and then used him as leverage to get others to follow.

However, Mike is not a person I want to offend. I relent. I will not rock the boat.

Instructors divide 20 of us into teams. I am in Mike's group. We receive our certificates in May 2007 after completing 18 postgraduate credits. The benefit I gained from networking with peers and understanding the Army's perspective makes my participation worthwhile.

I participate in lead and asbestos abatement training, and learn landfill regulations so I can appropriately audit associated work.

George's words ring true. "Be professional. You'll receive better cooperation if you don't surprise people." I schedule visits to field operations and, once again, wear a hard hat and high-topped boots when auditing demolition and remediation activities.

Work crews demolish the 1,400 wood-frame buildings by designing procedures under the watchful eyes of the State. The concrete pads and firewalls remain. There is no funding to remove them because the concrete is not contaminated.

Things change when Army higher-ups see the odd-looking structures pointing out of the ground, like Stonehenge. A mutual agreement between the Army and the State to crush the concrete pads and firewalls commences. The State uses the stockpiled gravel as aggregate for area highways.

During the wars, workers hosed down buildings between shifts to prevent the accumulation of explosive material. The drain system under Badger handled the wastewater. Using historical design records, our geologists bore soil samples along the underground drainpipes to check for contamination caused by deteriorated pipes. The lab receives these soil samples. Most samples test clean. When test results show contamination, our crews remediate and restore that area.

During busy summers in the lab, the Army funds hiring two technicians to help prep samples. Both are teachers. In the fall, the high school teacher arranges for me to talk to his classes about our lab work on my regular day off. He wants to encourage young people to study and pursue the sciences. I enjoy the students. However, I find repeating my talk every hour during the day disorienting. It is a relief to return to my regular job.

Some test results find contamination that is not the result of manufacturing propellant. Nitrates found in sludge from an outfall area was not from Badger. It came from the surrounding agricultural community. Resourceful remediation is implemented, none-the-less. Crews place the sludge in geotubes on Badger property. As liquid drains from the tubes, Dairy Forage uses it to fertilize their crops.

Polychlorinated biphenyl contamination found in a pond in the northwest part of the facility did not come from Badger. PCBs were not part of the manufacture process. Research reveals that water pumped from the Wisconsin River into the plant during production years fed this pond. Over the years, that water evaporated, concentrating PCBs that came from papermills upstream from Badger. It does not matter where the PCBs came from. The Army remediates the sludge on the bottom of the pond.

Our crews efficiently use landfill space by running wood that cannot be sold through a chipper, thus minimizing the Army's costs. Placing large, random pieces of buildings in a landfill is significantly more costly than reducing that wood to chips for disposal, because the chips occupy less space.

The Army addressed stopping the flow of contaminated groundwater after the first offsite hit was detected in the early 1990s. They drilled deep extraction wells with overlapping vortexes at the southern boundary of the plant in the path of the plume. The overlapping area of the vortexes are as deep below ground as the advancing contamination. These wells capture and redirect groundwater to an onsite remediation system specifically designed for Badger. The system uses activated carbon and air strippers to remove contaminates and can treat up to three million gallons daily.

The lab collects and tests water samples from the deep extraction wells and from throughout the new remediation system. Engineers track these test result to monitor the system's efficiency. Test results also indicate when activated carbon must be changed out.

Other military or federal organizations acquire some of Badger's production equipment. The Army commissions SpecPro to sell everything not scheduled for disposal, including uncontaminated structures. Bid packages are prepared and distributed to the public on a regular basis.

New owners dismantle buildings and haul them away, like when the Army sold houses and outbuildings after the farmers left the prairie in the early 1940s.

Amish woodworkers acquire many of these structures. It is unusual to see them at work in their white shirts, black pants, and straw hats while using none of the safety equipment required for our people. Their religion exempts them from some government rules.

The Army receives proceeds from selling metal, poles, pipes, clocks, motors, engines, tools, switches, graffiti walls dating back to WWII, fencing, railroad tracks, and thousands of other items put out for bids. The current price for sorted metal is high, an advantage for the Army.

The 7,500 acres are divided into parcels to manage and facilitate cleanup. By 2010, parcels in the southern part of the plant are ready for transfer from the Army to other government agencies.

When I retire, there is nothing left of Badger Army Ammunition Plant. The 1,400 buildings are gone. Industrial utilities no longer exist. The main electrical power was cut years before. The pumping station on the Wisconsin River that supplied over 80 million gallons of water daily for drinking and manufacturing—gone.

The feeling of satisfaction for work well done mingles with the ache of losing a magnificent resource that served our country in a time of need.

I walk across the parking lot at Badger for the last time in August 2014 after working over 30 years at the facility. The last of the property is being released from the Department of Defense when I depart. At 67 years old, I am the exceptional person who experiences their planned retirement date coinciding with the disappearance of the place where they spent their entire professional career.

I am one of the few people, the only woman, who worked the entire Vietnam War and demolition, remediation, and restoration at *The Powder Plant.* The end is bittersweet. Seeing the project through to closure is satisfying. On the other hand, I will miss my coworkers and the dynamic challenges of my job.

But like Badger—I AM GONE.

During three wars, workers drew graffiti on production building walls. The photograph is an example of these drawings. It is displayed in the Museum of Badger Army Ammunition on the west side of the old facility. A picture of Rusty, one of the more prolific artists, is shown with her work. Sections of graffiti walls were salvaged and sold when the facility was demolished.

Images: Badger History Group, Inc.

Structural integrity inspections were conducted to assure buildings such as the one pictured were safe to enter before equipment was removed for sale or disposal. *Image:* Carolyn Dallmann, 2006.

Many production buildings had to be wet down before demolition work commenced for safety reasons. *Image:* Carolyn Dallmann, 2006.

The pointed structures at the top of the long building with the green roof in the background are concrete firewalls that separated hazardous operations. *Image:* Carolyn Dallmann, 2011.

After demolition of contaminated buildings, concrete firewalls and slabs remained because they were not contaminated. *Image:* Carolyn Dallmann, 2011.

Concrete firewalls and slabs were crushed. The State used the aggregate for roadbeds. *Image:* Carolyn Dallmann, 2011.

Sludge containing nitrates was placed in geotubes. As liquid drained from the tubes, Dairy Forage used it to fertilize crops. *Image:* Carolyn Dallmann, 2006.

Random pieces of wood were run through a chipper before placing them in the landfill. This minimized consumption of landfill space and reduced disposal costs. *Image:* Carolyn Dallmann, 2010.

Multiple landfill cells were constructed at Badger in conjunction with the State to hold demolition debris. *Image:* Carolyn Dallmann, 2011.

This photo was taken from the laboratory. Multiple excavators simultaneously sorted debris during demolition. The staged material is from the ball powder manufacturing area. *Image:* Carolyn Dallmann, 2011.

After the huge tubs were removed from this building, it was disassembled for sale or disposal. *Image:* Carolyn Dallmann, 2006.

6

EPILOGUE

2024

In the 1940s, families sacrificed their property and homes on the Sauk Prairie. The toll it took on their lives haunts me. It did not have to be. But given Washington's political chicanery and the local history of the time, it happened. Regardless, the community and dedicated workers at Badger soldiered on to provide a vital resource for our nation.

John and Elsie Shimniok's grandchildren, my second cousins, live in the area. They tell me stories about what happened to their grandparents. Especially vivid are the negative feelings held by their fathers, John and Elsie's sons, about a country they trusted that took their land.

Friends and relatives of people who also lost property tell their stories through the Badger History Group, which operates the Museum of Badger Army Ammunition on the site of the old facility. Others talk about their personal experiences working at Badger or that of parents, siblings, relatives, or acquaintances. Everyone has a story.

At my fiftieth high school class reunion, we honor classmates who joined the military. More than a quarter of my Baraboo Class of '65 are veterans. I am embarrassed that I did not know at the time how many of my classmates served. I think our work at *The Powder Plant* contributed to the safe return of those who fought overseas.

I was a teenage kid when I started at Badger in 1966. I grew up there and became a wife, mother, and grandmother. Attaining my undergraduate degree in mathematics while I worked was a significant achievement, but it came at a cost. I most regret losing intimate time with the Artist and Actress. My husband David continually sacrificed his time and energy to help with the girls and support me. His only compensation was my gratitude. My hair is gray now, not dark brown, each strand earned by challenges on the job, with family, and with age.

Badger appears different today from when I worked there. It is a flat, open prairie except for a few wooded areas and the bluffs to the north. Dairy Forage continues farming controlled crops on the southern part of the property, land they previously rented from the Army. The northwestern part was transferred to the Native American Ho-Chunk Nation. The Sauk Prairie Conservation Alliance, under the Wisconsin Department of Natural Resources, regulates the property's northeast and central regions.

I am fortunate to be a part of Badger's vast, blended stories; the experience helps me understand the reasoning behind what seems unreasonable about WWII, the Korean Conflict, and the Vietnam War. When I first stepped onto the facility, I had no idea that most of my career would be at Badger. Many of my coworkers and their families remain friends; however, their number is dwindling.

When I visit today, I walk the new trails established on state land, including the Great Sauk Trail, and reflect on the history that unfolded here. Soldiers fought overseas. But farmers who gave up their land and people who worked at Badger were soldiers, too. Their sacrifice and effort brought troops home from the wars and peace for me and my family to continue living in this great community and country.

ACKNOWLEDGMENTS

To the soldiers who fought on the battlefield to keep our country safe and secure during WWII, the Korean Conflict, and the Vietnam War, especially those who paid the ultimate price, "Thank you for your service."

Thank you to the men and women who were employed at Badger since the 1940s, especially those who worked in the powder laboratory. You were not on the battlefield, but you valiantly upheld your country and our soldiers.

Special recognition goes to Badger employees whose sons, daughters, husbands, wives, fiancés, brothers, sisters, or best friends were fighting while you supported them at Badger.

To those who lost loved ones during the wars while working at Badger, your battles are different than those fighting on the ground, but you are soldiers, too.

The farmers who lived on the Sauk Prairie before WWII are recognized. They lost land after the government took their property to build the powder plant. With no money and no immediate place for their families, animals, machinery, and household goods, their sacrifice during a cold winter supported our country in a time of need.

The Native American, Ho Chunk nation, who, like the Sauk Prairie farmers, lost their land, your pain is not forgotten.

I am eternally grateful to the following people, who contributed to this complex story and supported my writing. They exceeded anything I expected or could have anticipated.

My brother Allen, mentor and confidant, read my original work, a jumbled mess about a subject outside of his expertise. His questions and comments compelled me to narrow my approach to a mass of information. Allen continued to read revisions early on.

Carol Fleishauer and Marc Seals slogged through the unedited manuscript with little background on what happened inside Badger. Marc reread the manuscript.

Richard S. Brown, a published author, provided content and copy reviews. His military experience and familiarity with munitions provided a professional critique. His questions and prodding about internal happenings at Badger compelled research and added dimension to my story that would otherwise be lacking.

Frank Wolf worked for over 30 years at Badger as a chemical process engineer and served as Chief Modernization Engineer. He was my boss's boss when I returned to work in 1988. He continued working in the industry in Canada for 14 years after he retired from the powder plant. Frank read my manuscript first for accuracy. Then he read it several more times.

The Naples Writers Forum was a tremendous help. I joined this group of 11 authors in 2016; half are published. Special recognition goes to Liz Bosco, Gilda Franklin, Kija Kim, Sal Marici, Gary Melhart, Anne Picone, and Larry Rogers. I especially appreciate Larry Rogers and new member, Linda Saether, for their final readthroughs.

People who granted me interviews concerning their personal experiences at or about Badger deepened my understanding of events that are part of my personal history. Thank you to Richard S. Brown, Shirley Cummings, Dan Hiller, Tom Pollard, and Frank Wolf.

Special recognition goes to Paul Young and Jim Horman for the many conversations we've had over the years about the powder lab and Badger. Bob Crary and Larry Hudack offered tidbits, which I have tucked into my stories. My husband, David Dallmann, shared his unique experience of the 1966 explosion and provided details about Badger's maintenance operations.

Many thanks to the Badger History Group board members Verlyn Mueller, Orie Eilertson, Frank Wolf, and Sandra Stiemke for providing historical data and photos. Board member, Michael Goc's book, *Powder, People and Place*, was an incredible resource.

I appreciate Carol Baumgarten and Verla Klingenmeyer for providing research material and pointing me to pertinent resources.

I am indebted to the entire team at Cornerstone Press, a gem that shines at UW-Stevens Point. They guided me through the publication process and made my book a reality. Thank you to Managing Editor Lillian Kulbeck and her editorial staff, Karlie Harpold, Eleanor Belcher, John Evans, Brett Hill, Asher Schroeder, Nathan Pearson, Aja Woolley, Jazmyne Johnson, and Christiana Niedwiecki. I owe a special thank you to Dr. Ross Tangedal, the director and publisher, for his confidence in me and for acquiring my manuscript. And thank you to Scott Miller for the cover design.

To my late parents, Harold and Pearl Schroeder, thank you for being the example and for supporting me even when we did not always agree. You taught me to do and be my best. I continue to rely on the wisdom and common sense you instilled in me. I wish you were here to read my stories.

Harold and Virginia Dallmann's experience with the interwoven history of the farming community and the powder plant, along with their candid photos, added to my story.

My talented daughter, Kyla Herbes, built my website. I was lost without her help. To my late daughter, Kassi, loved and remembered by many, you sit on my shoulder, always present in the best way. To Kyla's husband, Thorsten, I appreciate your interest in history. To Cooper and Zoe, my grandchildren, thank you for keeping me grounded. All my love to my husband, David, for your patience, your support, and for fixing things that break. You are all the lights in my life!

REFERENCES

Interviews

Brown, Richard, Retired Human Resource manager with the Department of the Army. Earlier, while at Letterkenny Army Depot in Pennsylvania his office serviced the Headquarters, Depot Systems Command, which included Army Ammunition Storage Facilities throughout the country. Author: *Going Off the Rails* and *Push Back Choson.*

Cummings, Shirley, Retired Administrative Assistant for Olin Corporation at Badger Army Ammunition Plant, in the Environmental Laboratory, Interview, July 9, 2019

Crary, Robert, Retired Accountant, Olin Corporation at Badger Army Ammunition Plant, conversation at author's presentation at the Reedsburg Public Library, concerning the explosion of 1966 and other plant trivia, July 10, 2023

Fisher, Gayle, Retired Plant Manager for Olin Corporation at Badger Army Ammunition Plant, Electronic conversation, December 4, 2023.

Hiller, Daniel, Retired Sheriff, Sauk County Sheriff's Office, Interview, concerning bombing of Sterling Hall, November 11, 2023

Horman, James, Retired, Wegner CPAs, previously a Chemist at Badger Army Ammunition Plant during the Vietnam War, conversations over many years and while writing this book, most recent was October 2, 2023

Hudack, Lawrence, Retired Supervisor of Ball Powder Area, Olin Corporation at Badger Army Ammunition Plant, conversation at author's presentation at the Reedsburg Public Library, concerning the explosion of 1966, ball powder operations and other plant trivia, July 10, 2023

Orie Eilertson, Board member of The Badger History Group, Museum of Army Ammunition Baraboo WI, Details from archives

Pollard, Thomas, Retired Lieutenant, Sauk County Sherriff's Office, Interview, concerning bombing of Sterling Hall, November 11, 2023

Sandra Stiemke, Board member of The Badger History Group, Museum of Army Ammunition Baraboo WI, Details from archives

Verlyn Mueller, Retired Project Engineer at BadgerAAP, Archivist and Board member of The Badger History Group, Museum of Army Ammunition, Baraboo WI, Details from archives

Wolf, Frank, Retired Chief Modernization Engineer, Olin Corporation at Badger Army Ammunition Plant, Interview on September 8, 2024, following earlier correspondence, discussions, and presentations at the Badger History Group lecture series, October 10, 2024, and others. Local historian from Mazomanie for over 40 years. Author of eight local history books on topics that include early settlers, founding of Mazomanie, the early railroad and the Civil War.

Young, Paul, Retired Senior Chemist, Badger Army Ammunition Plant, numerous conversations over 60 years and while writing this book.

Organizations

Sauk County Historical Society, Photograph of the Rudolph Schlag home

The Badger History Group, Inc., The Museum of Badger Army Ammunition, Baraboo WI, Photographs of Badger Army Ammunition Plant

Wisconsin Historical Society, Photograph of Leo T. Crawley

Books and Documents

Author not identified, Badger Army Ammunition Plant Historical Overview, 1941-2006, *U.S. Army Joint Munitions Command, AMSJM-HI (History Office),* Date is not shown.

Author not identified, Four Workers Killed Thursday In N.G. Explosion, *Badger Ordnance News* Baraboo, Wisconsin, Friday, July 27, 1945

Author not identified, The Interim Remedial Measure (IRM), *U.S. Army Toxic and Hazardous Materials Agency*, May 1990

Bates, Tom, *RADS, The 1970 Bombing of the Army Math Research Center at the University of Wisconsin and Its Aftermath*, HarperCollins, 1992

Crown, Deborah L., Bear Creek Archeology, Inc., and Peter, Duane E., Geo-Marine, Inc., U.S. Army Corps of Engineers – Fort Worth District, U.S. Army Materiel Command Historic Context Series, Geo-Marine, Inc. Plano, Texas, May 1996

Dallmann Family, photographs and handwritten records

Deborah L. Crown, Bear Creek Archeology, Inc., U.S. Army Materiel Command Historic Context Series, Report of Investigation, Number 2A, Principal Investigator, Duane E. Peter, Geo-Marine, Inc., US Army Corps of Engineers – Fort Worth District, *The World War II Ordnance Department's Government-Owned Contractor- Operated (GOCO) Industrial Facilities: Badger Ordnance Works Transcripts of Oral History Interviews*, May 1966

Goc, Michael, Badger History Group, Rifle Ammo For Vietnam, *Badger Ordnance News*, Winter 2019-20 Edition

Goc, Michael, *Powder, People and Place, Badger Ordnance Works and the Sauk Prairie*, New Past Press, Inc., Friendship, Wisconsin, 2002

Knoop, Dave, Water Testing at Badger, *Badger World*, January 1974

Mueller, Erhart, A. *Only in Sumpter*, Worzalla Publishing Co., 1977, Stevens Point, Wisconsin

Parkinson, Arlene (Groth), *A Biographical Sketch of Ella Anna Groth and the Kuhnau/Bethscheider Families*, Private family publication, April 15, 1998

Scott C. Shaffer, Deborah L. Crown, Bear Creek Archeology, Inc., U.S. Army Materiel Command Historic Context Series, Report of Investigation, Number 2A, Principal Investigator, Duane E. Peter, Geo-Marine, Inc., US Army Corps of Engineers – Fort Worth District, *The World War II Ordnance Department's Government-Owned Contractor-Operated (GOCO) Industrial Facilities: Badger Ordnance Works Historic Investigation*, February 1996

U.S. Army Joint Munitions Command, AMSJM-HI (History Office), 1 Rock Island Arsenal, Rock Island, IL 61299, Badger Army Ammunition Plant, Historical Overview, 1941-2006, accessed at https://www.jmc.army.mil/Docs/History/Badger%20Army%20Ammunition%20Plant%20-%20V3%20Internet.pdf, May 2018

Weiss, Stuart L., *The President's Man: Leo Crowley and Franklin Roosevelt in Peace and War*, Southern Illinois University Press, 1996

Newspapers

Author not listed, Army to Test Wells, *Baraboo News Republic*, July 27, 2001

Author not identified, CSWAB, DNR tangle over Badger, water tests, *Sauk Prairie Star*, September 15, 1994

Author(s) not identified, *CSWAB Newsletter*, April 1995 Issue

Author not identified, Open House, *Olin Extra*, March 13, 1997

Author not named, Proposed Open Burning of Hazardous Waste at BAAP, *Shopper Stopper*, September 15, 1992

Author not named, What is SMES?, *Shopper Stopper*, September 29, 1992

Ambelang, Jerry, Badger plant 50 years ago, *Capitol Times*, July 13, 1992

Avelleyra, Lisa, BAAP chemists put water through the works, *Baraboo News Republic*, Date not available

Avelleyra Treichel, Lisa, Cleaning water, *New Republic*, October 27, 1992

Avelleyra Treichel, Lisa, The Cleaning up of Badger, *Sunday News Republic*, October 25, 1992

Avelleyra Treichel, Lisa, Turning Badger to Industrial Park Receives Mixed Reviews, *Baraboo News Republic*, March 25, 1994. (and dozens of other articles concerning the Reindustrialization of Badger, 1994-1997)

Chickering, Pam, Controversial BAAP restores prairies, *Baraboo New Republic*, October 16, 1992

Fazen, Terri, Army, DNR to test village well, *Baraboo News Republic*, May 19, 1990

Fazen, Terri, Badger water purifying starts, *Baraboo News Republic*, June 1, 1990

Fazen Terri, Badger Well Testing on Third Round, *Baraboo News Republic*, July 19, 1990

Fazen, Terri, Prairie Water Tests Negative, *Baraboo News Republic*, May 31, 1990

Fazen, Terri, Water Problems Mirror Neb. Project, *Baraboo News Republic*, May 24, 1990

Grunig, Tara, Guard Unit at Badger for Training, *Baraboo News Republic*, February 13, 1995

Hillock, Darren, Cancer Study Shows No Badger Link, *Baraboo News Republic*, July 12, 1990

Howard, Joseph B., Badger Pollution Spreads, *Wisconsin State Journal*, May 18, 1990

Marquardt, Mike, 3 Wells Show Contamination Near Badger, *Baraboo News Republic*, May 1990 (specific date unknown)

Marquardt, Mike, SMES Manager Refutes Claims, *Baraboo News Republic*, August 8, 1990

Marquardt, Mike, Stop SMES Marches at BAAP, *Baraboo News Republic*, August 7, 1990

Marquardt, Mike, On-Plant Testing at BAAP Expected by Dec. Delayed, *Baraboo News Republic*, 1990, specific date unknown

McGrath, Jim, Army Calls BAAP Wells Safe, *Baraboo News Republic*, December 13, 1992, and dozens of other articles in the *Baraboo News Republic* relating to groundwater contamination at Badger.

McGrath, Jim, SWAB questions reservoir project [SMES], *Baraboo News Republic*, September 21, 1992

Klestinski, Lee, S-P students tour ammunition plant, *Baraboo News Republic*, May 10, 1991

O'Connell, Mike, Army to Study Badger Role in Defense, *Baraboo News Republic*, January 28, 1997

O'Connell, Mike, Army Won't Shelve Badger, *Baraboo News Republic*, January 30, 1997

O'Connell, Mike, Olin Engineers Stop Plan for Alcohol Facility, *Baraboo New Republic*, January 16, 1997

Riggles, Steve, Working at Badger, *Baraboo News Republic*, July 31, 1992

Satran Jr., Dan, Badger officials defend their lab's work, *Sauk Prairie Star*, Date not available.

Treleven, Ed, After 50 years, ammo plant still subject of controversy, *Wisconsin State Journal*, July 12, 1992

Treleven, Ed, Ammunition plant turns 50, *Wisconsin State Journal*, July 12, 1992

Treleven, Ed, Archaic chemical handling leaves polluted legacy, *Wisconsin State Journal*, July 12, 1992

Taylor, Steve, Scandal And Deceit In Dioxin Cleanup, *St. Louis Post-Dispatch*, September 19, 1996.

Vande Sande, Matt, Bus Tour Guides – Open House, *Olin Intel Office*, July, 28, 1992

Internet

Shackell, Steven, Superconducting Magnetic Energy Storage (SMES) could Revolutionize how We Store Electricity, *Arrow*, January 18, 2024, https://www.arrow.com/en/research-and-events/articles/superconducting-magentic-energy-storage, Retrieved September 14, 2024

Carolyn Dallmann is the author of *North Freedom* (Cornerstone Press 2022), a memoir of her time growing up on a family farm in North Freedom, Wisconsin, ten miles from Badger Army Ammunition Plant. Prior to writing fulltime, she worked at the ammunition plant for over thirty years. Her writing has appeared in *The Wisconsin Magazine of History*.

www.ingramcontent.com/pod-product-compliance
Lightning Source LLC
LaVergne TN
LVHW040044080526
838202LV00045B/3480
* 9 7 8 1 9 6 8 1 4 8 4 8 5 *